EUROPE:
A CONSTITUTION FOR
THE MILLENNIUM

To Professor Buchanan

With regards

EUROPE:
A CONSTITUTION FOR
THE MILLENNIUM

Frank Vibert

Dartmouth

Aldershot • Brookfield USA • Singapore • Sydney

Published by
Dartmouth Publishing Company Limited
Gower House
Croft Road
Aldershot
Hants GU11 3HR
England

Dartmouth Publishing Company
Old Post Road
Brookfield
Vermont 05036
USA

British Library Cataloguing in Publication Data
Vibert, Frank
  Europe: Constitution for the Millennium
  I. Title
  321.04094

Library of Congress Cataloging-in-Publication Data
Vibert, Frank.
  Europe : a constitution for the millennium / Frank Vibert.
    p.   cm.
  Includes bibliographical references.
  ISBN 1-85521-521-7
  1. European Union countries–Politics and government. 2. European
federation. I. Title.
  IN PROCESS
  320.94–dc20

95-13292
CIP

ISBN 1 85521 521 7

Printed and bound in Great Britain by
Ipswich Book Co. Ltd., Ipswich, Suffolk

Contents

Acknowledgements

Thanks are due to Professor Dr Joachim Rückert of the Institut für Rechtsgeschichte, Johann Wolfgang Goethe University of Frankfurt and to Professor Roland Vaubel, Lehrstuhl für Volkswirtschaftslehre, University of Mannheim for their comments on an earlier draft; to Richard Challoner for his assistance on research; and to Ruth Martin for preparing the manuscript.

Introduction

'I have in my contemplation the civil social man and no other'. Edmund Burke, *Reflections on the Revolution in France*, 1790.

The time for a European constitutional settlement

As the twentieth century closes, the focus in Europe is on political integration. For most of the period since the Second World War Europe has been divided. Following the collapse of communism, the countries of eastern and central Europe are looking not merely towards economic integration with the countries of western Europe but also towards political integration. At the same time, for the Member States of the existing European Union, the agenda has already begun the shift from economic integration to political union.

Behind the existing European Union there had indeed always existed an underlying political agenda – the binding together of France and Germany. Economics was seen as the way forward because the benefits of cooperation could easily be identified. Political union was correctly seen as involving a much more contentious agenda. It seemed prudent to western Europe's postwar leaders to see political union as following in the slipstream of economic union. Political union could gather its own momentum in a natural sequence behind the success of economic union.

The assumption that there could be a seamless transition from economic integration to political integration now looks highly questionable. The first attempt to address openly the successor agenda of political union was made with the Maastricht Treaty on European Union (negotiated in 1991). It awakened deep divisions. The institutions and procedures suited for the building of the original Economic Community are not necessarily well suited to political union. Moreover the arrangements developed for a group of twelve Member States are not easily adapted to the larger Union of twenty five or more Member States now possible in bringing all of Europe together.

The momentum towards further economic integration in Europe is irreversible. However, disputes about political union could lead to a quite unnecessary re-emergence of political divisions in Europe. Neither is it likely that a well functioning European economy could be sustained for long in the face of dysfunctional European institutions.

The assumption behind this book is that the best way to approach political union in Europe would be to put in place a well considered constitutional framework. Existing treaties act as a surrogate constitution. But because they have not been approached as constitutional documents they are seriously defective as a basis for political association in Europe. Attempts to achieve political union by indirect means, for example through monetary union, are likely to be viewed with suspicion. There may be a strong economic case for monetary union. However, it does not provide a means to avoid discussing the quite different questions that must be answered in a political union. Open ended processes are also likely to provoke unnecessary and destructive anxieties. A constitutional settlement would give clarity and stability to the main features of political union and allay undefined fears about unclear goals.

Proposals for a European constitution are being brought forward.[1] What however, has been largely absent from debates about Europe's future is a discussion of relevant constitutional theory. There is an appeal in pragmatism – taking events step by step on the basis of what works. Unfortunately, what is presented as pragmatism often conceals unrecognized theory. Even worse, much of the hidden theory is mistaken. By being concealed it cannot be questioned and debated. The purpose of this book therefore is to provide an explicit discussion of a theoretical basis for a European constitution. The intention is to try to illuminate some of the important questions which need to be considered as Europe moves towards an embracing political union.

The nature of constitutions

Individuals in society depend on each other. Constitutions are about the organization of these reciprocal relationships.[2] This does not mean an automatic jump to a discussion about rulers and the ruled or about the sovereign and the subject. Instead, it involves a discussion about the rules and institutions that help define relationships within society.

The ways in which individuals, associations and communities in society relate to each other can be characterized in three different ways:

- cooperative relationships are possible wherever tastes and preferences are the same or when participants perceive that they make mutual gains by acting together;
- relationships characterized by exchange are possible wherever participants

find that their differing preferences can be aligned through bargaining;
- conflicting relationships must be recognized whenever the gain of one individual or community results necessarily in a loss for another and where differing preferences cannot be aligned.

It is the function of a constitution to establish the rules within which the full range of these relationships can be worked out successfully within a civil order.[3] It is not sufficient to characterize the role of constitutions as dealing with just one type of dependency – to present relationships exclusively in the single terms of exchange, or conflict, or more idealistically, as cooperation.

Europe's constitutional challenge

An essential feature of any constitutional order is that it provides a means of enforcement. Individuals feel free from government when they can satisfy their aspirations through their own endeavours and through individual exchange in the market place. But the market does not work without a framework of rules backed by sanction, without enforceable contracts, or without enforceable property rights. Nor have societies yet found a way to satisfy human wants and needs simply through individual exchange. Collective provision involves the mobilization of resources and the enforcement of a tax regime. Moreover, it is impossible to discuss rules, collective provision and enforcement without taking account of such criteria as fairness and equity.[4] The institutions of the market are themselves about reciprocity.

The two central questions of a constitution are:
- how to express and justify coercive powers in a system of government and
- how to respect differences in preferences and relative values within the rules that orchestrate relationships in a civil society, at the same time as expressing common values such as fairness and justice.

The approach to these two questions is sometimes presented as involving an irreconcilable clash between those who stress the individual as the basic unit of society and those who stress the collective – the community as a whole. This is a false perception.[5] Those who stress the importance of the individual are unlikely to wish to be open to easy refutation as ignoring the value of the community. Those who stress the community are equally unlikely to wish to be open to the accusation of ignoring the individual. The coercive powers of government can be as much a threat to any community as they can be to any individual. A failure to respect differences in society can damage any association or any community as well as individuals.

The difficulties of transposition

The enduring problems of constitutional order are greatly magnified when transposed to Europe as a whole. Until now, constitutional questions in Europe have been resolved, with varying degrees of success and failure, within the context of what is loosely termed 'the nation state'. The transposition raises new questions:

- the new European order has to achieve legitimacy. The old nation state had an inherited legitimacy. The coercive powers of a European constitution have to be newly expressed and freshly justified.
- there is no common approach across Europe to constitutional order. Traditions, structure and practice differ widely. The new European order appeals to shared values and to the evident benefits of cooperation. But the constitutional order must also allow for the expression of differences in values and must be able to handle conflicting relationships.
- it is unlikely that the constitutional order in any one country of Europe can simply be applied to Europe as a whole. It is entirely possible that the right constitutional arrangements for a European political union will differ in important ways from the arrangements within any individual Member State.
- the old constitutional order of the nation state cannot simply be ignored. The nation state can be seen as an aid to legitimizing the new order, as a help to the expression of preferences and as assisting the clarification of relationships between different jurisdictions in Europe. Conversely, it can be viewed as an obstacle to each. Whichever view is taken, the new order has to redefine the role of the nation state.
- there is an unresolved tension between viewing the new European order as knitting together the peoples of Europe on the basis of egalitarian principles or on the basis of principles of association that recognize inequalities. Under egalitarian principles, differences between preferences would be resolved, in most cases, by simple majority voting in arriving at political decisions. It is population size that will mainly determine the balance between the large nation states and the small. However, principles of political association that recognize the Member State in the processes of the Union have to take into account the enormous inequalities between Member States. There is also a case, in a political association where preferences are as diverse as they are in Europe, for recognizing that not all collective choices will be seen as equal – that some will be seen as more important than others. The two approaches lead to quite different ways of structuring political processes in the Union.

Constitutional economics

In looking at constitutional theory for possible answers to the pivotal questions about a European constitution, there is only limited help to be obtained from traditional federal or confederal theory. This is because federalism is practised in so many different guises that it has ceased to have a core meaning. The term is used to describe states with widely different degrees of centralization or decentralization. It is also used to describe states with wide variations in civic and political freedom.

The analytic insights of political science are subject to other limitations. Many are based on the analysis of particular institutions in particular settings (for example, the workings of the Bundesrat in the German system of government). However, simple transpositions from individual nation states are unlikely to be applicable to Europe as a whole. Moreover, there is a shortage of relevant models. There are insights to be gained from the lengthy constitutional experience of systems as diverse as Switzerland on the one hand and the United States on the other. There are also insights to be gained from the much more recent experiences of Germany and Spain. But it is misleading and possibly dangerous to separate institutional form from the historical setting, the cultural context and the habits and conventions of the societies to which they belong and which have given them life.[6] Arrangements for political union suited to Europe as a whole will have their own special features.

This book therefore draws more extensively from what is known as constitutional economics. Constitutional economics uses the methodology of economics to examine rules and institutions in society. It has the advantage over much conventional political science that its insights do not depend on generalizing on the basis of the experience of a particular country, or on the basis of particular institutions in their own special settings.

Constitutional economics looks at:

- the interrelationships between individual and collective choice, and the boundaries between choices that can be resolved in the market and choices that are resolved through political processes;
- the costs of transactions in the market and accounts of market failures which lead societies to look to government processes, as well as accounts of government failures, and the costs of collective arrangements which lead societies to look again at what can be achieved through the market;[7]
- the effect on the choices of one actor of expectations about the behaviour of another actor and how this affects the rules guiding collective choice;
- rules for the appropriate distribution of collective powers;
- the rationale for non-market institutions and explanations for their behaviour;
- the performance of rules and the relationship between institutions and rules.

Constitutional economics goes back to a much earlier intellectual tradition in Europe.[8] It goes back to a time when the study of politics, ethics, the law, philosophy and economics was not divided by the demands of specialization.[9] It has re-emerged both in the United States and in Europe.[10]

The structure of the discussion

The discussion of the theoretical questions essential for arriving at a firm structure for European political union is divided into three parts. The first part explores how the purposes and underlying values of a constitution for a European political union are best expressed. The second part discusses key processes in a European political union and how the rules that govern them should be framed. The third part discusses the relationship between the processes desired and the shaping of Europe's political institutions. The first part is entirely theoretical and the third part entirely institutional. Those readers whose interests are mainly about institutional arrangements in a European political union may wish to skip the earlier discussion and pick up the threads around chapter 5.

(i) Constitutions and coercion

The first part of the discussion, in the opening three chapters of the book, leads up to the central problem of coercion in a constitution:

(a) Europe's constitutional quest (chapter 1) Constitutions express purpose. It is tempting therefore to specify constitutions in terms of the political outcomes that are intended to flow from a political union. The first chapter discusses this approach. It suggests that to specify the features of a political order on the basis of intended outcomes is a mistaken approach. It leads to a focus on powers without proper consideration of the limitations that are needed on powers. Constitutions should put their primary focus on processes.

(b) Rules (chapter 2) Constitutions that emphasize process rely on rules as a way of entrenching and protecting processes. The essential elements of rule based constitutions are therefore discussed next. The areas of disagreement over the content of a rule based constitution in Europe are described and the underlying causes of disagreement set out. There are two roots to the disagreement – a dispute about what is necessary to give legitimacy to rules and a dispute about the relationship of rules to values. The chapter discusses the view that the normative element is in the process itself but concludes that there has to be an appeal to values external to the rules. This leads to the discussion in the next chapter of the possible values that should underlie a political order in Europe.

(c) Values in the constitution (chapter 3) The most important values in a constitution are 'process values' – those that define how things are to be done and how people

in a political association are to work together. The discussion of the alternative ways in which constitutional values can be framed leads to the introduction of the 'non-coercion' principle as the key way to express values about processes. This principle means that the rules of political association are legitimized to the extent that they minimize the imposition of choices. The justification of this principle is discussed in relation to rules of prudence.

(ii) Processes and coercion

The second part of the book discusses the application of the 'non-coercion' principle to three crucial areas on which the success or failure of political union in Europe will hinge: how differences in values and preferences within Europe are to be approached, how powers are to be distributed, and how collective decisions are to be taken.

(a) Value differences (chapter 4) European political union will be built on shared values. The constitution however has to provide for ways of handling differences in values as well as differences in the relative weights and intensity of feelings attached to the same values. The fourth chapter examines the extent to which such differences can be expected to be resolved through political processes. Political processes are crude. Minimizing coercion means that normative boundaries must be set on the political process (for example, through declarations of individual and civil liberties). These normative boundaries limit the application of politics where the methods of political choice are at their weakest.

(b) Powers and their distribution (chapter 5) This chapter examines the case for saying that the principal public policy choices in Europe should be decided by the Union. It is a case that rests very heavily on the view that various types of market 'failure' can only be resolved by the collective action of the Union. This view is rejected. Instead the alternative case is accepted that theories of 'optimum domain' establish convincing reasons for preserving multiple jurisdictions in Europe.

The chapter continues by discussing the different ways in which multiple jurisdictions can be organized in relation to each other. It suggests that this is best achieved by a system where powers devolve up and not through a system either of hierarchy, where powers devolve down from the centre, or from a system where the centre has independent powers. This means that the powers of the centre should be limited to those delegated by the contracting parties to the constitution – the Member States and their peoples. Coercion is minimized in a system of diversified jurisdictions where power devolves up because such a system provides the most likely way in which the true costs of public policies can be established and true preferences expressed.

(c) Rules for taking decisions in the Union (chapter 6) Two different perspectives on decision taking in the European Union are discussed in the sixth chapter. One approach looks at decision rules from the perspective of choosers. The other approach looks at the subject matter of the choice.

The central problem for Europe is of inequalities. Some collective choices are more important than others and some Member States carry more weight than others. This means that there is no simple decision rule to be developed such as moving towards simple majority voting. On the contrary, the system will need to be built around concurrent and qualified majorities. In order to minimize coercive decision rules where choices are imposed, decision rules should be graduated to minimize the risk that damage could be done to the most strongly held preferences.

(iii) Institutions and processes

The third part of the book discusses institutional choices in a European political union. Institutional choices cannot be regarded as free standing choices within a constitution. On the contrary, institutions interact with processes and other constitutional rules. Thus the remaining chapters in the book consider the institutional arrangements for Europe's constitutional order that are consistent with the values and processes described in earlier chapters.

(a) Responsibility for the rules (chapter 7) This chapter starts by reviewing general ways of looking at the organization of institutional responsibilities. In particular the old doctrine of the separation of powers is presented as a valid admonition to define core functions and key relationships in any system.

The chapter continues by discussing how constitutional oversight is to be achieved. The task is defined and the methods outlined.[11] Two models are then discussed. The first is a judicial model – that of the US Supreme Court. The second model is a representative model. It looks at the arrangements necessary if oversight is to find a place not only for judicial methods of review but also a continuing role for the contracting parties to a European constitution – the Member States, their people and their representatives. The discussion concludes that the American model is not appropriate for Europe.

(b) The Government of Europe (chapter 8) This chapter discusses whether the Council of Ministers or the Commission should be seen as the governing body that determines the direction of public policy in European political union. The potential of the Commission to develop as the 'Government of Europe' is examined, both in its current form as an appointed body, as well as under alternative arrangements under which it would become an elected body. The different ways of looking at the Council as a form of coalition government are then examined. The

discussion concludes that it is the Council of Ministers that should be looked to as the Government of Europe.

(c) Assemblies (chapter 9) This chapter discusses the functions of the representative assembly in a European political union. The analysis suggests that the basic role of a representative assembly – to legitimize or challenge the legitimacy of a system of government – cannot be carried out by the Union assembly by itself. The representative assemblies of the Member States will also have a continuing role. Therefore the chapter goes on to discuss how the relationship between the Union assembly and the parliaments of Member States is best organized.

The main theme: minimizing the imposition of choices

The theme of this book is that a European constitutional order must be based on a clear expression of values. The most important values in a constitution are those that define political processes – the way in which the peoples of Europe are to act together. Enshrining the values that define the ways in which political processes are to work is far more important than trying to define the intended political outcomes of political association.

The processes incorporated in the constitution must be able to bring harmony to each of the different types of relationships involved in a European political order. They must encourage cooperation where similar preferences can be coordinated; they must encourage exchange where different preferences can be aligned through bargaining, and they must be capable of handling differences where interests and preferences conflict.

It is the way of handling differences and conflicts of interests and preferences that is critical in political association. In a European constitutional order that treats processes as a value and that values processes above outcomes, the key value is that processes should minimize coercion. This means that political processes in a European political order should minimize the extent to which choice can be imposed.

Justification

The justification of a European constitutional order that puts the emphasis on minimizing the coercive powers of the Union rests on the view that the rules of a constitution are akin to rules of prudence. Prudential values are not the same as moral values. But they are congruent with the moral order of society. Thus a European constitution can gain its ethical legitimacy to the extent that it minimizes the coercive powers of Europe's system of government to impose choices.

Application

What does a 'non-coercive Union' mean in practical terms for key political processes? It has three crucial aspects.

First, the limitations of the political process as a way of settling differences in Europe should be recognized. The role of politics must itself be circumscribed by rules whose function is to act as correctives to the weak points of the political method.

Second, power must be distributed in Europe between multiple jurisdictions with the place of Union jurisdiction determined by the functions that the other jurisdictions choose to delegate. Other jurisdictions should not depend for their role on the receipt of powers from the Union. Neither should the Union have powers independent of the Member States of the Union. The role of the nation state is redefined in terms of its place in a system of multiple jurisdictions.

Third, decision rules should recognize inequalities both between choosers and choices. Not all choices are equal. In addition, any system of decision taking that involves the Member States has to deal with inequalities between choosers. The standard decision rule in these circumstances will be one where the majority is qualified in a way which reflects both sources of inequality.

Institutions consistent with processes

The institutional arrangements in the European Union must be consistent with the intended processes. The need for consistency between processes and institutions means that:

- the arrangements for protecting the rules of the constitution must try to identify where the rules are likely to be most vulnerable and which institutions are likely to have the greatest incentive to wish to challenge the rules. A Union court cannot be regarded as the 'least dangerous' source of challenge to a system where the Union exercises delegated powers. The contracting parties themselves – the Member States, their peoples and their institutions – must maintain their role as the highest authority over the constitution.
- the arrangements for the Government of Europe must be consistent with maintaining multiple jurisdictions and non-majoritarian methods of choice. This means that the Council of Ministers, in conjunction with the heads of the governments of the Member States (the European Council) should be seen as the Government of Europe rather than the Commission.
- in order to maintain accountable government in a system of multiple jurisdictions, the relationship between the Union assembly and the parliaments of the Member States should involve a sharing of certain functions and a bicameral relationship in others.

Over the coming years Europe will establish a political union. Europe's clouded political heritage urges caution. This is not a reason to pull back from a constitutional settlement. It is however a reason to root the constitution in values that protect the individual citizen and the associations of society from the aberrations of government that scar Europe's past.

Notes

1   The European Constitutional Group published *A Proposal for a European Constitution* in December 1993. The Institutional Committee of the European Parliament tabled its report on a *Draft Constitution of the European Union* in February 1994.

2   Edmund Burke's concept of the 'civil social man' expresses this position. 'Men cannot enjoy the rights of an uncivil and of a civil state together'. Burke, E. (1790), *Reflections on the Revolution in France*.

3   Hume seems to have been the first to express rules within 'the general societies of men' in these terms and to draw a comparison with the rules of games. 'In societies for play, there are laws required for the conduct of the game; and these laws are different in each game. . . The comparison. . . is very imperfect. We may only learn from it the necessity of rules, wherever men have any intercourse with each other'. Hume, D. (1748), *An Enquiry Concerning Human Understanding*.

4   'Human nature cannot by any means subsist, without the association of individuals; and that association never could have place, were no regard paid to the laws of equity and justice'. Hume, ibid.

5   Adam Smith followed Hume in rejecting Hobbes' contractarian theory of the political order, like Hume seeing dependent relationships as the key. In his account of the historical stages of society he saw government becoming necessary in the 'age of shepherds' because at this point, in his view, exchange became important, inequalities arose and people became dependent on each other.

6   'Nations are not primarily ruled by laws; less by violence. . . Nations are governed. . . by a knowledge of their temper'. Burke, E. (1770), *Thoughts on the Causes of the Present Discontents*.

7   'My conclusion: let us study the world of positive transaction costs'. Coase, R.H. (1991), 'The Institutional Structure of Production', in *The American Economic Review*, September 1992.

8   'Constitutional political economy is best interpreted as a. . . rediscovery of basic elements of earlier intellectual traditions. . . These traditions are those of classical political economy and contractarian political philosophy'. Buchanan, J.M. (1990), 'The Domain of Constitutional Economics' in *Constitutional Political Economy*, vol. 1, no. 1, winter 1990.

9   Adam Smith's *Wealth of Nations* was intended only as one part of his account of the social order. In his theory of moral sentiments he explored why one kind of conduct should be preferred to another and in his lectures on jurisprudence he addressed the question of why we should obey the laws of society.

10   Germany's neo-liberals decried specialization of the individual sciences. They declared that their 'fundamental principle. . . consists in viewing individual economic questions as constituent parts of a greater whole'. Bohm, F., Eucken, W. and Grossmann-Doerth H. in 'The Ordo Manifesto of 1936'. See Peacock, A. and Willgerodt, H. (eds) (1989), *Germany's Social Market Economy: Origins and Evolution*.

11   Edmund Burke's well known dictum applies, 'A state without the means of some

change is without the means of its conservation. Without such means it might even risk the loss of that part of the constitution which it wished the most religiously to preserve'. Burke, E. (1790), *Reflections on the Revolution in France.*

Part I
CONSTITUTIONS AND COERCION

1 Europe's constitutional quest

'Why create magistrates, where there never arises any disorder or iniquity?' David Hume, *An Enquiry Concerning Human Understanding*, 1748.

I The motivation

The twentieth century has been the cruellest century in the often cruel history of Europe. In the disasters of earlier centuries, the transience and uncertainties of existence had been accepted with the solace of religious belief. By contrast, the nineteenth century inherited a new belief in the perfectibility of human nature and instilled hope in the idea of individual and social progress. The twentieth century exposed the fragility of that presumption. Just under 50 million people have been killed in two great wars. At least a further 40 million have been victims of ideology. In total in this century there have been over 90 million deaths in Europe from war and civil strife. Even for the survivors of war and civil conflict there has been the wider devastation of families shattered, individual endeavour destroyed and lives made apparently meaningless. For almost half the century the peoples of Europe have been physically divided. It has been an outside power, the United States of America, whose intervention has been decisive, not only in bringing two wars to an end, but also in bringing the communist division of Europe to an end.

As the next century approaches, the disasters of this century are being rapidly forgotten. Western Europe has achieved unprecedented levels of prosperity which the countries of central and eastern Europe attempt to emulate. The old ideological divides have perished; new ones have not yet taken their place. Armaments are being reduced. The United States is able to wind down its European involvement.

Yet an old problem remains. The countries of Europe have yet to find a sure way to live harmoniously together. The differences in their sizes, in their preferences, in their relative economic strengths, in their different perceptions of their national interest and in their different historical experiences and national myths, remain both a source of strength and a source of friction.

The sources of tension in Europe have not gone away. They have simply changed their form. The simple east-west ideological divide, frozen by superpower confrontation, has vanished. In its absence other differences can rise to the surface. Ethnic rivalries are no longer suppressed and are a potential source of friction wherever the sense of ethnic identity lacks congruity with the boundaries of the nation states within Europe. Immigration and mobility are a constant irritant to the politics of identity. There are important differences in social preferences at different income levels. Different social traditions have also bred differences in relative values. Dissimilar approaches have been taken to social and political organization. There exist differences in the approach to international rules (for example, on trade and the environment) and on the enforcement of international rules (for example, in peace keeping operations).

The new sources of tension, unlike the old, do not threaten instant cataclysm. But their total effect is corrosive. Moreover the sources of dissension cannot be dealt with by old structures. The old structures are those of the nation state in Europe. The nation state looked inward. It was built on the myth of national self-sufficiency. The new tasks in Europe lie in organizing the mutual dependencies within Europe – between states, between societies and between the peoples of Europe. The role of the nation state will be redefined.

There is therefore a search for a new political order in Europe. The right framework will itself promote greater harmony in Europe. The wrong framework will only aggravate differences. If the means of reconciling divergent views cannot be found Europe will be vulnerable, once again, to the politics of frustration, intolerance and ideology.

The start of a European constitution

Within a single country, differences within society are accommodated and resolved partly through habit and convention, partly through the law and partly through the political and constitutional framework. The more homogenous the society and the more stable its history, the greater the role for habit and convention. On a European scale, the habits and conventions of a cooperative society are not yet entrenched, law remains fragmented and constitutional construction is in its infancy.

The infant construction is the Treaty on European Union, ratified in 1993 by the then twelve Member States of the European Community. The Treaty on European Union itself incorporates two earlier treaties – the Single European Act (1987) and the Treaty of Rome (1956). Together they comprise a surrogate constitution. To its supporters, this treaty base provides the nucleus of a constitutional order that can be extended over time to cover the rest of Europe. Others see it as already dated, suited at best only for cooperation on a limited number of fronts by a limited number of countries and at worst as a deeply flawed approach to building a constitution for Europe – one that is likely to aggravate tensions in Europe rather than provide a mechanism to mediate and resolve them.

There is an urgency to sorting out the divisions of opinion about the future political order in Europe. Left unresolved, the divisions will block the voluntary acceptance of a new order while leaving in place the malaise provoked by the shortcomings of the existing order.

The strong historical motivation behind the search for a new political order in Europe does not justify any European order. If a new form of political association is to be a success, it has to command popular support in Europe and its main features must be able to be validated.

The case for a constitution for Europe (and for a debate centred on constitutional questions) is based on the belief that a constitution can provide the framework for a successful political association between the peoples of Europe and assist the validation of a new order. This means not only identifying the institutions and the procedures of political union but addressing also the more fundamental issues concerning validation – what procedural principles and what underlying values will give legitimacy to the arrangements for political union. The debate about the shape of a constitution is thus a way to put in focus the key questions about the future political order in Europe.

The emergence of divisions

Despite the strength of the motivation to put a new political order in Europe into a constitutional form there are major divisions of opinion emerging on the shape of a European constitutional order.

At first sight, the differences about the shape of a new political order in Europe appear to be simply about the proper development of institutional responsibilities in the European Union, for example, over the correct evolution of the role of the present European Parliament or the Commission. The differences are, however, more fundamental.

The differences centre on questions of constitutional process – how powers are to be defined, how they are to be distributed and how decisions are to be taken. If the countries of Europe are to come together successfully in a full political union there needs to be clear agreement on the ways in which the processes of political association are to work. Once processes can be agreed, then the role of the different institutions can be more easily defined.

Underlying the central question of the processes of a full European political union is yet a further source of difference. It revolves around the alternative ways in which the purpose of a constitution can be defined. This in turn leads to different approaches to constitutional construction. One approach emphasizes the importance of agreement on the specific political outcomes to be obtained from the new political order. The other approach sees outcomes as less important than getting the processes of association right. This difference is not simply a question of mechanisms. It is a question of the values to be reflected in Europe's political order. If Europe's new political order is to achieve legitimacy, it must not only incorporate processes which command assent, but also express values that command support.

In order to initiate a discussion of these questions, this chapter centres on the different ways in which the purpose of a constitution can be defined and the two different approaches that can be taken to constitutional construction. However, before doing so, it considers the starting point of the constitutional quest itself.

The divisions of opinion over a possible new order for Europe are not simply about different views as to what form that new order should take. There is also a body of opinion that the search to design a new order is a mistake. Throughout Europe the old political order built around the nation state is under stress. Nevertheless there is a body of both conservative and liberal theory that warns strongly against any attempt to design a new order. This view – that the search to give a constitutional shape to a new political order for Europe is a mistaken quest – must first be considered.

II A mistaken quest?

The warnings against the attempt to design a constitutional order in Europe are sometimes simply dismissed as nostalgia for the nation state. They are discredited too by the remnants of an ideological nationalism.[1] It would however be a mistake to brush the cautions aside on these grounds. The warnings have nothing to do with nostalgia and still less to do with extreme nationalism. They are a warning against the dangers of approaching the task of building European political union in the wrong way. The warnings come from within both the conservative and the liberal tradition in Europe. According to the one, the attempt to put in place a constitutional structure for Europe is a fallacy of 'rationalism'. According to the other, the mistake is one of 'constructivism'.

(i) A rationalist fallacy?

The raison d'être of conservatism is to preserve. However, the conservative objection to the building of a new political order in Europe is not based simply on a desire to preserve the existing political order built around the institutions of the nation state. The root objection stems from a view about the source of our knowledge of the social and political order.

(a) Knowledge and the constitutional order The conservative view is that our knowledge of the political order is acquired knowledge.[2] It accumulates over time through a myriad of social interactions, through trial and error and through the pursuit of small scale practical improvements or the attempt to eliminate practical inconveniences in relationships. The knowledge is imparted by experience and not by appeal to abstract principle. The social order that emerges is a product of experience and circumstance, not of deliberate design. Conserving the existing order is both a way of preserving this acquired knowledge and a way of transmitting it.

According to this view, constitutions themselves are to be regarded with suspicion. The codification of procedures, rights and institutions is justified only as the entrenchment of existing practices and forms that have proved their worth. Entrenchment itself has dangers. It can lead to rigidities which impede the further peaceful evolution of society.

From this view about the nature of our knowledge of the social order there flows the deepest suspicion about attempts to design any social and political order. It is a fallacy of 'rationalism' to suppose that a political order can be designed.

Attempts to construct a new constitutional order in Europe fall under these same suspicions. A European constitution too must suffer from the inherent defects of conscious design. It will be based on imperfect knowledge and on an appeal to abstract principle. The attempt puts at risk the evolution of a pragmatic step by step approach to a new political order in Europe.[3]

The conservative caution about the perils of 'rationalism' can be accepted without necessarily drawing the conclusion that an attempt to define a new political order in Europe commits the rationalist fallacy. The weakness in the conservative case against an attempt to give constitutional form to a new European order lies in the incompleteness of the conservative view of change.

(b) Change under conservatism The conservative approach to constitutional order must include an account of when and how change is to take place. If it cannot provide a mechanism for change then it becomes simply a defence of the existing order – 'whatever is, is best'. Even if particular circumstances were to warrant such an assertion, it would remain only an assertion. There would be no means of resolving counter assertions. Once the possibility of change is acknowledged, the conservative tradition faces the need to distinguish between 'good' change and 'bad' change.

Two criteria are typically advanced. First, the need to show that the relative performance of the existing order is faltering and second, the need to show that change corresponds to the permanent interests of the society.[4]

The effect of such criteria is to move opposition to a new European order away from perceptions about the fallacies of 'rationalism'. The criteria for change transform the question. The question for conservatives becomes whether a new order in Europe might indeed be warranted by the falterings of the old order built around the nation state. Thinking in terms of a new order might equally be justified by consideration of the permanent interests of the members of the existing political and civil societies.

The case for a constitutional order in Europe is precisely that the habits of a civil society, conceived so far within the structure of the nation state in Europe, can now be conceived within a much wider European association. Existing national institutions are not performing well and are under challenge throughout Europe. It can indeed be argued to be in the permanent interests of the peoples of the individual nation states to develop the possibility of a new political order.

The conservative tradition must face not only the question of when change might be justified but also how it is to take place. Because of the weight given to acquired knowledge, conservative criteria stress the significance of the embedded inheritance of knowledge and the importance of gradual change based on clearly identified defects. Measured against such criteria, the shortcomings of the individual nation state as the basis for political association are indeed increasingly evident. Thus, the conservative case against a constitution is reduced in the end to an argument about whether thinking in terms of a constitution for Europe provides the right way of moving towards a new order.

The conservative reservation is that constitution making places too much reliance on theory and abstract principle. Yet, the existing treaty base already is beginning to act as a surrogate constitution for Europe. In considering whether it is appropriate as the basis for the new political order in Europe, or whether it should be amended or changed, it is very difficult for the conservative tradition to avoid any reliance whatsoever on abstract principle.[5] It is possible to give great weight to what actually exists. But in considering change, it is difficult to have a view that rests entirely on past experience and does not turn, in one way or another, to more abstract considerations. Pragmatism is often a delusion.[6] Moreover, since those who argue in favour of a new European order deploy theoretical arguments, or carry theoretical assumptions into the debate, conservatives must themselves be ready to argue on theoretical grounds.

(ii) A constructivist mistake?

The conservative view that there is a civil order that emerges as the product of unplanned social interaction and which can be distinguished from a consciously designed product is shared by some recent proponents of the classical liberal tradition.[7] Since such liberals regard themselves as part of a rational tradition, they have preferred to label the mistake of constitutional design a 'constructivist' mistake rather than a mistake of rationalism. The basic objection remains the same. The civil order is not amenable to planned design. It follows that constitutions fall under the same suspicion. They are seen to embody belief in a designed order.

(a) Knowledge in the social order This strand in liberal thought is also based on a perception about knowledge and the social order. It claims that the knowledge available to a designer is always deficient. The designer can only make use of centralized knowledge. Knowledge, on the other hand, is spread throughout society. What emerges from countless individual decision makers who act on the best information available to them is going to surpass design based on the crude approximations of knowledge gathered at the centre.[8]

According to this view, not only is the knowledge available to the individual actor in society superior to that of a centralized designer but, in addition, the incentives to act for the individual on the information available are much more direct. Thus a designed order is always going to be less robust than the 'spontaneous' order.[9]

This liberal objection to the design of a new constitutional order in Europe is similar to the conservative objection in that both are based on a view about knowledge. Equally, however, this particular view from within the liberal tradition is also vulnerable to criticism about its account of change.

(b) Change Evolution plays an important role in both the conservative and liberal account of change and distrust of the designed order. The conservative emphasizes evolution because it embodies past knowledge. The liberal values evolution because it reflects the workings of the spontaneous order.

Beyond this common point of departure, at first sight the liberal has less difficulty than the conservative in the account of change. The spontaneous order is not a static concept. On the contrary, one of the assumed strengths of the spontaneous order is its superior adaptability. However, the liberal is placed in the position of defending an existing order because the spontaneous order is embodied in the inherited order. Rules of conduct that have survived have proved their worth through their survival. The more efficient will have prevailed over the others.[10]

One pragmatic difficulty with a reliance on the superiority of the spontaneous order is its very passivity. A belief in the shortcomings in knowledge available to any designer, combined with the assumed inherent superior strength of the spontaneous order, makes it appear irrational to engage in debate about the design of any political order. Any attempt at design is not only misguided but will inevitably fail. Such passivity watches on the sidelines as possibly highly undesirable changes take place in the political order.[11]

A second pragmatic difficulty arises from the possibility of conflict or interference between a designed order and the spontaneous order. One possible position to take in the face of such a conflict is the view that over the long run the spontaneous order will always prevail, precisely because it captures superior knowledge and has superior responsiveness. The difficulty with this position is that the long run may be very long indeed (as has been the misery associated with communism). Historians will no doubt debate for many decades to what extent Soviet communism collapsed because of its internal contradictions and to what extent the external resolve of the United States played a decisive part. All theories about the 'inevitability' of the collapse of different social orders have become rather tarnished.

More important than the pragmatic difficulties are the logical difficulties.

If the spontaneous order is held in some way to represent a superior order and its functioning is impeded by a designed order, then it is irrational not to wish to see change in the designed order. This in turn means that there has to be some view of changes that will bring the civil order as close as possible to the spontaneous order.[12]

Once the possibility of change is acknowledged, it becomes very difficult to deny any place at all in the process of change to conscious design. It is more in keeping with historical processes to see design and principle as one component of institutional change.[13]

If a place for design is admitted in the process of change then the question becomes one of defining its role. Here the liberal is in difficulties similar to that of the conservative. The emphasis is on evolutionary change. Yet design has to be accommodated.[14]

These difficulties make any further objection to a place for constitutional design depend on the adoption of a more extreme position. Either passivity can continue to be justified by denying a logical connection between holding a belief (in the superiority of the spontaneous order) and undertaking actions in support of that belief. Or, alternatively, the link between belief and action can be accepted but the rationality of action can be denied.[15]

(c) The spontaneous order   The difficulties for this strand of the liberal tradition in giving a logically consistent account of the role of design in the process of change stems from an ambiguity in the account of the 'spontaneous' order. Is the spontaneous order a hypothetical state – an abstraction – or does it purport to represent reality?

The practical robustness of the concept of the spontaneous order seems to be vindicated in the real world. Despite the efforts of the authorities, there are many cases where spontaneous forces overcome or circumvent governments. The collapse of communism, the spread of global markets despite, and in part stimulated by, government barriers, as well as the advances of modern communications technology, all provide the liberal account of the superiority of decentralized knowledge with a real world underpinning.

Nevertheless, if the spontaneous order is meant to reflect reality then it seems an incomplete account. It is difficult to present the real world order as simply the product of the unplanned interaction between individuals. The role of government has been far too pervasive in the history of society to be eliminated from any account of inherited reality. While much of the social framework may have evolved without conscious design it is difficult to ignore the role of ideas or the role of design in that part which reflects the impositions of government. The recognition that the spontaneous order rests in part on an imposed order (or a reaction to it) thus reintroduces the question of design.[16]

If, therefore, the concept of the spontaneous order represents a hypothetical state and not an account of reality, then its role is a different one. It stands together on a par with other accounts of hypothetical states of nature, such as those of Hobbes or Rousseau or Montesquieu, to illuminate some particular aspect of the social order. Abstract exemplars of this kind often possess enormous value as a way of making a point about the real world order.[17] If, however, the concept of the spontaneous order is employed as an abstraction, at best an account of only a particular aspect of reality, its role seems to be limited to that of cautioning against the pitfalls of design. This is far from a justification of passivity.

There is however one more fundamental objection to thinking in terms of a constitutional structure for Europe. This objection comes from the libertarian tradition.

(iii) The libertarian critique

The libertarian tradition also warns against constitutional design in Europe. The elaboration of this tradition has taken place mainly in the United States.[18] But its roots are in Europe.[19] Its essential message is about the validation of rules in a social order.

The libertarian perspective puts the spotlight on the inherently coercive nature of government. In contrast to anarchism it does not reject the need for rules in society. What it challenges is the need for government to define the rules or to provide the sanction behind the rules. It offers the alternative model of a social order where individuals are the providers of order. Its apparent kinship with anarchism arises because an order that is based on individual behaviour claims to be less intrusive than any form of collectively defined and imposed order.[20]

The libertarian view rests on strong assumptions about the superiority of individual choice in all circumstances. An individual that chooses, is always going to choose rationally because the reasons, whatever they are, will be rational for that individual. The only valid laws for human action are based on the individual actor.[21] Constitutions are likely to be inherently flawed because they rest on visions about society as a whole and assertions about universal values rather than on knowledge of the individual.[22] Constitutions assume that a civil order requires government and the state rather than exploring the possibility of a civil order based on the individual.[23]

If the view that there is an order that can be provided by individuals is accepted, then the pursuit of a collective order such as provided by a constitutional framework is unnecessary. Worse than that, the attempt to put in place such an order is an affront to liberty. It necessarily sanctions coercion over the individual.[24] The search for a European constitutional order is thus flawed from the start.

The libertarian case looks as though it can be quickly dismissed. It appears to defy the whole weight of human history. Order in society appears to require government in some form. The idea that individuals can be the providers of order appears to conflict with the need for rules to be known to all participants in the social order, to be stable rather than uncertain and to be uniformly applied.

There is however a different perspective. The libertarian reminds us of the distinction between the social order and the political order. The two are not the same. The political order must always be validated.

III Defining purpose

In the end, the various objections to the putting in place of a constitutional order for Europe are not compelling. Conservatives have to face the possibility, under their own criteria for change, that a broader form of civil association in Europe might correspond to the permanent interests of those who have hitherto found the advantages of civil association best expressed within the political order of the nation state. Liberals have to face the possibility that those spontaneous forces that are eroding the nation state may themselves be impeded by design in Europe unless they themselves participate in debate on that design. It is very difficult for conservatives to deny any place for abstract principle in the way that civil associations have evolved. It is equally difficult for liberals to deny any role for design in the way that a spontaneous order evolves. Thus in looking at the changes taking place in Europe it is legitimate to consider both a role for principle and design. Placing the new order in Europe within a constitutional context does not necessarily commit either a rationalist or a constructivist error.

The warnings about the dangers of constitutional design in creating a new political order in Europe do however serve an important role in focusing on the question of the purposes of constitutional design in Europe.

Constitutions are purposive documents. This is why they include action oriented provisions about institutions, procedures and, possibly, declarations of basic liberties. They are purposive also in a more fundamental sense. They express the underlying purpose of why the political association has been formed. Purpose, expressed in these various ways, aims to rationalize and legitimize the entire construction.

The ways in which constitutions express the overall rationale for the political order they describe can have important implications for the practical provisions they subsequently include. Many causes of disagreement about the practical aspects of a constitutional order stem from unrecognized differences in views about the way in which the overall purpose of the political order has been expressed. The debate about a constitutional framework for Europe must avoid a false start. Thus it is important to try to identify the different ways in which a constitution can convey the fundamental purpose of the political order it describes.

(i) Ways of expressing 'purpose'

There are three ways of expressing the purposes of a political order in a constitution.

One approach is to build the constitution around a declaration of the goals and intended outcomes of political association. If the goals and intended outcomes can be agreed, they thereby provide a rationale for the practical arrangements of the political order. They serve as a legitimizing device.

A second approach is to build the constitution around processes. The underlying purpose of the political order is to establish the ways in which people can come together, act together and sort out any differences together. Purpose can thus be expressed in rules of procedure or by statements of principle that provide a guide to procedures. These too can be seen as legitimizing the constitution.

A third way of expressing constitutional purpose is to look for a statement of the overarching values on which the political order is based. If these values can be agreed then again they give guidance to the subsequent practical content of the constitution and they too serve to validate its overall content.

These different ways in which the overall purpose of a political order can be expressed in a constitution are not necessarily in conflict. Typically, examples of each may be found in the opening provisions of a constitution.[25] Statements of overarching values can be related either to goals or to processes. If the goal is an ethically 'good' goal it can be seen as helping to validate the order. If the processes of working together in the political order are consistent with the ethically good, they provide a different route to validating the constitutional construction. Moreover, processes must not consist of empty formalities. The quality of the processes and their results are both important.

(ii) Conflicts over purpose

However, these different ways of expressing purpose can also be in conflict. From this conflict, subsequent difficulties can arise about the practical content of the constitutional order. Even more important is that if there is conflict over the expression of constitutional purpose, then the role of a constitution in validating and legitimizing a political order is undermined.

The warnings from within the conservative and liberal tradition about the perils of constitutional design are important because they identify the sources of conflict. The warnings essentially emphasize the fundamental importance of process in a political order – the way in which things are done. They point to the potential conflict between trying to focus on goals and outcomes at the expense of processes. They also point to the potential conflict between statements of overarching values and processes. This potential conflict arises when the values are tied to the ends to be achieved and can be used to override processes.

One reason why these warnings may not be sufficiently heeded has already been mentioned – the concept of the spontaneous order gives only a part characterization of reality. Its promise of superior outcomes lacks total conviction in the real world.[26] So too does the appeal to rely on the virtues of evolution. A second reason arises from the treatment of the ethical.[27] It is not possible to equate the ethical with what has evolved. A reliance on spontaneous forces appears to leave out entirely the ethical. The relationship between processes and values needs to be clear.

The role of values in a constitution and their relationship to processes will be discussed in more detail in a later chapter. The discussion which follows takes up the contrast and potential conflict between viewing constitutional purpose primarily in terms of outcomes as compared with putting the emphasis on processes.

IV   Two approaches to constitutional order

Disagreements about how to express the fundamental purposes of a constitution, or a new political order, stem from two very different perceptions about where to place the emphasis in the building of a constitutional order. One approach stresses the importance of prior agreement on specifying the goals and intended outcomes of the constitution. By contrast, the other approach puts the stress on constitutional process.

Common to both approaches is an attempt to provide a solid base for a political order. Each aims:

- to define the interests of the participants in the political order;
- to establish an approach to the structure of constitutional arrangements;
- to provide measures of success and failure against which the performance of the arrangements can be judged and the need for change assessed;
- to pave the way for the legitimization of the political order.

The two different approaches give quite different answers to how this solid base is to be provided. The divergences reflect fundamentally different views of what is important in a constitution.

(i) The identification of interest

When constitutional arrangements emphasize the hoped for end results of union, the aim is to identify the common interest in the construction by defining common goals. If the proposed outcome of a constitution is clearly specified then participants can identify their own self-interest in the arrangement. The identification of interest is seen to be particularly important where the participant is relinquishing an independent power or agreeing to share power. Other things being equal, an individual or a nation state is likely to prefer independence. A reason needs to be given for sharing powers with others. This reason can be found through specifying the objectives and planned outcomes that participants can identify with.

By contrast, when constitutions are viewed as centring on process rather than on outcomes, the common interest of participants is identified by the manner of working together. The sharing of powers becomes possible if all parties are agreed on how powers will be exercised and in what way they will be shared and divided. End results are important but they cannot be divorced from process. The identification of the interests of the participants has to extend not only to the hoped for realization of goals but also to how those goals are to be attained in common.

(ii) The approach to structure

The specification of outcomes in a constitution is seen to provide a basis for structure because institutions and powers can be measured against the proposed outcomes. The specification of outcomes helps achieve coherence between means and ends. Institutions and procedures must be consistent with meeting the intended aims. Some options can be excluded as incompatible. This appeal of defining intended objectives goes beyond the structuring of particular institutions or particular powers consistent with reaching the objectives. The specification of goals provides a basis for a unified theory of the constitutional construction. The parts can find their place within the greater whole. The intended goals serve as a coordinating mechanism.

By contrast, a focus on process may take into account the aspirations of the political order, but gives the central role to such qualities of political association as democratic participation, consensus and consent without which a political order is unlikely to endure. If processes are well founded it will be possible for the political order to accommodate to the changing goals of political association and to address specific goals as they arise. Such qualities may not lead to the most effective of political orders in terms of the quick attainment of goals. The political order would however have other more stable qualities.

(iii) Measuring performance

The setting of goals appears to offer a simple way of measuring the success or failure of constitutional arrangements and the adequacy of institutions, powers and procedures.

By contrast, the emphasis on process measures progress by the entrenchment of the methods and habits of association. The calculation of self-interest of participants in particular goals becomes less important than the acceptance of the merits of the rules of association including, for example, the acceptance of the rule of law.

(iv) Legitimization

The specification of planned outcomes is seen as a way of legitimizing the construction because the structure is 'good' when it aims to produce 'good' results. The securing of external boundaries, the attainment of social harmony or the pursuit of sustainable development, are all among the objectives that many would count as representing good ends. Constructions that have these good ends among their objectives are seen to gain legitimacy as a result.

By contrast, the emphasis on process argues that the values incorporated in the processes of a political order are the key values in a constitution. It is these which legitimize a system of government. If the attainment of outcomes alone – even 'good' outcomes – legitimizes a form of government, it could legitimize the benevolent despot or the enlightened elite. Even if a constitution were to achieve the outcomes it targets, the validation of a constitution involves more – it also involves the validation of procedures used to attain ends.[28]

V The superiority of process

(i) The appeal of defined goals

Despite the warnings about the importance of process, constitutional construction in Europe is most often seen in terms of a design to achieve specified outcomes. The attractiveness of this route appears to outweigh the reasons why civil and political association should be viewed in terms of process.

There are three apparently persuasive reasons why, despite the warnings, it seems attractive to view constitutions primarily as instruments to achieve defined outcomes. It has been the method used by the Economic Community in the past, it draws on an analogy with business behaviour, and it appeals also to analogy with the behaviour of individuals.

(a) The success of the past The first reason for looking at political union in Europe in terms of the specific goals to be achieved draws on the historical experience of the Economic Community. Historically, each of the successive treaties in the existing treaty base has been built around the attainment of specified desired objectives – the orderly build up of the postwar coal and steel industries; the construction of a common market and a common agricultural policy; the attainment of a single internal market; the goal of a single currency. The method of setting goals – even ambitious goals – has been the 'Community method' to date.

This approach of building a European union by the setting of increasingly ambitious objectives has appeared to work well in the past. The common objectives have served to identify the interests of the participating Member States and to help suppress national rivalries. The desirability of these objectives has been used to justify the arrangements in the treaties to public opinion in the Member States. It has helped to get the treaties accepted and thus helped to legitimize the arrangements.

Nevertheless, public reservations about the Maastricht Treaty raise questions as to whether this way of proceeding can be carried over successfully into the creation of a political order. In part, the difficulties of addressing political union can be expected. The sensitivities are quite different from those involved, for example, in production sharing in coal and steel. But in part, the difficulties may also stem from the overemphasis on setting goals and too little emphasis on the processes of getting there. There is a suspicion of setting goals of one sort (for example, for monetary union) for the purposes of reaching goals of another sort (political union). Moreover, the historical Community method involves a constant search for new public policy goals in order to achieve a different underlying purpose. For example, an increased stress on developing a common security and defence policy is seen, by some, as replacing economic goals, as a new means for driving forward the fundamental aim of political union. The danger is that suspicion of the ulterior motive may weaken what is otherwise a good public policy objective while further increasing suspicions about fundamental aims. The case for looking at processes is thus not merely of theoretical interest. It could be of crucial practical importance if European political union is to move ahead with popular support.

(b) Political association as enterprise A second reason for the appeal of looking at political union in terms of goals is through the analogy with business behaviour. Corporations draw up plans and targets as a way to organize, rationalize and explain their activities. Political union can be seen as analogous on a grand scale with corporate enterprise and benefiting from the same methods.

The shortcoming of the analogy is that it overlooks the ways in which civil and political association differ from a corporate enterprise. The ties within society are not simply or even mainly those formed by the pursuit of common goals.[29] A robust political association must be able to mediate differences of opinion within society about political goals and survive despite such differences.[30]

(c) Individuals as planners A third reason which may underlie the potent appeal of specifying outcomes as the key to specifying the shape of a political order is through analogy with individual behaviour. Individuals set objectives and goals for themselves. Such behaviour reflects individuals as purposive in their choices and actions.[31] Plans connect present circumstances to future goals and help individuals to achieve coherence between the ends they pursue and the means to get there.[32] Goal setting for the political order can be viewed as a way to capture for society as a whole this aspect of human rationality.

The analogy is a powerful one. It serves as a reminder that the setting of goals and the drawing up of plans cannot automatically be identified with collective behaviour or with values that put the collective ahead of the individual. Nevertheless, like the analogy with the behaviour of business, it is a limited analogy. It captures only one aspect of individual behaviour.

(ii) The case for process

The persuasive appeal of looking at constitutions in the light of the ends to be attained is open to fundamental objections in addition to the reservations already made. The emphasis on ends cannot serve to legitimize the construction of a political order. It provides a false guide to structures. The measuring rod it offers for the performance of a political association is illusory. The solid basis it appears to provide for defining the interests of participants is a mirage.

The rock on which outcome oriented approaches to constitutional order founder is the rock of government failure. The prevalence of government failure means that if self-interest is identified with the outcomes of government, the constitution is inherently fragile. No system of government can guarantee outcomes. If the outcome is not attained the proposed basis for the association is necessarily weakened or destroyed.

(a) Defining the interest The idea that identifying the interests of the participants with the ends to be attained can provide a solid base for a constitution is the first idea to founder on the problem of government failure. Governments may set out with the best of objectives but their programmes frequently fail to accomplish their goals and sometimes have unintended and adverse consequences. At most, constitutions can express aspirations about desired outcomes.

The analogy with individuals as planning agents is the analogy of the language of intention. Such language is conditional and recognizes that goals may change if individuals change their preferences or acknowledge certain goals as beyond their reach.[33] Any goals expressed in a constitution must similarly be viewed in highly conditional terms.

The aspirations expressing the intended outcomes of a political order can be framed in general terms within the opening provisions of a constitution through references to objectives such as 'peace', 'happiness', 'prosperity', and 'independence'. Despite their generality they still perhaps can serve a purpose in generally identifying the aspirations of participants with the objectives of the association. But the interests of participants have to be identified with more than aspirations. The alternative approach is to try to define the common interest in terms of the ways in which people can work together successfully in political association. If there is agreement on how to work together, that agreement can rest in place and be consolidated even if the political goals of association change and even if aspirations are not always met.

(b) The approach to structure Looking at structure in terms of the end objectives to be achieved appears to provide a clear guide to structure. After the goals have been set, the institutions and their powers can be designed to meet those goals. Once however those intended outcomes are seen as aspirations, that might or might not be attainable, and as reflecting goals that might change over time, they can no longer give a clear or durable guide to structure. The connection is too loose. Stating the goals of a political order in the conditional and general language of aspirations is not merely a point about the logic of such statements. It means that there is no tight or lasting connection between statements of goals and the practical structures and arrangements to be set out in a constitution.

By contrast a focus on process leads to an emphasis on structuring the rules of political association. The rules leave fluid the outcomes to be attained. Rules about procedures provide a more stable basis for structure because the rules of association can remain constant even though political goals can change. When a political association does face common problems the habits of association may make the society adapt more successfully to meeting the problems. In addition, a rule based approach to political order avoids any predisposition to see government as the only solution to social problems or politics as the inevitable answer. Rules can be framed to recognize that the boundaries between what the market can do and what governments do well are also subject to change in the light of experience and innovation. Accordingly, institutions cannot be structured just as instruments to achieve goals. They must be structured instead to support the more lasting rules of association and be able to adjust to changing goals.

(c) Measuring performance The idea that if constitutions specify outcomes they provide thereby a measure of performance and success or failure is mistaken. On the contrary, if constitutions are specified in terms of outcomes, it becomes extremely difficult to acknowledge failure. Failure means the whole venture is thrown into doubt. So too are the institutions associated with the failed outcomes. The result of identifying the common interest and political structures with the attainment of specific goals is that the ensuing political order will always attempt to deny failure. This corrupts the core of government. It stifles one of the most important ways of attaining social progress – the willingness to acknowledge failure and make changes as a result.

The dynamics of failure are well illustrated in the history of the European Community by the Common Agricultural Policy (CAP). The objectives of attempting to maintain employment and income in rural and remote areas are objectives all governments can agree with in principle. The reality is that the policies adopted have been expensive failures. At least part of the reason for the difficulty in acknowledging the failure and trying alternatives, including measures within the Member States, is because this is perceived to weaken the European structure. Failures have to be denied because of the challenge they present to European institutions. Rather than attempt to validate the institutional framework on other grounds, it appears easier to deflect criticism of the CAP as criticism of the structure.

If policies fail then procedures can also be questioned – possibly deservedly so. But since the procedures have been formulated in the light of more general criteria such as the need to ensure participation or consent or to distribute powers, the failure of policies does not remove these other elements underpinning the rules. They can stand on other grounds or change if desired.

(d) Legitimization A focus on outcomes sees legitimization in terms of the desirability to society of the intended objectives. One objection to this view of legitimization arises simply from the variety of objectives that can be claimed on behalf of a political order.[34] They lose credibility because of their ubiquity. A second objection has already been mentioned – in reality, claims to achieve objectives can only be regarded as aspirations and with a certain measure of scepticism. Moreover, attempts to legitimize the state by stressing what the state can accomplish, diminish the value of civil association and the many ways in which individuals and non-state organizations can achieve social objectives.

The most fundamental objection to trying to legitimize a political order by appeal to the attainment of desires or even by an appeal to end objectives that are 'good', is that the normative or ethical component of legitimization is linked in some indissoluble way to conduct rather than to outcomes.[35] This view was expressed in Kant's belief that political systems have to be grounded in relation to the moral law rather than the pursuit of happiness or end states that are linked to happiness.[36] In this respect he followed Rousseau in connecting civil association with moral values.[37] Both looked for a regulatory principle that would establish the connection between the ethical qualities of civil association and the processes of the political order.

The implication of this tradition in political thought is that there is no short cut to the legitimization of a political order by an appeal to the 'good' ends it hopes to achieve. Not only can there be no assurance that such ends will be achieved, in addition, such claims miss the key element of a normative justification of a political order. Validation is not to be found in specifying desired outcomes but in looking to the link between the procedural qualities of the political order and the associative qualities of civil society.

(iii) The implications of an emphasis on process

The idea that constitutions can be approached by defining the intended outcomes of the political order appeared to promise a way to define the interest of all participants, a guide to the subsequent structuring of institutions, powers and procedures, a way of measuring performance and a help to legitimizing the political order. On closer inspection this proved to be a false promise. No system of government can guarantee outcomes. The intentions of a political order can at best be seen as aspirations. The connection is too loose to provide a durable guide to structure. An emphasis on outcomes instead of providing a measure of performance is more likely to lead to an attempt to conceal failure. An appeal to the intended ends of political association – even 'good' ends – cannot provide any shortcut to the legitimization of a political order.

This is not to say that the goals and intended outcomes of political association have no role to play in the shaping of a constitution and its institutions. They do. But they must be checked against the more important procedural elements in a political order. The more robust way for a European constitution to define the interest of participants in political association is through codifying the ways in which the political order will carry out its business. Goals may change. Procedural qualities such as consent will always be critical. Moreover, it is in these procedural qualities that a normative validation of a constitution is to be found.

The difference of emphasis between these two approaches is of more than simply theoretical interest. They lead to quite different ways of formulating the key components of a political order:

- When the emphasis is on outcomes, law becomes the instrument by which government can achieve its objectives. When the emphasis is on process, the focus is on the rule of law – government has to operate under the law.
- When the emphasis is on intended goals of association, key procedures tend to be seen in hierarchical terms since hierarchy appears the most simple way to disseminate pre-specified objectives. When the emphasis is on process, procedures have to be formulated to capture other qualities such as an accurate reflection of different preferences in society.
- When the emphasis is on outcomes, institutions are seen simply as instruments to attain ends rather than as wielders of powers that must be placed in a framework consistent with processes.

A constitutional approach that stresses the primary importance of processes rests on the concept of a rule based political order. The constitution sets out the leading principles that should guide the formulation of procedures, codifies the key procedures themselves and defines institutions and their powers in a manner consistent with the desired processes. The leading principles of a rule based approach to political order are discussed next.

Notes

1   See Minogue, K.R. (1967), *Nationalism*, for a brief description of the varieties of nationalism. Ideological nationalism can be defined as the belief that the nation is the ultimate unit of political organization to which all societies tend (a belief usually sustained by

the cultivation of various national myths).

2   The criticism of constitutional design as a 'rationalist' error is associated with Michael Oakeshott whose views are drawn upon in this section. See Oakeshott, M. (1975), *On Human Conduct*.

3   Burke crystallizes the conservative view about the importance of pragmatism. 'Circumstances. . . give in reality to every political principle its distinguishing colour, and discriminating effect. The circumstances are what render every civil and political scheme beneficial or noxious to mankind'. Burke, E. (1790), *Reflections on the Revolution in France*.

4   These are the two criteria advanced by Oakeshott, op. cit.

5   The difficulties of denying any role to abstract principle are well illustrated by Edmund Burke's account of the 1688 revolution in the United Kingdom. On the one hand he attempts to dismiss it as, 'a small and temporary deviation'; on the other hand he refers to the Declaration of Right as, 'the corner stone of our constitution'. Burke, op. cit.

6   The criticism made by J.S. Mill of trying to base all social knowledge on individual experience remains valid. 'It is impossible. . . that mankind in general should form all their opinions for themselves: an authority from which they mostly derive them may be rejected in theory, but it always exists in fact'. 'De Tocqueville on Democracy in America II', *Essays on Politics and Society*.

7   The critique of constitutional design as an error of 'constructivism' is associated with Hayek's criticism of socialist design. It is not a view inherent in the classical liberal tradition. J.S. Mill, for example, specifically attacked certain theories of his time that governments are not made but grow. 'Because governments, like other works of human contrivance, may be constructed with insufficient foresight and skill, does it follow that foresight and skill are utterly unavailing, and that no governments can hope for the support of the people's affections in times of civilization, but those produced by the fortuitous concourse of atoms in ages of barbarism? The doctrine is not only philosophically, but even historically false'. 'The Rationale of Representation', ibid.

8   Hayek acknowledged the similarity between his critique of constructivism and the conservative critique of rationalism in comparing his distinction between taxis (the man made order) and cosmos (the order independent of any human will) with the distinction made by Oakeshott between teleocracy and nomocracy. See the discussion in 'The Confusion of Language in Political Thought' in Hayek, F.A. (1978), *New Studies in Philosophy, Politics, Economics and the History of Ideas*.

9   'While the complexity of activities which can be ordered. . . is necessarily limited to what can be known to the organiser, there is no similar limit in a spontaneous order'. Hayek, ibid.

10 Hayek tried to distinguish this aspect of the liberal tradition from the conservative tradition by arguing that the liberal is not committed to defending all traditional values. Every single value can be questioned; but not all values at the same time. See Hayek, 'The Errors of Constructivism', ibid.

11 The German neo-liberals were particularly critical of passivity in the face of the rise of national socialism: 'This confidence in the inner silent forces seemed innocuous but, in reality, as later events demonstrated, it proved extremely dangerous'. Bohm, F., Eucken, W. and Grossmann-Doerth, H. in 'The Ordo Manifesto of 1936'. See Peacock, A. and Willgerodt, H. (eds) (1989), *Germany's Social Market Economy: Origins and Evolution*.

12 In his work on constitutional order, Professor Buchanan accepts that such a criterion is necessary. He offers the following criterion for constitutional change consistent with movement towards the spontaneous order. 'Alternative structures may be compared,

and evaluated, in terms of their abilities to facilitate the accomplishment of the separately determined individual objectives'. Buchanan, J.M. (1991), *The Economics and the Ethics of Constitutional Order*.

13 See for example Professor Berman's account of the origin of law as combining custom, authority and ideas. Berman, H.J. (1983), *Law and Revolution*.

14 Hayek defines the area for design as lying within a system of rules, not themselves the product of invention, and with the aim of improving an existing order. ('The Errors of Constructivism', op. cit.). This is ambiguous to say the least. If the effort to put in place a constitutional order for Europe is seen as 'improving an existing order' then clearly liberals of a Hayekian persuasion should be involved in the debate on the European order.

15 It may be considered irrational to act to participate in constitutional change because the individual actor may simply feel powerless. It is for this reason that Professor Buchanan introduces ethical considerations as a motivator of the individual: 'Each one of us, as a citizen, has an ethical obligation to enter directly and\or indirectly into an ongoing and continuing constitutional dialogue that is distinct from, but parallel to, the patterns of ordinary activity carried on within those rules that define the existing regime'. Buchanan, (1991), op. cit. For a more general discussion of the relationship between holding a belief and the commitment to act see Benn, Stanley I. (1988), *A Theory of Freedom*.

16 This is ultimately admitted by Hayek: 'A spontaneous order may rest in part on regularities which are not spontaneous but imposed'. Thus Hayek himself seems in the end to have to introduce a further distinction between the 'spontaneous' order and what he calls the 'existing factual order of society'. Hayek, 'The Confusion of Language in Political Thought', op. cit.

17 Milton Friedman defends these kinds of usually economic abstractions by distinguishing between 'descriptive accuracy' and 'analytic relevance'. 'Ideal types are not intended to be descriptive; they are designed to isolate the features that are crucial for a particular problem'. Friedman, M. (1953), 'The Methodology of Positive Economics' in *Essays in Positive Economics*.

18 Its main proponents are the followers of Ayn Rand and Murray Rothbard.

19 The link is with the individualism of Austrian economics – particularly with Ludwig von Mises.

20 'All of the services commonly thought to require the State. . . can be and have been supplied far more efficiently, and certainly more morally, by private persons'. Rothbard, M. (1982), *The Ethics of Liberty*.

21 'The assertion that there is irrational action is always rooted in an evaluation of a scale of values different from our own. . . If we do not wish to pass judgement on the ends and the scales of value of other people and to claim omniscience for ourselves, the statement, 'He acts irrationally,' is meaningless'. 'Action is, by definition, always rational'. von Mises, L. (1933), *Epistemological Problems of Economics*.

22 'We must start from the action of the individual because this is the only thing of which we can have direct cognition'. von Mises, ibid.

23 'The great non sequitur committed by defenders of the state. . . is to leap from the necessity of society to the necessity of the State'. Rothbard, op. cit.

24 'the crucial point is that in the Utopia of limited government and laisser-faire, there are no institutional mechanisms to keep the State limited'. Rothbard, op. cit.

25 See, for example, Articles 2, 3 and 4 of the Swiss constitution which refer to the aims, distribution of powers and individual values intended by the arrangements.

26 Having recognized that the spontaneous order is in part a reflection of the imposed order (a benchmark rather than a reflection of reality) Hayek justifies his choice of the spontaneous order because of its superior capture of knowledge and flexibilities, i.e.

superior outcomes.

27   The ethical is downplayed when the emphasis on process is justified exclusively in terms of the superiority of outcomes under an evolutionary regime or from the spontaneous order. Such arguments run the risk of confusing 'is' propositions from 'ought' propositions. They also run the risk of appealing to the same grounds for support as those who would prefer rule by an enlightened elite as a means to achieve superior outcomes. Hayek recognized both these traps. 'The success of rational striving. . . is largely due to the observance of values, whose role in our society ought to be clearly distinguished from that of deliberately pursued goals'. Hayek, 'The Errors of Constructivism', op. cit.

28   Both Rousseau and Kant looked to processes in order to establish the regulatory principle that connected the ethical qualities of civil association with the ethical legitimization of the political order:

'The formal condition under which nature can alone attain this its real end is the existence of a constitution so regulating the mutual relations of men that the abuse of freedom by individuals striving against one another is opposed by a lawful authority centred in a whole, called a civil community'. Kant I. (1790), *Critique of Teleological Judgement*.

For Rousseau the 'regulatory principle' was 'the general will'.

'The body politic,. . . is also a moral being possessed of a will; and this general will, which. . . is the source of the laws, constitutes for all members of the State, in their relations to one another and to it, the rule of what is just or unjust'. Rousseau J.J. (1762), 'A Discourse on Political Economy' in *The Social Contract and Discourses*.

29   Oakeshott, for example, draws a fundamental distinction between civil society and an 'enterprise association'. 'Civil relationship is to be identified as association in terms of moral considerations'. Oakeshott, op. cit.

30   Max Weber also distinguished between political association (*Anstalt*) and enterprise which he defined as rational activity of a specified kind.

31   A view of the individual as a 'project pursuer' is given in Lomanski, L.E. (1987), *Persons, Rights and the Moral Community*. Raz also characterizes the well being of individuals as a function of the individual as goal setter. Raz, J. (1986), *The Morality of Freedom*.

32   The concept of the individual as planning agent is explored by Bratman in the context of his investigation of the use of the language of intention as a device to signal consistency between means and ends. 'There is a strong pragmatic rationale for means-end-coherent plans: plans that are means-end incoherent are typically doomed to failure'. Bratman. J.E. (1987), *Intention, Plans and Practical Reason*.

33   For an account of the conditional language of intention see Bratman, ibid.

34   'It is not possible to define a political organization, including the state, in terms of the end to which its action is devoted. . . there is no conceivable end to which some political association has not at some time pursued. . . there is none which all have recognised'. Weber, M. *Economy and Society*, Roth, G. and Wittich, C. (eds) (1978).

35   This 'non instrumentalist' view of morality is expressed by Oakeshott. 'A morality may be defined as a practice without any extrinsic purpose; it is concerned with good and bad conduct, and not with performances in respect of their outcomes'. Oakeshott, M., op. cit.

36   'A state of being bound by a certain given end which I have preferred to all others of the same kind, is a comparatively better state in terms of happiness. . . but that state of consciously preferring the moral law of duty in cases where it conflicts with certain of my ends is not just a better state, but the only state which is good in itself'. 'On the Common Saying: This may be True in Theory, but it does not Apply in Practice' in *Kant's Political Writings*, (ed) Reiss H.

37 'In all social contracts, we find a union of many individuals for some common end which they all share. But a union as an end in itself which they all ought to share. . . is only found in a society in so far as it constitutes a civil state'. Kant, ibid.

2 Rules

'Civil Societies are not meer Meetings, but Bonds, to the making whereof, Faith and Compacts are necessary'. Thomas Hobbes, *De Cive*, 1651.

I Process and rules

The central focus of constitutions that emphasize the processes of political association is on rules. Rules provide the framework for processes. They define what is correct process. They attempt to define the powers and roles of institutions in a manner consistent with the desired processes. They try to identify the likely sources of challenge to the rules and to protect processes from such challenge. Hence, a constitution for Europe that emphasizes process should be seen and framed as a rule based constitution.

There are two central pillars of a rule based approach to the political order. One is the concept of 'the rule of law'. The other central element is the market order. They play a central role because they provide the setting for many of the more detailed rules relating to particular aspects of the system. While some of the more detailed rules may fail without bringing down the concept of a rule based order, the rule of law and a properly defined market order are core elements. Their failure, or their erosion over time, can lead a rules based political order to fail. They provide standards against which many other rules can be judged.

The idea that Europe's governance should be seen as a rule based system lies uneasily with the traditions of many Member States. Its application gives a much more prominent place to the written constitutional framework and to the judiciary than is the practice in a number of countries. Its emphasis on the need for a clearly defined market order is a challenge to the unfettered discretionary powers to intervene in markets and society that governments like to exercise. An emphasis on the way that powers can be distributed territorially, or in other ways, among different jurisdictions, is also a challenge to those Member States that have centralized practices of government or, that have difficulties in their own regional articulation. Its application is also in contradiction to the uniquely British notion of the sovereignty of parliament, where parliament is the source of law. More generally it is a challenge to all those countries in Europe that have, in practice, seen law as the servant of government rather than government obliged to operate under the law.

The challenge to a rule based concept of government comes historically from two sources – from rulers (those governments that incline to disregard processes) and from ideology (values that are held to override process). There is no government in Europe that has not succumbed to these temptations in this century. It is to Europe's credit that the concept of rule based government has a long history. It is to Europe's discredit that the theory has been so disregarded in practice. The actual practice of rule based government in Europe has shallow roots.

The constitutional challenge for Europe is both to define correct government processes in the new European order and to protect them against the inevitable challenges. Communism has collapsed but ideology has not vanished. Personal dictatorship has gone but elitism is strongly entrenched. The advantages of a market order are widely accepted but the temptation to turn to the state as the remedy of all ills in society remains strong.

The organization of the discussion

This chapter discusses the leading features of a rule based political order, the areas and sources of dispute and opens the discussion of how the rules of a political order can be justified.

First, the central elements of the rule based approach are discussed with a particular focus on the rule of law and the rules of the market order.

Second, there is a discussion of the disputed aspects of these central elements. The main area of dispute in the concept of the rule of law concerns the relationship between the rule of law and government as the source of law. The main area of dispute in relation to the market order is how to express the social dimension of the market order. Cutting across both the central elements of the rule of law and the market order is a third source of dispute – the question of whether to recognize private power as well as public power as representing a possible source of distortion to a rule based political order.

Third, the analysis identifies different views about the legitimization of rules as a common feature of disputes about the content of rules. Divergent accounts of the relationship between rules and values emerge as a key reason why differences arise over the right rules for Europe.

This leads, fourthly, to a summary of the different approaches that can be taken to justify the procedures of a rule based political order. The chapter discusses in particular the view that the justification lies 'in the process' and does not require an appeal to 'outside' values. Finally, the chapter discusses why the justification of the rules requires an appeal to outside values. The view that justification is to be found 'in the process' is flawed because of its reliance on the concept of 'utility' and because it cannot capture the sense in which the rules of a political order are rules of 'constraint'.

II The central components

The concept of a rule based political order is wider than that of rules established and enforceable by law. Not all rules in a rule based system depend on the law. The law itself finds its place within a broader system of rules. The idea of a rule based order is also wider than that of the market order. The market order deals with only part of a rule based order. Not all preferences can be settled through the market. Nevertheless, these two elements have a central role.

(i) The rule of law

Law plays a central role in a rule based system of government for four reasons. It is the means through which much that is abstract about social relationships is made concrete. It conveys the crucial notion that government itself must operate within the law. It provides an alternative channel to politics for the redress of grievances against government. Its procedural criteria have a wider relevance for the qualities sought in the rules of the political order.

(a) *Tangibility* Law provides an essential underpinning of a rule based constitution because law helps translate abstract freedoms into tangible freedoms. Habits and convention play an important part in defining relationships in society, but the rule of law adds the crucial element of enforceability. Law establishes the institutional setting within which exchange takes place within society.[1] It defines the scope for market exchange by, for example, crystallizing the rights of individuals to negotiate and enforce contracts and the rights of ownership.[2] In addition, by defining the procedural standards to which government must adhere, it also helps condition political exchange. As a social mechanism, important both in market processes and political processes, it is a crucial unifying force in a rule based system.

(b) *Government under the law* Central to the idea of a rule based constitution is that the government too should be seen as operating within the law. The idea that government should operate within or under the law is reflected in constitutional terms, in part, in the idea of the independence of the judiciary. The early conception that the execution of the law and the administration of justice could be seen as part of the executive functions of government gave way to the view that the judiciary should be seen as independent. The judiciary must not be a tool of government.[3]

Concurrent with this view of government under the law is a rejection of the view that authority in a political order necessarily has to be viewed in terms of a search for the sovereign power. Instead, a rule based system sees power as being able to be distributed between different branches of government, territorially or otherwise segmented, while law can be seen as having an independent or coordinate authority with that of the political order.[4]

(c) Law as a channel for grievance Law is crucial to a rule based constitution for a third reason – it not only provides a means of holding government in check, it also provides an alternative to action through politics for the settling of grievances in society. A rule based system of government does not view politics as the only means by which preferences can be expressed in society. The market provides an alternative. So too does the law. Like the market, but unlike the collective processes of politics, the law can be instigated by individuals and small associations and does not require the mass mobilization of opinion. It is thus a particularly crucial channel in any large political association where individual actors may often feel powerless. The larger the political association the more litigious it is likely to be.

(d) Procedural standards Law is central to the idea of a rule based constitution in a final sense through the procedural standards it sets. The rule of law conveys such procedural values as predictability, consistency, reliability, the absence of arbitrariness, as well as the sense of equality before the law.

These are all desirable attributes of a rule based system in the wider context of the political order. At its best, the law aspires to reflect procedures that are rational, fair and accessible. The rules of the political order too must reflect such values.

The idea of procedural standards, combined with the idea of power exercised under the rules, applies in a rule based system to electoral politics. Procedural standards insist on the importance of participatory democracy. Government must rest on consent. The people must be free of arbitrary government. In a fundamental sense, sovereignty, if it can be said to reside anywhere in society, rests in the final analysis with the people. But electoral politics too must also operate within a system of rules. While consent is a necessary condition for a free society it is not a sufficient condition. Popular opinion may wish to disregard the constraints that are set upon government and disregard the concept of government under the law. The procedural context places democratic participation within a broader setting of rules and not as a political force to operate outside the rules.

(e) Rules and legal systems Discussion of the relationship between a rule based constitution and the rule of law are confused by two factors. One is that the concept of a rule based political order is wider than the concept of a legal system. The rules establish the basic limits and conditions of political association. While government is seen as having to operate under the law in the sense of 'within' the law, the legal

order is not seen as being elevated to a position that is itself outside any limits. In the rule based view of constitutions, all powers (including those of judicial bodies) need to be defined and placed within a broader system of conventions, rules, checks and balances. The concept of rule based government is that all power, wherever it is exercised in society, including when it is exercised by a judicial body, should be exercised within the rules. A constitution is a vehicle for expressing these 'meta' rules.

The second factor that confuses the discussion of the relationship between a rule based system of government and the concept of the rule of law is that government is itself often the source of law. Moreover, particular legal systems may operate as an arm of government rather than to enforce the rule of law. These distinctions were recognized at an early point in the German *Rechtsstaat* tradition. It is a tradition that remains relevant for Europe today.

(f) The Rechtsstaat tradition The *Rechtsstaat* tradition in nineteenth century Germany combined the idea of procedural safeguards together with the idea of judicial independence, to insist that all exercise of the administrative power of government over the person or property of the citizen should be made subject to judicial review. Together with constitutionally imposed limitations on government, it aimed to make sure that government was brought firmly under the law.[5]

The two concepts of *Rechtsstaat* and *Staatsrecht* illustrate the different sides of the rule of law – that the authority of law makes freedoms tangible but that governments are often the source of law. There is an inherent tension between these two aspects that the earlier classical economists of the market order had failed to resolve.[6]

The *Rechtsstaat* tradition remains relevant in Europe in part because its particular target was bureaucratic government.[7] But it remains relevant for another more important historical reason – the concept of government under the law was subverted, in Germany and elsewhere, by a succession of political leaders, to the view of law as the instrument of government.[8] The warning remains to be heeded.[9]

(ii) The market order

In a rule based political order, the market is seen as performing a constitutional function, as well as being seen as a mechanism for economic exchange. Because the market enables individuals to realize their own preferences without interference by government in their choices, the market provides a check on government. It provides a means of dispersing power in society. It establishes a permanent test of the claims of government to act in the public interest.

If the market is viewed in this way then it is important for the constitution to entrench market rules and those elements needed for the market order such as the right to private property. Constitutional references to the market order define the relationship between the market order and the political order and have a crucial impact on each.

(iii) Relationships

In a rule based system of government, law and the market have to be seen together as interactive systems. The law sets the terms on which the market operates. However, the market can operate outside the formal law as a 'black' market. It may perform a socially and politically important function in so doing. But the qualities provided by law – the enforceability of contracts and the definition of property rights are also needed in a black market. A black market is accompanied by a parallel system of unofficial law enforcement. The suppression of a recognized market order will lead not only to a parallel market but to a parallel law. In civil or in uncivil society, law and the market go together.

The interdependence of the market order and the concept of the rule of law can be illustrated in a different way. If the government takes over the market, in whole or in part, the allocation of resources in society takes place through political processes and is reflected in administrative decisions. A whole additional range of transactions become part of the political process and administrative machine. Since there will be that much more power vested in the political order and since the law will be called upon to enforce administrative decisions (where they can be enforced) it is correspondingly likely that the law itself will become simply the instrument of government. The concept of government under the law thus gets subverted. Thus, again, the rule of law and the rules of the market order go hand in hand. In Europe there is now little serious opposition to a market oriented economy. There are however differences in how to express the market order. The idea of law as the instrument of government also lives on. There are also different ideas about participatory standards. These areas of disagreement are outlined next.

III Disagreements on the central elements

There is disagreement within Europe about how to express each of the two central aspects of a rule based constitution. Unless agreement can be reached, the search for a constitutional base for European political union that will provide for a participatory form of government operating under the rules, may be in vain. The areas of fundamental dispute concern both how to specify the role of law in a European political union and how to express the market order.

(i) The law as the instrument of government

Historically in Europe there has been a strong opposition in practice to the idea that government must itself operate within the rules. In the real world this is because governments do not like to live up to the procedural standards expected of them.

There is also a more theoretical reason alluded to earlier. If the political order and the constitution is viewed as a goal oriented means to an end, then it becomes all too easy to see law mainly as an 'instrument' to achieve these ends. Law as the instrument of government has its origin in viewing the political order as about achieving outcomes.

Unfortunately, the view of law as an 'instrument' remains alive in the context of the development of the European Union. Community law is often seen (and practised) as one of the instruments to achieve European integration. In practice, ensuring the uniform application of Community law in the areas in which it applies does have an integrating effect. However, the role of European law has to find its place in the broader system of rules, including those rules which specify the scope for Union jurisdiction. If the rules intended to define Union authority are interpreted to extend the scope of jurisdiction, then European law risks being viewed as the servant of higher political purposes or as the servant of other branches of a European system of government. The concept of *Rechtsstaat* risks becoming undermined by *Staatsrecht*.

(ii) The social market

The dominant concept of the market order in Europe is that of the social market. It suggests that while the market should be accepted as the least inefficient way of wealth creation in society, its shortcomings should also be recognized. The role of government is to adjust for these shortcomings. The government cannot be indifferent to the rules of exchange.[10] Neither can it be indifferent to the social outcomes of exchange. The willingness of the government to act as the 'adjuster' makes the rules of the market order acceptable to all.

The key question is how to recognize this role of the government as market 'adjuster' together with a clear definition of the relationship of the market order to the political order.

The perceived need to recognize the shortcomings of the market can be framed in two fundamentally different ways.

In the first, the role of government as adjuster is through the provision of compensation for those who cannot flourish in a market system. It places an emphasis on the role of government in providing income support for those who cannot manage.

The emphasis of the second approach is quite different. It suggests that governments should play the role of adjuster by being prepared to modify market rules wherever they are associated with economic or social distress.

(a) Rule Changes The rule modification approach to the social market involves being prepared to modify the rules of the market order whenever their operation appears to lead to social distress or hardship. In order to head off undesired outcomes, market rules can be changed. For example, price and wage signals can be modified by price support schemes or by subsidies. It involves the carrying out of state investments that would not meet the investment criteria of private investors or private lenders. It involves administrative and regulatory restrictions on choice rather than allowing for individual choice, and involves rationing rather than market clearing.

From the perspective of a rule based constitution, the rule modification interpretation of the social market is a damaging one. The rationale against modifying market rules does not rest simply or even mainly on the weakening of wealth creation in society, important and corrosive though this effect may be. More important are the implications arising from the weakening of the rules based approach. The rule modification approach:

- removes the external test on government to prove its claims that its interventions actually provide benefits;
- removes any independent measure of government failure;
- reintroduces uncertainty into the market framework which rules are meant to cure;
- introduces conflict between the rules in the market place;

To the extent that rule modification involves a pre-set idea about desired patterns of distribution it can be used to justify continual interference in the rules and thus continuous instability.[11]

(b) Compensation The compensation principle recognizes that markets can produce great inequities and that there are those who cannot thrive in the market place. It suggests that there should be a sharing of both the benefits and the burdens of a market economy. The benefits of the market can be attained through leaving intact the rules of individual exchange and contractual autonomy. The burdens of the market can be recognized by a collective acceptance of income redistributive schemes financed through the tax system. This is the role of government.[12]

The compensation interpretation of the social market concept has been attacked by some liberals. It is difficult to demarcate where compensation should stop. Resources have to come from somewhere and this gives free licence to the coercive power of government to tax and dampen income incentives. Redistributive policies may trigger divisions in society rather than healing them and will spark a race between interest groups to capture the redistributive mechanism. It sets up dependency relations in society. It tends to assume that government is benign.[13]

These various objections to the compensation principle suggest the dangers inherent in it. Nevertheless it is important to distinguish between effects of the compensation principle and the principle itself. The compensation principle is a limited one.[14] It is a function that can be exercised mainly through income support and the tax system without interfering with other aspects of the market. Neither does it necessarily assume that the government has to be the provider of goods and services through a large public sector. Moreover, there are other checks and balances that can be provided in the constitution to set a limit on the government as compensator. Monetary rules can remove its power to print money. Fiscal rules can limit its powers to tax and spend. Constitutional provisions on the distribution of powers can help ensure that decisions on income support are taken close to those who may need it.

In a rule based system therefore, the emphasis in defining the market order is on the role of government as a compensator, rather than as a rule modifier. The concept of the social market is thus not necessarily in conflict with a rules based order. It can achieve a clear definition of the relationship between the rules of the market and the role of government in viewing the government as the 'adjuster' of the market through the compensation approach.

(iii) Private and public power

Cutting across disagreements about how to express the social dimension of the market and how to express the relationship between the legal and the political order, is a third area of disagreement about the central rules of a rule based political order. The disagreement turns on the question as to whether, and to what extent, a rule based constitution should see the private accumulation of power in society as a threat to a rule based system. Is it simply the accumulation of power in the public sector that is a threat? The debate can be seen as about how to frame participatory standards in a rule based system. The market order, even with the government playing the role of 'compensator', can be viewed as likely to upset the procedural requirements of fair participatory standards.

The German neo-liberal tradition fully accepted the need to be concerned by the tendency of private power to accumulate. Private monopolies were not only undesirable in themselves but provided a platform for the capture of the legislative role of government. The market became a system of state capitalism rather than free enterprise. Accordingly, neo-liberals have stressed the need for constitutional rules to adopt an integrated approach to private and public power.[15] It is a view that is not exclusive to Europe.[16]

Historically, Europe has approached the question of the private accumulation of power in two ways – as a problem to be handled through social partnership and corporatism or to be kept in check by an insistence on strong competition laws adjudicated by a body independent of government.

(*a*) *Corporatism* The debate on corporatism was revived in the last century in Europe, partly as an indulgence in nostalgia for medievalism looking back to the days of guilds, and partly as a reaction to the perceived powers of owners of capital.[17] In its modern manifestation in European institutions, it shows itself in such bodies as the Economic and Social Committee of the European Community (ECOSOC) and in the view that all measures of economic and social legislation should be framed in consultation with the 'social partners'.

Corporatism rests on three assumptions:

- each profession or sectoral interest should have a body representing its interests;
- these associations should have a say in influencing economic and social policy;
- such functional representation should have a part in government.

The benign aspect of this tradition is its recognition of the importance of the many intermediate associations in society.[18] Such interest groups can be an expression of voluntary association and cooperation; can stand for an expression not only of economic interests in society but for values; can provide a means for self-help; can be important advocates for minority interests and can stand up for the disadvantaged or the inarticulate. In a modern democratic society, where individuals and groups often feel remote from being able to influence the decisions of government that affect them, the role of intermediate associations is vitally important.[19]

There is however another side. Such groups can operate at the expense of those excluded and to protect particular interests and it is often difficult to assess the claims of such groups to be representative. Giving them formal recognition may freeze the ability of society to adapt to change. The establishment of dependency relationships will, over the long run, make them clients of government or government the client of interests rather than true intermediaries.[20] The focus of their advocacy tends to encourage more government – in part because their access enables them to influence the shape of the government interventions.

The recognition of such interests in any formal way is not only unnecessary but it is likely to be damaging to society. It invites such interests to capture the power of government to legislate in their favour.[21] It ignores the fact that private power in the postwar period has drawn its support not from the market but from governments. The main threat to the market order in postwar Europe has not come through the accumulation of private power but from government intervention in the market. It has been state aids and state protection that have distorted the market's ability to restrain private power. Corporatism entrenches such distortions. Voluntary associations must retain their private identity.

(b) *Competition* According to the neo-liberal view, the correct approach to the accumulation of private power lies not through corporatism but through ensuring that markets remain competitive. As long as markets are contestable, private power will always be disputed and likely to be short lived. To the neo-liberal tradition, the key to the ensuring of competition and to breaking any connection between private and public power, lies through having independent authorities to ensure that competition prevails in the market and not through corporatism. In the same way that an independent judiciary is essential for the rule of law, an independent competition authority is seen as essential in overseeing the rules of competition.

Not all liberals believe that strong competition institutions are needed to keep private accumulations of power in check.[22] Some believe that the market alone leads to the rise and fall of private power. As long as markets are free and open, the growth of private power will always be subject to competition. As long as markets are contestable, no private interest will be able to exploit monopoly power without inviting new entrants attracted by the excess profits. The ultimate guarantor of the dispersion of power in the market is through free trade so that domestic participants can always be challenged. Free trade will make any government sponsorship of private enterprise increasingly onerous to the tax payer and increasingly open to challenge.

Nevertheless, the distinction made by the German neo-liberals between state capitalism and a rule based market order remains valid. Within Europe, state capitalism is not dead and the relationship between governments and private power is often too close. In the case of Italy, the connection brought a system of government to collapse. Within the European context, an independent competition authority will be an important and necessary part of the constitutional order.

IV   The origin of disputes

It could well be concluded from these differences that the whole idea of an agreed European approach to a rule based constitution is doomed in advance. Different views about the meaning of the rule of law, the content of the market order and over how to treat powerful interests in society, represent very fundamental differences.

Such differences however exist and are reflected already in Europe's surrogate constitution – the treaties. They need to be brought into the open if the political order is to have a more solid foundation. Unless such fundamental disagreements are cleared up, they will cripple attempts at building political union in Europe. Political failure will be deserved.

Underlying each of the areas of disagreement are questions about legitimization. The origin of theoretical disagreements over the basic rules in a European political union lies in different views about how to legitimize the key elements. An essential step in clarifying these underlying disputes is therefore to identify the arguments about legitimization.

(i) Corporatism and legitimacy

The rejection of the corporatist approach to private power is partly based on the existence of an alternative route, and a more accurately focused approach, to curbing private power through competition policy. The more fundamental objection to corporatism is that the proposed partners will inevitably lack legitimate standing. In a fast moving world there is no durable basis for selection. Both the government and the interests selected are likely to abuse the relationship. The participatory standards of a rule based regime are thus likely to be undermined.

(ii) The rule of law and legitimization

The idea of law as the instrument of government lives on not just because some of Europe's leaders in politics and the law, wittingly or unwittingly, adopt a naively 'instrumentalist' view of the role of European law as a means to achieve the political end of European integration. Closely connected with the view of law as a means to achieve ends is a false theory of legitimization – a legitimate political end is seen to help legitimize the law.

In addition, the legitimization of Europe's system of law is sometimes seen as identical to the legitimization of Europe's system of government. It is a connection made plausible, first, by the link between the authority of government and the enforcement of law and, second, by the legislative role of government as a source of law.

One such approach to the law is outlined in the next chapter – that of Kelsen. It is singled out because it remains apparently influential in some legal circles in Europe. In his approach, Kelsen attempted to develop a 'pure' theory where the explanation of legal concepts were to be found exclusively in the legal material itself. Kelsen shares with many other legal theorists a desire to separate legal concepts from natural law theories. However, by linking the 'basic norm' (from which all else in the legal system flowed) to the original constitution, Kelsen in fact linked the legitimization of the law to the legitimization of the political order. This too is a false connection.

(iii) The social market and legitimization

Underlying the different concepts of the social market are also divergent views about how to legitimize the rules of exchange in the market order.

(a) The entitlements approach One approach (an entitlements approach) attempts to justify a market order by pre-set concepts of fair starting points, or just outcomes, of a market order. Rules should be modified, if necessary, to adjust the starting points or to modify the outcomes, in order to fit these preconceptions. Not only does this lead to constant modification and thus defeat the purpose of a stable system of exchange, but it also involves having to justify these pre-set criteria.[23]

(b) Rules for oneself A second approach (that associated with Rawls) is that legitimate rules are those that would be chosen by individuals for themselves from a hypothetical starting point and in a state of ignorance of outcomes (behind a veil of ignorance). According to Rawls, such rules will incorporate a standard of fairness and social justice centred around the distance between the best off and the worst off (the difference principle).

This approach also opens the way to rules modification. Rules can be modified to try and head off the anticipated impact of the market on the worse off, in all those cases where we can anticipate where disadvantages are going to occur. In other cases, where we are in a state of ignorance of likely outcomes, we can still modify rules by introducing what is thought in the abstract to produce 'fair' results.

The force of this approach is in linking the concept of consent to rules to the fairness of the content of rules, and in trying to avoid fixed preconceptions about 'end states' by a concern for relative differences. However, it does not avoid the problem of bringing in views about what is 'fair' or what is 'right' distribution. These views about what is 'fair' in turn have to be justified. The Rawlsian approach, in common with the entitlements approach, is a recipe for constant interference with the rules of a market order.

(c) Contract as expectation and promise A third approach (that of some of the German neo-liberals) is that legitimization resides in the nature of contract in a system of voluntary exchange. A system of voluntary exchange is fair because of the expectation of mutual gain and satisfaction from the exchange.[24][25]

This neo-liberal view of the market rests on a theory of contract. The market framework is seen as a framework for the assignment of rights. These rights are encapsulated in contracts. It is of the essence of contract that there must be the possibility of reciprocal gains and that there is also a voluntary acceptance of the exchange. Sometimes the party to a contract will be disappointed by the actual outcome. It is not however the expectation at the time of entry into the contract.

In the case of the market, it is known in advance that the market will create losers as well as winners. The neo-liberals therefore faced the difficulty of how to justify rules of exchange when there would be a challenge to any general expectation of satisfaction. They saw compensation as the answer. Compensation did not mean attempts to eliminate income differentials. It did mean the government stepping in where people could not use market mechanisms to help themselves.[26]

The expectation theory of compensation is sometimes supplemented by a 'promise' theory. The suggestion is that a system of voluntary contract cannot be explained just by the expectation of satisfaction but essentially relies on trust backed by the moral force of 'promise'.[27] The compensation principle can thus be seen in terms of a promise of compensation for losers given in association with the acceptance of market rules. If rules are accepted by virtue of promises then those promises must be kept. Compensation must be paid.

(iv) Legitimization and values

There is a common element in these debates about the legitimization of the basic components of a rule based order. The common element is a debate about the relationship between the rules and values. There are three aspects of this debate. One is the question of which values are relevant (for example, corporatism affronts standards of participatory fairness). A second aspect is whether the values are in some way intrinsic to the rules or whether an appeal to outside standards of value are necessary (for example, Kelsen's entanglement of the legitimization of a system of law with the legitimization of the political order was the result of a search for a positive theory of law not based on outside values).[28] The third aspect is how the values, whether intrinsic to the rules or external to the rules, relate to ethical standards (for example, the 'promise' principle introduces moral obligation into compensation).

Thus, in order to start the process of building agreement on the central aspects of a constitutional order for Europe, the different approaches to the legitimization of rules need to be clarified. In particular the relationships of rules to values needs to be made explicit. The legitimization of the rules of a political order cannot avoid questions about the role of values in a constitution.

V Legitimizing the rules

Europe is in the unusual historical situation of being at the start of setting the rules for political union. It provides an opportunity for all the potential rules of the system to be examined. It inevitably brings in, explicitly or tacitly, different assumptions about what qualities legitimize a political order. It opens up a constitutional setting that is usually closed.[29]

(i) Is legitimization necessary? The acquis

While the current situation in Europe is, by historical standards, most unusual in representing the start of a new political order, there are still powerful voices who would wish to limit the debate. They are the voices not only of the old order – the nation state – they are also the voices of the existing institutions of the European Union that could lose their position in any thorough examination of constitutional principles.

The device to limit the scope of the debate rests on the concept of the *acquis*. The doctrine states that whatever exists in present arrangements for the distribution of authority in the European Union should be preserved. Powers and responsibilities can be added but not taken away.

The doctrine of the *acquis* can be rested on three different grounds. One is that it represents contracts (treaties) freely entered into by the contracting parties which thus provide a legitimate base for political union. This argument however overlooks the fundamental transition from arrangements for a part of Europe to arrangements for Europe as a whole, as well as the transition from arrangements mainly concerned with economic integration to arrangements whose primary focus will be on political union.

The second basis for preserving the *acquis* is simply to protect what has already evolved. This appeals to the important place that evolution holds in both conservative and liberal thinking. The difficulty is simply that one cannot move from a statement about what has evolved, to a value judgement that what has evolved is good. The statement that 'what has evolved is good' needs justification.

The third possible basis for justifying the *acquis* as the starting point is that what has been put in place has proved its worth by the history of integration that it has fostered. It is equivalent to an argument that the present arrangements have demonstrated their utility and that this validates their continuance. This assumes that what has been of utility in the past will go on being of utility in the very different circumstances that Europe now faces. More fundamentally, it confuses utility as an explanation for the historical evolution of rules and institutions and utility as a justification.

Any attempt to curtail a full debate about the legitimization of the framework for European political union based on the *acquis* is based on false premises. Moreover, a debate about the fundamentals of a European political order can be an important means by which that order can gain support.

(ii) Approaches to legitimization

The main approaches to the legitimization or justification of a political order focus on the issue of consent to authority. The relationship is traditionally expressed either in terms of contract, or of the conformity of authority to perceptions of a just society, or in terms of the utility of the rules and institutions of the social and political order.[30] These traditional ways of looking at the relationship continue in their modern versions.

The discussion which follows departs from these conventional divisions in order to focus on the question of the treatment of values in the legitimization of the political order. This approach is taken because:

- a central aspect of any constitutional order concerns the values reflected in that order.[31] A rule based approach to constitutional order must make clear the relationship of those rules to values.
- a different treatment of values is a source of division within otherwise related approaches to legitimization (for example, accounts that rely on modern versions of contract theory).
- although 'utility' is no longer followed as a general theory for the legitimization of a political order, the notion of utility remains crucial in theories of the origin and acceptability of rules. The treatment of values in the concept of utility therefore needs explanation.[32]
- values are crucial in any attempt to articulate the relationship between the political order and the ethical order in society. The idea that the 'moral' is reflected in the rules of society is a feature of several accounts of legitimization.

(iii) Rules and values

There is a long-standing tension between the concept of a political order based on rules and a justification that appeals to values. The sources of tension are as follows:

- values are often seen as conflicting. A rule based system is looking for consistent rules.
- disputes about values are likely to be difficult to resolve and therefore stable and predictable rules may be difficult to obtain.[33]
- rules may appear to be vulnerable to being overridden by appeals to values. Values can thus be seen as a potential source of challenge to a rule based order.

Because of these sources of tension, it is therefore all the more important to be clear about the relation of rules to values and to address the sources of tension. As the starting point of the discussion, the view is considered that values can be found in the processes themselves of a rule based order. According to this view there is no need to consider external values. The risk of conflict between rules and values can be averted.

VI Values in the process

The view that the legitimacy of a political order can be judged in terms of process without an appeal to external values sees politics in terms of exchange. The analogy is with exchange in the market place.[34]

In this account, constitutional agreement represents compromise between separate individual interests. Individuals carry their own values into the bargaining or trading process.[35] Agreement carries normative significance in and of itself. What is agreed is legitimate. The normative significance of 'agreement in itself' is stressed because agreement is the ultimate test of mutually beneficial exchange. The criterion for agreement is a rigorous one. It is associated with the principle of unanimous agreement. All participants have to be satisfied. Different constitutional arrangements can be compared by reference to this process of agreement among individuals.[36]

(i) The explanation of rules

The underlying assumption behind this account of a rule based order is that the conventions, rules, laws, ethics and institutions of a social order can be explained as a result of the simple interaction of individuals.[37] The view is taken that it is possible to make assumptions about individual motives and then deduce consequences for the system. Statements about the normative in society can be reduced to statements referring solely to individual human beings, their actions, and the relations among them. The rules can be justified in these terms. There is no need to appeal to outside values.

Following this methodology, two explanations can be given of the emergence of social rules. One explanation rests on the assumption that agreement on rules will emerge through a process of individual utility maximization. The other account is that rules will emerge through a process of individual bargaining.

(a) Individual utility maximization The first approach argues that individual utility maximization alone is able to lead to a 'natural equilibrium' in the distribution of rights and boundaries in society. Agreement will be reached on rules that set boundaries because individuals will want to reap the gains of secure boundaries rather than incur the costs of defending them.

The significance of this account is that no normative elements are required. Individuals start from some status quo and simply calculate their individual gains and losses in order to arrive at agreement.[38]

(b) Bargaining The second approach argues from games theory that cooperative behaviour and rules could emerge from the rational choice of individuals in bargaining situations. The motivation behind such behaviour occurs whenever individuals see a potential for a mutual gain from cooperative behaviour (a cooperative surplus).

The significance of this approach is that it means there is no need to suppose that a central authority in society needs to exist in order to achieve social rules.[39] Norms emerge as a means by which individuals deal with these bargaining situations. They represent the outcome of successfully repeated bargaining solutions.[40] Norms bring the benefit of stable behaviour in bargaining situations.

These two accounts of how rules can spring from individual behaviour appear to get rid of the need for explanations of rules for a social or political order that depend on authority. An outside authority is not required to explain the origin of rules. Neither are external values needed to establish and validate rules of behaviour. Agreements are reached. The normative is in the agreement.

(ii) Constitutions as mutual gain

One important aspect of this account of the emergence of a rule based order lies in the setting. The setting involves the key assumption of mutual gain. There is an assumption of mutually beneficial exchange in utility maximization. The settings chosen from bargaining theory are also those 'positive sum' games where there are cooperative gains to each party.[41]

This assumption clearly gives an incomplete picture of social relations. There are bargaining situations where one party's gain is another's loss and there are also situations where both parties lose whatever the outcome.[42] Any complete account of the emergence of rules and agreements has to be able to deal with this wider setting.

Because the setting of individual utility maximization and bargaining is a setting limited to an appreciation of mutual gain, doubt is cast on whether the account is able to deal with situations where there is conflict. In such cases the resolution of conflict requires the existence of rules that override the preferences of some participants who will see the outcome in terms of loss. In this wider context it is implausible to suppose that all conflicts of interest in social relationships can be settled through bargaining and exchange. An explanation has to be given of the enforcing powers of government in cases where disputes cannot be bargained away.

The explanation offered is that the constitutional framework is a grand overall bargain. People agree to be overruled on particular occasions (within the rules) because they still believe in the expectation of overall mutual gain at the time of setting the rules. Enforcement is agreed in the context of the constitutional bargain because it is recognized, in striking the bargain, that rules with sanctions attached are needed to make government work – in the same way as they are needed to make markets work. Nevertheless, it is the expectation of overall gain that enables participants to agree to rules that allow their preferences to be overruled, disputes settled and rules enforced. The constitutional bargain represents the point in political exchange where all are satisfied, comparable to the idea of competitive equilibrium in the market place where all mutual gains from trade have been exhausted.

The account allows for the continual refreshment of the grand constitutional bargain after the rules have been agreed (in the post constitutional setting) through the provision of 'opt outs'. If participants no longer see the possibility of gain from the association they are entitled to secede.

Clearly the model captures an important aspect of political relationships. If there were no expectation of mutual gain, participants would not associate. Unless there is an overall expectation of gain, a political order would never be agreed.

Nevertheless, the question remains whether the idea of the continuous calculation of net gain really captures the 'glue' that holds together successful civil and political associations.

Can the rules of a constitution, and the enforcing powers of government, be seen and justified simply in terms of a grand bargain centred on an overall expectation of mutual gain? Can a European political order be explained and justified simply in these same terms?

VII Reinstating external values

Both the exchange account and the bargaining account of the emergence of rules, and the emergence of constitutional agreements about rules, rest on the concept of utility satisfaction. This leads to difficulties in the account of the constitutional bargain in two vital areas: first, in defining the relationship between rules and values, particularly moral values, and second, in expressing rules as rules of constraint. As a result, although the concept of mutual gain stands as an important explanation for the emergence of a rule based system, it is an incomplete explanation and it cannot serve as a justification for the rules that do emerge.

(i) Norms and values

Not all rules in society need be rules of morality. The idea that there are norms which are instruments for social choice without the use of 'oughts', 'rights' and 'duties' is important.

The nature of these 'norms' however needs to be clear, along with their relationship to ethical standards. Otherwise, they are vulnerable to challenge by rival norms or on ethical grounds.

An account of rules that relies on utility can claim that the normative is ethical only in so far as utility is ethical.[43] Alternatively the claim is that what emerges through utility maximization is 'good' in some other sense.[44] These claims do nothing to clarify the relationship between the rules and the ethical or any other kind of value judgement. The reason is because the concept of utility in bargaining theory and in economics is a broadly inclusive measure of satisfaction.

Utility in games theory has a specialized meaning about measuring preference rankings and outcome probabilities.[45] It does not characterize the quality of the measurement scale.[46] In particular its strength as a measure lies in the variety of factors that can be taken into account: motivations – good or bad; goals – good or bad; preferences – strong or weak.

Utility in the context of economic exchange is also a very broadly inclusive measure. It makes no distinctions between ends, and motivation is unimportant.[47] It tends to be seen as a measure of materialist satisfaction but this is because most of its applications are in the context of physical markets. It can be extended to cover, for example, altruistic motivation.[48] The values that an individual carries into the constitutional trade and bargain can be anything.

The breadth of what can be included in the concept of utility – either in bargaining theory or in economic exchange – means that the relationship between the norms or agreements that emerge from utility satisfaction and the ethical or other values can never be clarified.[49] Thus, what emerges in the way of norms that are complied with, or generally agreed, can always be challenged by rival values or on ethical grounds. This is because what is generally complied with, or what is agreed, may not be 'good'.[50]

The defence of the idea of utility satisfaction as 'good in itself' rests on the view that the constitutional bargain is the one that maximizes value to the individual participants themselves. In order to 'second guess' this bargain, an outside observer applying external standards of value is 'playing God'. In other words, outside observers are implying that their own standards are better than those of the individuals reaching an agreement based on whatever values they have brought to the bargaining table. In short it is improper to question the bargain.

There is however no reason to accept that someone questioning the bargain is playing God, or necessarily questioning standards of behaviour that reflect the interactions of individuals. What is being demanded is that the reasoning, the motivation and the values that individuals carry into the bargaining be exposed to view and debate. This cannot be done in the utility model because utility encompasses all values in a single function so that they cannot be examined.[51] Utility satisfaction hides from view the values that have gone into the bargain.

(ii) Maximization

This general lack of clarity between rules, values and the ethical which arises when the explanation of rules relies on concepts of utility becomes a more specific weakness in looking at the rules of a political order as a system of constraints. In a crucial way the rules of a political system are rules of constraint. They impose constraints on the authority of government, on the role of politics and on the way in which relationships are conducted between the participants in a political order.

One way in which the use of maximization behaviour can be reconciled with the idea of rules as constraints is through a belief in the free market. If all are agreed on a model of the market where exchange is as free as possible, an emphasis on rules is an emphasis also on minimizing rules in the political order that allow for market preferences to be overridden and thus in favour of rules that constrain government.

It seems, however, a weakness to rest the idea of rules as constraints just on a particular view of the market. If the favoured version of the market is one that supports the need for various forms of market management then the analogy becomes one of managed political systems. Rules start allowing for governments to exercise wide discretionary powers. The concept of rules that constrain governments is fatally weakened.

Another attempt to reconcile the idea of rules as constraints with the maximizing assumptions of utility satisfaction, is through the idea of 'constrained maximization'.[52] The attempt is to look for reasons why individuals that are 'maximizing' should accept rules that are 'constraining' without looking for explanations that rely on altruism or ethical norms that override the individual. It is held to be rational to choose constraints on our own behaviour and that of others. It is also seen to be rational to choose rules that are coercive as long as others are also constrained.

The idea that individuals will rationally choose rules of constraint is not an issue. The difficulty is that 'constrained maximization' is difficult to reconcile with the concept of utility as used in exchange or bargaining theory. A possible avenue is to suggest that individual participants will carry into their agreement on the constitutional bargain the values associated with constraint. In particular they may choose rules as if 'risk averse' and wish to protect themselves either from the grant of governmental powers without constraint or from unconstrained behaviour more generally.[53] Individuals will do their own calculations as to how much weight to give to constraint as compared with other values.

This response is again unsatisfactory. 'Risk aversion' is being used as a proxy for the value to be attached to prudent behaviour. If the bargainers are striking agreements on the basis of rules of prudence and not utility maximization this change in assumptions needs to be made clear.

The underlying difficulty is to give an account of constraint that does not rely on outside standards of value (such as prudence) or relate in some way, directly or indirectly, to the ethical.[54] It is difficult to deny any relationship between constrained behaviour and outside ethical values.[55]

In the final analysis, the rules in a rule based constitution cannot rest solely on assumptions about behaviour that are rooted simply on the basis of utility satisfaction. Utility is too broad a concept. It leaves the justification of process oriented rules vulnerable to attack on the grounds of the unclear relationship to values and ethical standards. Rules of process emphasize the importance of such features as consent, impartiality and procedural fairness and it seems very difficult to anchor these qualities without justifying them by reference to external values that are themselves procedural values.[56] Neither is it satisfactory to claim that procedural values might likely be taken into account by individuals.[57] If they are, they must be open for inspection and validation.

Values that are held to be relevant to the justification of a constitutional order need to be able to be examined and debated. Procedural values need to be justified in relation to their rivals.[58] A debate cannot be finessed by claims that all possible values have been weighed by individuals in the process of reaching agreement and are immune from inspection.

If, therefore, a constitutional order for Europe is to be grounded on rules that emphasize process, there is a need to examine relevant constitutional values. Some rival values, if adopted, might lead to the downplaying of process and of rules. They could, if adopted, undermine the concept of a rule based constitution. This is a risk that has to be run. Attempts to base a constitutional order without reference to explicit standards of value cannot succeed. Procedural values have to be justified in relation to other values. The next chapter therefore takes up the question of values in a constitution.

Notes

1 'What are traded on the market are not, as is often supposed by economists, physical entities, but the rights to perform certain actions, and the rights which individuals possess are established by the legal system'. Coase, R.H. (1992), 'The Institutional Structure of Production', *The American Economic Review*, September 1992.
2 'Justice. . . is the main pillar that upholds the whole edifice'. Smith A. (1778), *The Theory of Moral Sentiments*.
3 'In order to make every individual feel himself perfectly secure in the possession of every right which belongs to him, it is not only necessary that the judicial should be separated from the executive power, but that it should be rendered as much as possible independent of that power'. Smith A. (1776), *An Inquiry into the Nature and Causes of the Wealth of Nations*.
4 Hobbes is the arch exponent of the conflict between the concept of government under the law and the power of the sovereign. He attacked the idea 'that they who bear Rule are Subject also to the Civill Lawes,' as one of the ideas adverse to civil society on the grounds that enforcement was necessary. 'All judgement. . . in a city belongs to him who hath the swords (i.e.) to him, who hath the supreme authority'. He can also be seen as an exponent of the view that if law sits above government (the sovereign) then the law is assuming political power. 'For if his power were limited, that limitation must necessarily proceed from some greater power; For he that prescribes limits, must have a greater power than he who is confin'd by them'. Consistent with these views Hobbes also attacked the idea of shared or distributed powers. 'That the Supreme Authority may be divided, is a most fatall opinion to all Common-weales'. Hobbes T. (1651), *De Cive*.
5 The best account in English of the *Rechtsstaat* tradition is that given by Dietze, G. (1973), *Two Concepts of the Rule of Law*.
6 Despite his emphasis on the importance of the independence of the judiciary, Adam Smith continued to look at power in terms of sovereignty. 'The sovereign power is in all

things absolute, and as soon as the government is firmly established becomes liable to be controuled by no regular force. . . we must always end in some body who have a power liable to no controul from a regular power'. Smith A. (1762–4), *Lectures on Jurisprudence*.

7   Hayek referred to *Rechtsstaat* conceptions as 'Perhaps better adapted to the problems of our time than many of the older institutions', because of the threat to liberty of the power of the professional administrator. See Hayek, F.A. (1960), *The Constitution of Liberty*.

8   The account of German experience is given by Dietze, op. cit.

9   Raz is a recent theorist who fails to distinguish between the concept of the rule of law and law as the instrument of government. 'A non-democratic legal system, based on the denial of human rights, on extensive poverty, on racial segregation, sexual inequalities, and religious persecution may, in principle, conform to the requirements of the rule of law better than any of the legal systems of the more enlightened Western democracies'. Raz. J. (1979), *The Authority of Law*.

10 'Every question which can possibly arise as to the policy of contracts, and of the relations which they establish among human beings, is a question for the legislator; and one which he cannot escape from considering, and in some way or other deciding'. Mill J.S. (1848), *Principles of Political Economy*, Bk. V.

11 'No end-state principle or distributional patterned principle of justice can be continuously realized without continuous interference with people's lives'. Nozick, D. (1974), *Anarchy, State and Utopia*.

12 This view of government is given, for example, in Fried, C. (1981), *Contract as Promise*. Nozick also provides a version of compensation theory based on a view that exchange is risky and some exchange prohibited. He admits 'The correctness of some principles, such as the principle of compensation, requiring those imposing a prohibition on risky activities to compensate those disadvantaged through having these risky activities prohibited to them'. Nozick, op. cit.

13 'The reason why many of the new welfare activities of government are a threat to freedom, then, is that, though they are presented as mere service activities, they really constitute an exercise of the coercive powers of government'. Hayek, op. cit. The way in which the limited concept of the social market was quickly distorted in Germany was criticized by Hamm in the 1981 Ordo yearbook. See Hamm, W. 'The Welfare State at its Limit' in Peacock, A. and Willgerodt H. (eds) 1989, *Germany's Social Market Economy: Origins and Evolution*.

14 Nozick suggests that the compensation principle is limited to apply only to the disadvantaged. '. . . the fact that we partially are 'social products'. . . does not create in us a general floating debt which the current society can collect and use as it will'. Nozick, op. cit.

15 Eucken expressed the German neo-liberal concern about the 'mutual dependence' between private and public power. See, Eucken, W. (1948), 'What kind of Economic and Social System', in Peacock and Willgerodt, op. cit.

16 'In the end, process strategies run up against very serious limitations. While they may well reduce the risk of governmental tyranny, they often increase the risk of private exploitation'. Ackerman, B.A. (1980), *Social Justice in the Liberal State*.

17 See the account in Black, A. (1984), *Guilds and Civil Society in European Political Thought from the 12th Century to the Present*.

18 The positive side of this tradition was represented in 19th century thought by von Gierke. See, Gierke, O.v. (1900), *Political Theories of the Middle Age*.

19 For a modern statement of this view, see Hirst, P. (1994), *Associative Democracy*.

20 The pitfalls of the client relationship is illustrated by Hirst's suggestion that such

associations should become the recipients of public finance. See Hirst, ibid.

21 'The state first encourages the formation of private economic power and then becomes partially dependent on it'. Eucken, op.cit.

22 'When technical conditions make a monopoly the natural outcome of competitive market forces, there are only three alternatives that seem available; private monopoly, public monopoly, or public regulation. All three are bad so we must choose between evils. . . I reluctantly conclude that, if tolerable, private monopoly may be the least of evils'. Friedman, M. (1962), *Capitalism and Freedom*.

23 Nozick suggests there are three components of entitlement theories of social justice; a theory about the original acquisition of holdings; about justice in the transfer of holdings and about the rectification of injustice in holdings. See, Nozick, op. cit.

24 Bohm's concept of the 'private law society' expresses a neo-liberal view of freedom of contract. See Bohm, F. (1966), 'Rule of Law in a Market Economy' in Peacock and Willgerodt, op. cit.

25 Nozick interprets Locke as attempting to combine holdings and exchange theory in associating property rights with the combination of land and labour. An individual has pure entitlement when there is no exchange and ownership is not based on exchange. 'The Lockean proviso is not an 'end state principle', it focuses on a particular way that appropriative actions affect others, and not on the structure of the situation that results'. Nozick, op. cit.

26 'The more that collective provision against risks is promoted the less interest individuals have in a self reliant mode of life'. Hamm, op. cit.

27 This view is associated with Fried. According to Fried, rules of contract need the support of moral obligation. 'Considerations of self interest cannot supply the moral basis of my obligation to keep a promise. . . neither can considerations of utility'. He argues that the trust necessary in the entering into of contracts is supported by promise. 'Trust becomes a powerful tool for our working our mutual wills in the world. . . The device that gives trust its sharpest, most palpable form is promise'. Fried, op. cit.

28 In relation to the social order, Rawls looks for outside standards. 'A set of principles is required for choosing among the various social arrangements which determine this division of advantages and for underwriting an agreement on the proper distributive shares'.

29 Montesquieu rejected Hobbes account of contract precisely on the grounds that it is the normal experience of persons to be born into a society whose rules and conventions are given and that must in large measure be accepted. In the terms of modern contractarian theory, Europe is in the unusual position of being in a 'pre-constitutional' setting rather than the more normal 'post-constitutional' setting. See Buchanan, J.M. (1975), *Limits of Liberty: Between Anarchy and Leviathan*.

30 Hobbes of course represents the contract tradition. His version of the original contract claimed to be an account of 'how and by what meanes the right of one may be transfer'd unto another to make their compacts valid'. Hobbes, op. cit.

31 For Montesquieu different value systems were the defining feature of different political and social orders.

32 Adam Smith attacked Hume for his account of rules based on utility. 'It seems impossible that the approbation of virtue should be a sentiment of the same kind with that by which we approve of a convenient and well contrived building; or that we should have no other reason for praising a man than that for which we comend a chest of drawers'. Smith A. (1778), *Theory of Moral Sentiments*.

33 Hobbes rejected accounts of 'rights' because of the potential for conflict between rights. 'Nature hath given to every one a right to all'. The state of nature thus leads to a state of war. Hobbes, op. cit.

34   The account of value 'in the process' in this section draws mainly on Buchanan, J.M. (1991), *The Economics and Ethics of Constitutional Order*.

35   'The source of values lies exclusively within the preferences of the persons who trade'. Brennan, G. and Buchanan, J.M. (1985), *The Reason of Rules*.

36   '. . . alternative structures may be compared, and evaluated, in terms of their abilities to facilitate the accomplishment of the separately determined individual objectives'. Buchanan, J.M. (1991), op. cit.

37   Representative of this general approach is Ullmann-Margalit, E. (1977), *The Emergence of Norms*.

38   See Buchanan, J.M. (1975), op. cit.

39   'Cooperation can evolve from small clusters of individuals who base their cooperation on reciprocity'. Axelrod, R. (1984), *The Evolution of Cooperation*.

40   According to Ullmann-Margalit the correlation between these bargaining situations and norms for dealing with them is 'offered as an account of the emergence of norms' not in the sense of a historical event but as a logical 'could have'. Ullmann-Margalit, op. cit.

41   Axelrod's setting where the reward for mutual cooperation is higher than alternative pay-offs involves a positive sum game with some conflictual elements. 'It is not safe to assume that the other player is out to get you'. Axelrod, op. cit.

42   Schelling emphasizes the diversity of bargaining situations. Games range from pure coordination to pure conflict. However, Ullmann-Margalit, (op. cit.) Axelrod (op. cit.) and Gauthier (see below) address coordination games with some conflictual elements. See Schelling, T. (1960) & (1984),*The Strategy of Conflict* and *Choice and Consequence*.

43   Ullmann-Margalit makes this point, op. cit.

44   Ullmann-Margalit defines a norm as 'a prescribed guide for conduct or action which is generally complied with by the members of a society'. Ullmann-Margalit, op. cit. Buchanan uses an evolutionary standard of value. 'That is 'good' which 'tends to emerge' from the free choices of the individuals who are involved'. Buchanan, (1975), op. cit.

45   'So far as game theory is concerned, there really are no 'utility scales' to compare. There are only preference rankings among outcomes that have to incorporate numerical probabilities when some of the outcomes themselves are probabilistic'. Schelling, *Choice and Consequence*, op. cit.

46   'To use this language is not to establish any special significance to a zero. . . utility or to a unit. . . utility; any result obtained will be independent of how the unit and zero are assigned; it will depend only on the ratios in which the. . . utility differences stand to one another'. Braithwaite, R.B. (1955), *Theory of Games as a Tool for the Moral Philosopher*.

47   Von Mises expresses these points very clearly, 'Modern economics makes no distinction among ends because it considers them all equally legitimate'. . . 'Catallactics does not ask whether or not the consumers are right, noble, generous, wise, patriotic or church going. It is concerned not with why they act, but only with how they act'. . . 'For the market, the motivation of the buyers' actions is indifferent. All that counts is that they are prepared to spend a definite sum'. von Mises, L. (1962), *Epistemological Problems of Economics*.

48   This type of extension is associated with Becker. See Becker, G.S. (1974), 'A Theory of Social Interactions', *Journal of Political Economy*, 82.

49   Arrow makes this point in relation to utility scales in social choice theory. 'This theorem does not, as far as I can see, give any special ethical significance to the particular utility scale found. . . what it does say is that among the many different ways of assigning a utility indicator to the preferences among alternative probability distributions, there is one method. . . which has the property of stating the laws of rational behaviour in a

particularly convenient way. . . This is a very useful matter. . . but it has nothing to do with welfare considerations'. Arrow, K.J. (1951), *Social Choice and Individual Values*.

50 Gauthier suggests further difficulties with the dependence of norms or agreement on utility. The implication of equating utility with ethics is that in a world of perfect competition in equilibrium, when there are no further gains from exchange, morality vanishes. Ethics becomes associated just with market failure. Gauthier, D. (1986), *Morals by Agreement*.

51 Simon criticizes the way the utility function loads all values into a single function, 'the utility function, in this way finessing the question of how different values are to be compared'. See, Simon, H. A. 'Alternative Views of Rationality' in Arkes, H.R. and Hammond, K.R. (eds) (1986), *Judgement and Decision Making: An Interdisciplinary Reader*.

52 This attempt is associated with Gauthier: 'In defending constrained maximisation we have implicitly reinterpreted the utility-maximising conception of practical rationality. . . A choice is rational if and only if it maximises the actor's expected utility. We identify rationality with utility-maximisation at the level of dispositions to choose'. His aim is to demonstrate that, 'A fully rational utility-maximiser disposes himself to compliance with his rationally undertaken covenants or agreements'. Gauthier, op. cit.

53 For a discussion of quasi-risk aversive behaviour, see Brennan and Buchanan op. cit.

54 Gauthier suggests that the connection between individual reason and morals lies in 'the rationality of accepting a moral constraint on the direct pursuit of one's greatest utility'. Gauthier, op. cit. This does not escape the need for the individual to justify the choice.

55 Adam Smith was drawn to stoicist theories of ethical restraint.

56 Ackerman points to the connection between the method of agreement and reasonableness. According to Ackerman the method of agreement has to meet procedural standards. Agreement by itself is not enough. 'The liberal state is deeply committed to the ideal of free exchange – provided that mutually beneficial trade occurs within a power structure legitimated by liberal dialogue'. Ackerman, op. cit.

57 The suggestion is made that individuals would likely agree on standards of fairness in much the same way that Rawl's individuals will agree on standards of fairness. '. . . to the extent that a person faced with a constitutional choice remains uncertain as to what his position will be under separate choice options, he will tend to agree on arrangements that might be called 'fair' in the sense that patterns of outcomes generated under such arrangements will be broadly acceptable'. Brennan and Buchanan, op. cit.

58 Buchanan's difficulty in avoiding an appeal to outside standards is shown when he suggests that, 'A 'good' or 'proper' process is defined as one that assures fairness or impartiality in the rules that emerge'. Buchanan, (1991), op. cit.

3 Values in the constitution

'But what is government itself but the greatest of all reflections on human nature? If men were angels no government would be necessary'. The Federalist, no. LI, Hamilton or Madison.

I The role of values

Political union in Europe must be founded on a clear statement of values. In turn, the relationship of these values to ethical principles also needs to be clear. The core principles of the union have to be able to command ethical assent. The question is how to express and justify the values that should underpin the rules of political union. One approach has already been discussed – the idea that in a rule based political order the normative element is contained within the rules themselves. This approach has been rejected. An appeal to external values is needed. This opens the way for a discussion of which values can help legitimize the political order in Europe.

(i) False approaches to validation

The validation of a European political order is sometimes approached in ways that echo earlier mistakes in Europe. One false approach that echoes these earlier mistakes is the appeal to history. The justification of a European political order is rested on arguments about historical processes in Europe. The trend of history is away from a Europe based on independent nation states. It might be argued from this evolution that the new order can be justified simply as the logical outcome of these trends. However, if European political union is presented simply as the historically 'inevitable' successor of political association based on the nation state, or as the 'logical culmination' of European history, then its proponents are falling into the same logical traps as those who earlier used the same arguments to justify the claim of the nation state to be the outcome of an inevitable process and the culmination of history. Our knowledge of history is not sufficient to support claims to knowledge of the future.[1] Even if it were possible to claim that a European political union is historically inevitable, it is a logical fallacy to step from an allegedly 'empirical' claim to a value judgement that a particular political union is justified.

The disasters of European history in this century appear to provide a historical rationale for a new European political order that has ethical validity. These disasters certainly explain the motivation behind a search for a new order. They also provide an ethical reason for the search for a new order. They can explain the ethical appeal of looking for a new political framework for politics in Europe. But they do not validate any new order. The justification has to be made in terms of the features of the political union itself.

It would equally be a mistake to see European union as a value in itself which requires no further justification. If European political union is put forward as a value in itself that has simply to be asserted in order to command respect, then, once again, the mistakes of nationalist logic are being repeated. The nation state was once presented as the moral idea that could not be challenged and the embodiment of the good. A particular form of the political order cannot be automatically identified with the moral order. Justification is needed. European political union requires validation in terms of its own features. It is not any political order in Europe that can claim legitimacy. It is not any political order in Europe that should be regarded as worthy of support.

The search for validation of Europe's political order in terms of its own features should not however be identified with looking for something that is held to be 'uniquely' European. Those who search for the 'unique' characteristics of a special European 'identity' that might be used to provide an ethical content to European political union are engaged in a false search. A European political union will indeed have its own characteristics. It might look unlike any other large political union, for example, the United States. In this sense it will be unique. But a search for a unique ethical character once again echoes far too closely the earlier search for the unique spirit of individual nation states that contributed to so much damage in Europe.

(ii) Values and the constitution

A key purpose of a constitution is to express the fundamental values of the political order. They provide a basis on which all can agree that the endeavour of political association is a good endeavour. They help legitimize the political order.

The expression of values is not only about legitimization. Values also provide a basis for structure. They provide the standard against which processes can be judged. Since institutions interact with processes, values also provide a benchmark against which institutions and their powers can be assessed. They provide a means to recognize the problem areas in political association where perhaps additional rules are necessary. They provide an ongoing test of rules and institutions as political practices evolve.

The importance of the values expressed and the way in which they relate to ethical principles is more than theoretical. The values expressed in a constitution resonate with values and beliefs held in society. They can thus affect perceptions and increase the acceptability of the political order[2]. This resonance can work either for good or for ill. By giving an ethical backing to the rules of a rule based order, values can work for the good by strengthening the force of the rules. A wrong choice of values can work to increase the acceptability of the wrong types of political regime. It is therefore of vital importance which values are expressed[3].

It is the practical resonances of values, as well as their role in legitimizing and structuring a constitutional order, that makes the choice of values and the justification of the choice so important. The fear of those looking at values to be associated with political processes is precisely that outside standards of value will be chosen which override right process or the right institutional forms or the right distribution of powers. Nevertheless, as discussed earlier, the debate about outside standards of value is not a debate that can be avoided. It is a debate about the right values.

(iii) The choice of values

In the analysis which follows, five different approaches to the choice of values in Europe's constitution are discussed:

(a) Supreme values – this is an attempt to find a value which is beyond dispute and which can stand as a measure against which all else can be judged. This approach is rejected, not on the grounds that the search is mistaken, but on the grounds that any supreme value or guiding principle must itself be capable of justification.

(b) The basic norm – this approach looks at the constitution as a legal construct and attempts to find the starting point beyond dispute from which legal and institutional structures flow. This approach too is rejected. The theory does not give an account through which the concept of the 'basic norm' can be validated.

(c) Precondition values – this approach looks for values which, either singly or in conjunction, are causally connected with the desired political order and are themselves part of it (for example, the right to private property may be held to be both part of any democratic order in Europe and necessary to achieve that order). This approach is also rejected. Such values either legitimize too little or too much. Moreover, there is a confusion over whether the force of such values is directed to processes or end states. The proper place for such values is in respect of particular parts of a constitution and not as general validating principles.

(d) Cooperative values – cooperative values attempt to give definition, and the promise of permanence, to cooperative procedures in a political union. They are rejected as a general approach to the political order because cooperative values characterize only part of the political process. They do not address effectively that part where the critical problems arise - those cases where interests conflict.

(e) Prudential values – finally, the rules of a political order are looked at as rules of prudence. They are rules that guard against types of political order or disorder that are feared in the formation of the political union. One issue is how to express the value of prudence as a guiding principle in the formation of rules. The 'non-coercion' principle – that the political order in Europe should be arranged so as to minimize the imposition of choice in the union – is set out.

The prudential approach holds that the most important values in a constitution are those that govern how things should be done by people acting together in civil and political society. It endorses the idea that rules should encourage cooperative behaviour and provide as well for the settling of differences through bargaining and exchange. But it addresses as well the issue that not all problems in political association can be settled either by cooperation or by bargaining. There is a particular need to focus on coercive powers in any system of government.[4]

II Supreme values

The search for a supreme value holds out the promise of a quick cut off to debate about the right values in a constitution. The purpose of a supreme value is to have a standard that is itself beyond dispute.[5] Once established, this standard can be used to resolve any other conflicts in the constitution.

Statements about supreme values seem, at first sight, to be rather remote from the current debate about political association in Europe. They do, however, lie just beneath the surface. The current treaty base of the existing European Union already contains references that could be interpreted as statements about supreme values. These are references to the European Union itself and to 'closer European union'. Either might be held up as the highest values in a European constitution.

If European union, by itself, is held up as a supreme value, then the claim is that it overrides any other competing value. It is an end state that is to be preferred above any other. It is also an unconditional or unqualified value. A qualified statement that a European union is to be preferred as a form of political association if, and only if, it meets other criteria, such as providing for a democratic form of government, is not provided for.

The difficulty in having a more elaborate form of supreme value is that the elaboration invites further questions (for example, about the requirements of a democracy). At this point the supreme value is losing its intended purpose as an undisputed standard of value.

'Closer European union' has somewhat different connotations when interpreted as a statement of a supreme value. It is a value not just about an end state to be held above all others but also about procedures for arriving at the end state. If 'closer European union' is held up as the highest value in Europe's constitutional framework then all processes, all rules and all exercises of power by European institutions could be judged by whether they fulfil the purpose of bringing about a closer union.

One objection to any attempt to establish a supreme value is that by attempting to subordinate other values to a single value the quest is inherently 'illiberal'. The supreme value is 'dictatorial'. This line of objection amounts to a counter-assertion, either of value relativism (that there is no way of determining between rival values) or of value pluralism (that there is no single standard of value to be found). It rejects a long line of liberal thinkers who have attempted to establish a guiding principle on which their concept of a liberal state could be based.[6]

The more telling line of objection seems to lie in the distinction that must be made between the two different reasons behind attempts to enshrine a supreme value in a constitution. One reason is to find a value that is itself beyond dispute. The attraction of such a value is that it would provide an unquestionable basis for legitimizing the political association. The second reason is the search for a higher value or regulatory principle against which others can be judged. The attraction is to provide a standard of value.

The two are not the same. If a value can be found that is beyond dispute it can indeed act as a standard of value against which others can be judged. However, it is also possible to look for a standard of value that is open to justification. There need be no attempt to avoid debate about its justification. The search for a guiding regulatory principle is a search for a standard of value which serves as a yardstick for other features of a political order. It need not be claimed that it itself is beyond dispute.

The fundamental difficulty with the first approach is to find a value that cannot itself be disputed. For example, European union is an important and worthwhile goal. Nevertheless its desirability depends very much on the form it takes. If it takes a form incompatible with personal freedom, those who place personal freedom above other values will dispute European union being held up as the highest value. Similarly, reservations could be expressed about 'closer European union' as a supreme value. Such a rule would work against any stable constitutional settlement because it entrenches a one-way dynamic. It would also work against any fixed distribution of powers because it would tend to encourage the continuous accumulation of powers by the union. Thus, it would fail the test of those who look to a constitution to provide a stable framework of rules and institutions.

A supreme value either has to be capable of being defended against other rival values or, it rests on assertion alone. Assertion is unsatisfactory as a constitutional base since it is open to the counter assertion of other values. Assertion therefore, cannot serve as a legitimizing principle because disputes about legitimacy can never be subject to rational argument or brought to a close. If there is a standard of value to be found which is to help legitimize political association, it must be capable of being justified and defended by more than simple assertion.

A particular trap in the search for an undisputed standard of value is to identify the supreme value with the political order itself. This is the trap in any attempt to identify European union itself (or closer European union) as the supreme value. Europe has experienced a time when the nation state was seen as the expression of the highest ethical ideal. European union may potentially provide a better framework for political association in Europe than the nation state. But a political order by itself can never be equated with the ethical ideal. The political dangers need hardly be stressed. But it is also a mistake in logic – a confusion of an empirical statement about a political order with a value statement about that order. The validity of a political order will always have to be defended by normative standards.[7]

Thus any attempt to establish European political union as a value beyond dispute leads down an erroneous and dangerous path. It tries to deny debate about the shape of that political union. It tries to avoid discussion of the values that should underpin European political union.

III The basic norm

Closely related to the search for an undisputed value on which the legitimacy of a constitutional structure can be rested, is the concept of the 'basic norm'. The concept of the basic norm is part of a 'pure theory of law' which focuses on political association as a legal structure.[8] It sees the law as giving practical reality to the state because the ultimate sanction of government is its legal powers.[9] Legitimization therefore depends on the legitimization of a system of law. It is the function of a constitution to provide this legitimization of a legal regime[10]. The constitution does this through the expression of a 'basic norm' from which all other legal norms can be derived. The basic norm thus serves a purpose analogous to a supreme value. It is the statement beyond dispute and the standard from which all else flows.[11]

This search for the statement on which all legal and state authority can be rested or derived is associated with the Austrian legal philosopher, Hans Kelsen. He himself saw his theory as developing several strands in Kant's earlier thinking, both about the relationship between the law and the state, and about the logic of legal statements.

Kelsen's search for the basic norm was a crucial aspect of his view of the law as reflecting a hierarchy of norms. For Kelsen the law is a system of norms.[12] The basis of a binding valid norm is the existence of an authorizing higher norm. He postulated the basic norm as a way to avoid infinite regress. The 'basic' norm is a norm where no further question can be raised about the basis of its validity.[13] This basic norm is to be found in the constitution. In order to avoid further regress as to which constitution is binding, Kelsen looks to whatever can be seen as the historically original constitution.[14]

Thus for a follower of Kelsen, a constitution for Europe would provide the basis for legitimizing a system of law based around European law. For those who see the existing treaties acting as a surrogate constitution for Europe and are of Kelsen's persuasion, the treaties would justify the instigation of a general hierarchy of norms. It would also validate the authority of European law as generally superior to other law in Europe.

Kelsen's theory has continuing appeal precisely because it appears to provide a practical basis both for a legal structure as well as for institutional structures.[15] The legal structure is hierarchical.[16] The institutional hierarchy parallels the legal hierarchy. The legal hierarchy, in conjunction with the institutional hierarchy, together provide a clear structure of authority and obedience. Kelsen's theory thus carries with it a particular formulation of federalism and relations between jurisdictions which is also hierarchical.[17] The purpose of the constitution is to legitimize this structure of authority.[18]

Kelsen's theories remain influential – although this is not always made explicit. Both the European Commission and the European Parliament have supported the concept of a general 'hierarchy of acts' (Maastricht Declaration 16) and a corresponding general hierarchy of institutions and layers of authority. The theory therefore deserves close inspection.

Kelsen's theory of the basic norm is open to two fundamental objections. First, the logical status of the concept of the basic norm is unclear. Kelsen thus fails to establish it as a validating statement beyond dispute. Second, Kelsen fails to provide a satisfactory account of a valid constitution.

(i) The logical status of the 'basic norm'

Kelsen presented his theory of law as a theory of positive law which derived its content from positive legal norms.[19] The logical status of the 'norm' is therefore crucial. Kelsen gave conflicting accounts. On the one hand he explained law as a 'social technique, not a problem of morals', and presented norms as having a content determined by facts.[20] But he also explained norms as being 'ought' statements (i.e. value statements).[21] Elsewhere Kelsen appears to confirm that norms are value statements rather than factual statements.[22] However, they are also, according to Kelsen, a peculiar kind of statement which has a factual basis in an act of will.[23] The result of this succession of accounts of the logical status of the basic norm is muddle. The muddle is whether the norm is a factual statement or a value statement and, if a value statement, what kind of value statement. The effect of this confusion is that it is impossible to bring standards of logical criticism to bear. The basic norm is beyond dispute, not because it is so logically, but because there is not a clear account of it that enables standards of logic to apply.

(ii) What form of government does it authorize?

A second fundamental criticism of Kelsen's theories is that they appear to authorize any form of hierarchical political order. All that appears to matter is the validity of a first constitution which contains the basic norm.[24] But just as the basic norm cannot be scrutinized, so there is no account of what makes a constitution valid. If it is simply what is historically first, then this seems a poor basis for legitimizing a constitution. Not only may a first constitution be highly imperfect, but, any constitution at any time must be capable of validation by more than 'because it is there'. For example, the existence of the treaties underlying the European Union provides a basis in practice for a legal order. But their existence does not in itself justify the legal order. The process by which the treaties have come into existence is part of the reason why they are accepted as 'valid'. Their content also has to be capable of justification.

The closest Kelsen comes to offering a theory of constitutional validation is in connecting an act of will with a simple majority vote.[25] Even if acceptance of a constitution by a simple majority vote is regarded as a necessary procedural requirement to validate a constitution, many will dispute the procedure of a simple majority as a sufficient procedure. Not only might different voting thresholds be seen as necessary, but other procedural requirements (such as ratification by a sufficient number of Member States in a union) might also be seen as relevant. Neither can it be assumed that what has been agreed, by whatever majority, is necessarily good or justified. The content of the constitution has to be justified by more than simply having been agreed.

Kelsen thus does not provide a theory which can validate a constitutional order, let alone one based on a general hierarchical distribution of law, institutions and authority. The theory of the basic norm and the hierarchy of norms does not provide the basis for, or any guide at all, to the structuring of powers in a European political union.

IV Precondition values

Instead of searching for a supreme value that is beyond dispute, or for a single validating legal norm that is beyond dispute, a different approach to justifying the rules of a political order is to look for values that are both the means to the end of the order desired and also essential components of it. These values are not only expressive of the desired order but also causally linked to the attainment of the desired order. For the purposes of this discussion they are referred to as 'precondition values'.

There are four values that traditionally have been put forward as serving the dual purpose of being both the means to an end of a political order that can be justified and necessary constituents of it. The first is the right of free expression; the second is the right of private property; the third is freedom of contract and the fourth is that of social justice.

At first sight, these different values seem only loosely connected as foundations for a constitutional order. Moreover, the concept of social justice is frequently presented as a collective value in conflict with the individualistic premises of private property and contract. In the analysis that follows they are not treated as necessarily in conflict. 'Contract' is closely associated with concepts of equity and fairness. Moreover, concepts of social justice can be based on individualistic premises. It would be foolish of those who expound social justice to present their case in a way that allows it to be easily demolished on the grounds that individual preferences are being overlooked. It would be equally unwise for those who affirm the value of the individual to expound it on a basis where it was similarly vulnerable to an easy objection that the social setting was being ignored.

Common to each of these values is the search for a principle that will validate rules that regulate relationships between what is public and what is private. The regulatory principle is procedural in the case of free expression and based on possession in the case of private property. Contract attempts to bridge both approaches – freedom to contract is procedural but intimately connected with possession. Contract also introduces related values of procedural fairness. The concept of social justice extends the emphasis on the fairness of rules.

(i) Free expression

The claim of freedom of expression to be the cornerstone of a constitutional order is that unless individuals are free to express themselves it is impossible either for the individual to feel free or for individuals in association with others in society to identify areas for cooperative behaviour or to find ways of accommodating their differences.

For Kant, freedom of expression was the essential means through which individuals could exercise their role as public citizens and help ensure the progressive alignment of the actual law of the state with what was found to be morally good. It connected the role of the private person with the public citizen and the actual state with the moral order.[26]

(ii) Private property

The right to private property as a basic constitutional value rests on two founda-tions. The first is that private property is essential for the market order. It is thus the foundation for choice through the market. In turn this helps define the area where choice must be exercised through political processes. It thus helps define both the political sphere for public choice and the place of the market for private choice.

Its second claim for consideration as a fundamental value in a constitution is the role it allows for the private life of the individual. It defines the boundary between what individuals can achieve for themselves and what must be achieved through association with others. The fact that the individual has the assurance of this private sphere may make the restrictions associated with life in association with others more acceptable.[27]

(iii) Freedom of contract

A third value that is sometimes held as fundamental to a political order is freedom of contract. The justification is close to that of private property. It is the foundation of a market order and thus of choice exercised through market processes.

Freedom of contract has certain advantages as a principle compared with the value to be attached to private property. It puts the emphasis on a process – the freedom to exchange – rather than a state, the ownership of property. It expresses the freedom of the individual as the free agent. It thus avoids legitimizing a particular structure of power in society which might accompany a particular structure of ownership. In so far as the concept and practice of contract carries with it certain values, such as 'fairness' and 'equity', it appears to offer a more immedi-ate link than private possession with the ethical qualities of civil association.

(iv) Social justice

There is one value in particular that is held to recognize more completely the importance of power structures and to give a fuller account of ethical relationships in a political association. This is the concept of social justice. As a constitutional value it might be expressed in the form of a stress in the constitution on such qualities as cohesion and social harmony, or more generally, by reference to the social dimension. These might be supported in a constitution by declarations of social 'rights'. The important claim of social justice to be a precondition value is that it provides an ethical basis for mutually acceptable rules.[28]

The value to be attached to social justice is sometimes held to be in complete contradiction to the value to be attached to private property and freedom to contract. This is because social justice appears to offer a reason why the individual right of possession is not an overriding right, and why contracts, freely entered into by individuals, might be overturned for other reasons. However, this assumed contradiction between the individualistic values of private property and freedom to contract is an oversimplification. In particular, it ignores a long tradition of basing a concern for welfare on individualistic premises.

Two different approaches can be taken to basing social justice on individualistic premises. One approach is that of Kant – that rules must meet the ethical standard of what would be chosen by individuals for themselves.[29] In modern form it is associated with the theories of John Rawls – that from behind a 'veil of ignorance' it would be rational for an individual to choose rules which are egalitarian and distributively fair.[30] The second approach is to associate the social dimension with concepts of the 'autonomous' individual. According to this line of argument, the individual will not be able to make full use of their rational choices unless social provisioning helps the individual achieve autonomy.[31] Rules should recognize the importance of individuals achieving their potential.[32]

Precondition values are sometimes interpreted as being inconsistent in their basic premises. As suggested above, this need not be the case – each can be based on individualistic premises. Precondition values also offer several advantages. Part of their appeal lies in the idea that the validation of a political order lies in a cluster of values rather than in the expression of some single or basic value. They focus also on the interrelationship between values in society. More generally, they attempt to delineate the relationship between private association and collective association and distinguish the role of the private citizen from the role of the public citizen. Unlike 'supreme values' that rest on assertion, they do not claim to be beyond dispute. They aim to justify their claims to be both part of a valid political order and a necessary means to attain it.

(v) Problems with preconditions

Precondition values nevertheless fail to serve as legitimizing principles for a constitutional order. They fail for two major reasons. First they legitimize either too little or too much; second, there is a fatal indecision as to whether legitimizing values should focus on process values or on end states. For both reasons they are open to ambiguous interpretation. This means that they cannot provide a clear general guide to a rule based constitutional order.

(a) *Legitimizing too little or too much* There are few who would doubt that a value such as free expression is a constituent of a democratic political order and a necessary means to achieve and maintain one. Since the collapse of communism there are also few who would doubt the key role of private property and freedom of contract in a civil and political order. What is however questioned is the sufficiency of these criteria. Because of their lack of sufficiency they cannot alone stand as legitimizing principles for a political order.

Freedom of expression is an insufficient ingredient of a political order because there are many other components such as free elections and free association which are needed to comprise a list of necessary freedoms. The right to private property is insufficient because it oversimplifies the interrelations between private and public power. Public power can be used to achieve private ends (state capitalism). Conversely private interests can capture the levers of public power. Competition provides a check against an overaccumulation of power in the private sector but does not (without enforcement by bodies independent of the government) provide an answer to privileges accorded to private interests by the state. Competition between jurisdictions may limit the discretionary powers of any one government. But at this point, the debate about the foundations of a constitution have entered into a discussion about structures needed to disperse power in society. They have gone away from the right to property to a broader set of considerations.[33]

Freedom to contract broadens the net of the necessary values in a constitution because it introduces notions of fairness in transactions. Nevertheless, because of the risk of too close a relationship between private power and public power, a rule based constitution that is founded just on the right to private property and freedom to contract is unlikely to command respect. Those with private means will be seen as being in a position where they may have an 'unfair' advantage in shaping the rules, or even be able to violate the rules. Those without private means may see their own frustrations as rooted in the rules.

If freedom of expression, the right to private property and freedom to contract legitimize too little, by contrast, concepts of social justice legitimize too much. The approach of legitimizing rules that could plausibly be chosen by individuals as rules to be generalized allows for open ended claims about the content of rules.[34] More fundamentally, the logical steps in moving from an individual conception of what is right, to a general conception of what is good for society, are open to question.[35] Concepts of social justice based on autonomy are equally difficult to close because of the many aspects that can be attributed to 'autonomy'.

(b) Procedural or end state Freedom of expression and freedom to contract are values that relate to processes. They suggest that the key values in a constitution are those that relate to the processes of association. By contrast, the right to private property and the value to be ascribed to social justice are values that relate to end states – a state of possession or individual self-realization that may or may not be justified according to concepts of social justice. They suggest that the key values in political association relate to the outcomes permitted.

It can be argued that in political association both outcome values and process values are equally important. This is the appeal of viewing the key values of a political order as a 'cluster'. But equality is not possible. If outcomes are the most important feature of political association then they override processes. If processes are the key value then they come ahead of the outcomes that may result.

One response to this problem is to establish an ordering between the cluster of values.[36] This could mean, for example, that the right to free expression, freedom to contract and to private property would rank ahead of the concept of distributive fairness and that a departure from the principles that rank first could not be compensated by additional elements of whatever ranks later. The difficulty is first to justify such an ordering.[37] The second difficulty is to prevent additional elements of, say social justice, being seen as compensating for the loss of freedoms which had been ranked ahead. Both will be presented as being about freedoms.

The indecision as to what category of values are important masks a deeper division about how to characterize the underlying relationships in a civil association. Values such as private property are frequently advanced as constitutional values because of an underlying assumption that the individual is in inherent conflict with the collective in a political order. Relationships are seen as conflictual. If so, this view of the political order must itself be justified. By contrast, values such as social justice tend to be built on assumptions about the importance of cooperative relationships. The adequacy of this assumption must also be justified.[38] The key values for a constitution must rest on a coherent view of relationships in a political association. The assembly of a cluster of values leads to fudge rather than coherency.

The result of these defects is that precondition values cannot serve as the foundation for legitimizing the rules of political association to be enshrined in a constitution. Values that legitimize too little will be challenged for their insufficiencies; values that legitimize too much will erode the concept of rules as limits on what needs to be done collectively. Conflicts will take place between rules of process and rules about end states.

This does not mean that such values do not have a place in a constitution. But it means they cannot serve either singly or collectively as general legitimizing principles or as general guides to constitutional structure. Their role is in the context of particular provisions, for example, freedom of expression will find its role in any declaration of rights; similarly, concepts of social justice may find their place in the powers reserved by Member States to decide on income transfers in their jurisdiction.

V Cooperative values

The expression of cooperative values in a constitution is one important way in which the key values in a political order can be seen to centre on process.

(i) The primacy of process values

The case for process values to be regarded as the fundamental values in a constitution rests on two foundations.

First, there are purely practical considerations. If participants in civil association are not accepting of the ways of doing things together, then there is likely to be constant challenge to the legitimacy of the association. The resulting uncertainties will weaken the foundations of the association and make rational behaviour difficult.

The second and more fundamental rationale is that the way in which people agree to work together reflects the most important normative assumptions on which political association is justified.

There are two different values that claim to lay the foundation for right processes in a constitution. There is first the value to be attached to cooperation and cooperative processes. There is second the value to be attached to processes that do not impose choice. This is referred to as the non-coercion principle. The key difference between the two lies in the way in which they characterize relationships in a social and political order.

The value attached to cooperation in a political association is sometimes assumed to involve putting the value of collective action above that of the individual. If so, cooperative values would be vulnerable to quick dismissal on the grounds that they legitimize too much in systems of government. However, cooperation can also be seen as the rational response of individuals to choice in a social setting. For example, one well known study has pointed to the rationality of coordination emerging by precedent based on regularities in behaviour, or through distinguishing features in the setting (salience) that lead to coordination.[39] Many of these patterns of coordination will be reflected in society simply as conventions. Constitutions provide for authoritative codification and for sanctions. It is from this perspective that cooperation has a strong claim to be considered as a value that can legitimize the rules governing the interactions in a political association – rules that rest on cooperative values reflect a basis for working together that people would rationally choose.

(ii) The case for cooperative values

The case for cooperative values as a rational response to social interactions can be rested on two different grounds. They reinforce each other. The first basis is one that, in its modern form, is derived from bargaining (game) theory. The proposition is that an agreed strategy for cooperation and a promise to behave cooperatively can lead to cooperative outcomes in practice.[40] Transposed to the context of a European constitution, the implications are that if Member States and their populations are committed to seeking cooperative outcomes in their association, and if everyone sticks to this understanding in their actual behaviour, the result will be cooperative outcomes in practice.

In an exploration of this theme it has been shown that a strategy based on reciprocity can thrive even where other strategies are being tried and that a cooperative strategy once established can resist less cooperative strategies. The study suggests also the importance of not being the first to break away from a cooperative strategy.[41]

A second basis on which cooperation can be rested is through the extension of orthodox theories of individual economic behaviour to take into account the interactions of individuals with others who may affect an individual's economic behaviour.[42]

A stress on cooperative procedures is closely related to the value to be attached to continuity. The same game theoretic structure emphasizes the importance of encouraging expectations of future cooperative behaviour.[43] Constitutions can be seen as encouraging these expectations by transforming cooperative procedures into the rules of the game.

By giving assurances about the continuity of behaviour, constitutions provide a way of meeting one of the key conditions under which cooperative outcomes are likely to be reached. Game theory suggests it may not pay to cooperate unless the participants have some assurance that they are engaged in an ongoing relationship rather than a one time interaction. Behaviour will differ if the situation is seen to be one that will be repeated. The incentive to cooperate is much reduced if there is to be no future in which to cooperate. Repetition will alter the behaviour of participants because it will alter their strategies.[44]

(iii) The weakness in cooperative values

The principle objection to legitimizing a constitution on the grounds that it enshrines the value of cooperation is that cooperation oversimplifies the setting of political association. Cooperative solutions apply to a particular range of social coordination issues – those where coincidence of interests predominates.[45] The bargaining settings which emphasize the value of cooperative strategies are usually positive sum settings. Even in these settings, cooperation is not a complete strategy.[46]

Civil and political association has to deal with a much wider range of settings. Not all instances of cooperation will be desirable. Some interests may collude. More important, it is not possible to abstract away the problems of conflict of interest. Some settings will not be positive sum settings (where all participants gain) but zero sum settings where one participant's gain is the loss of another, or may be non-zero settings where all are losers. Cooperation cannot change a zero sum setting to a positive sum setting. The cooperative setting is too limited.[47]

VI Prudential values

Pure political theorists tend to have been rather dismissive of the notion of the rules of a political order being seen as rules of prudence. It was those founding fathers of the American constitution, who were both theorists and practitioners, who emphasized the importance of a prudential approach. They took the view that the rules of social and political organization should be viewed as rules of prudence against the weaknesses in human behaviour in the political order, in much the same way that moral rules are sometimes seen as defences against the weaknesses of human nature in individual behaviour. In taking this view, they seem to have been influenced more by Hume than by Locke.[48]

What are the underlying characteristics of a rule based constitutional order when the rules are conditioned by prudential concerns?

First, the rules of political association must take a broad view of human nature, human motivation, preferences and choices. Individuals do not always act rationally, particularly when in association, and the ties of civil and political association are not simply the ties of rational self-interest. Rules that relate to the powers of government, or to those acting in association, have to take this broader perspective into account. This is particularly important in framing rules about the distribution of powers where different forms of ties and the multiplicity of different human preferences must be recognized.

Second, the rules of association must recognize the large gap that exists between individual choices and actions.[49] All these weaknesses will show up in collective action and in the actions of those with political power. The rules of political association must therefore be framed from a precautionary perspective. Good intentions may not always prevail. The rules must guard against the misuses of power, whether those abuses come from individuals in association, or from governments.

Third, political rules are viewed as ways to achieve consistency in difficult areas of collective choice. Individual choices are not always consistent. Politics, as a method of collective choice, will not always achieve consistency. Prudential rules address particular areas of weakness in political choice.

Fourth, prudential rules provide rational ways to relate to the future, even though human nature is not always rational. They accept that human nature will err. Ideally human nature can be corrected, but a second best strategy is one of pre-commitment. Politics too has a weakness in dealing with choices that relate to the future. Prudential rules in a political association embody a strategy of pre-commitment in areas where choices about the future are likely to be weak.[50]

Finally, prudential rules do not simply have to be seen as ways of limiting undesired aspects of human behaviour in politics, or just as ways to achieve consistency in difficult areas of collective choice, but also, more positively, as ways of helping to manage future choice.[51] Many future public policy choices in Europe are going to be taken collectively. A fundamental purpose of the rules of a

European constitution is to give assurance about the framework for these decisions. If rules are to provide this assurance about the way in which future choices are to be managed, there has to be a particular emphasis on the stability of the rules and clarity about the procedures for their change.

The difficulty in justifying the prudential approach has been, first, to express prudence in the form of a general principle helpful for shaping procedures and rules in a political order. Second, there is the difficulty of relating prudence to the ethical. Prudence is often casually treated as synonymous with utility or short term self-interest.

(i) Non-coercion as a prudential principle

The non-coercion principle is usually attributed to Knut Wicksell's use of the unanimity rule in choices relating to public expenditure.[52] However in the discussion below it is treated in a much broader way as a general principle for capturing the essence of prudential rules. In this broader interpretation it represents the principle that the rules of a political order can be legitimized only in so far as they minimize the extent to which choice is imposed. In practical terms this means that powers and procedures in a European political union can be validated only if they can be shown to minimize the imposition of choices on communities and citizens within Europe through the political order.

Formulated as a prudential principle, the non-coercion principle starts from the point that the rules of political association are about how to manage interrelationships in society. The individual is to be seen in association with others and not in isolation. Otherwise the principle would be open to the simple objection that it ignores the basic social setting – the community. The starting point is that emphasized by Hume.[53] Adam Smith took a similar view.[54]

From this point of departure, the rules that relate to systems of government are seen to be rules that reflect the different ways in which people depend on each other.[55] It thus becomes crucial to define the nature of these dependencies and approaches to them.

(a) The cooperative One aspect of the way in which people depend on each other is indeed the cooperative – those things that can only be done in association.[56] The important characteristic of such settings is that all participants gain from the association. They also gain from the rules formalizing cooperative association. Hume drew analogies with the coordination of rowing a boat and the gains from clear rules of the road.

Under the non-coercion principle the benefits of rules that allow for cooperative association through the political order are acknowledged.[57] However, cooperation is seen to characterize only part of the rules of the political order. The gains from cooperation break down when interests conflict. Depictions of the way people depend on each other have to deal with the setting of conflict and the rules governing conflict. This is the message of Hobbes.[58] The rules that facilitate cooperative behaviour can be permissive. However, if the rules of political association are characterized entirely in these terms, political association will be seen as entirely benign and the rules will take inadequate precautions in dealing with those settings where the conflict of interests requires the coercive powers of government to be used.

(b) Exchange and bargaining One approach to the conflict of interests in society is to point to the scope for exchange and bargaining as methods of resolving differences. This is the analogy discussed earlier between the methods of political association with the methods of the economic market place.

The characterization of political processes as ones of exchange in the expectation of mutual gain, clearly captures another important aspect of relationships in a civil association. It does not replace characterizing a part of civil association as a means to reap the gains of cooperation. Both are valid characterizations of particular aspects of political association. Under the non-coercion rule as a prudential principle, rules that enable the political setting to be used as a mechanism for exchange and bargaining are seen to be highly desirable. Again, however, the question is whether the exchange account is a sufficient characterization. As discussed earlier, the maximizing assumptions of the exchange and bargaining model do not give a convincing account of rules as constraints in dealing with situations of conflict. Moreover, utility is too broad a concept for the justification of the rules of a political order.

(c) The conflictual The prudential approach is compatible with cooperative solutions to coordination settings and with rules that encourage exchange and bargaining solutions to differences in interests. However, the main area of difficulty with shaping the political order is seen to lie in the rules that establish, and the principles used to justify, the powers of government to settle differences by coercion.[59] It is particularly important in this context to frame rules as a precaution against the misuses of power. The non-coercion principle suggests that the rules of a political order should give particular emphasis to constraining the powers of government to impose choices. It does not characterize the political order exclusively in terms of conflicts of interest. It does see it as the most difficult area in any system of government. The power of the political order to settle differences through coercion is where there is a particular need for establishing prudential rules and justificatory principles.

The reason why coercion is seen as needing special attention in the rules of government lies first in the potential for abuse. The government usually has a monopoly on certain kinds of power in society (armed forces and tax) or privileged access to power (the police) and these powers can be misused. Coercion allows not only individual preferences to be overruled but also those of communities. The coercive powers of government may allow the majority to misuse the authority of government against minorities. Conversely, in cases where dedicated minorities control the levers of government, the powers of government to coerce may be used to force the majority to acquiesce within a political association.

Second, it is particularly in the context of the coercive powers of government that the prudential values underlying the rules must be clear and the relationship with ethical principles established. Both Bodin and Hobbes, despite being exponents of sovereign power, recognized this in emphasizing that their sovereigns remained answerable to reason and (in the terms of their era) to the divine.[60]

(ii) Prudential values and the ethical

(a) The individual? One approach to justifying, on ethical grounds, the principle that choice should not be imposed is that it respects the individual as the basis of society. This line of validation has two weaknesses.

First, the prudential approach is not only consistent with the view that choices should not be imposed on individuals but also with the view that choices should not be imposed on communities or wider groupings. All imposed choices need justification.

Second, resting the principle on the value of the individual runs into the notorious difficulties of justifying the individual as the basis for political association. If the ethical value of the individual is simply asserted, then, it is open to the counter assertion of other supreme values (including those that would potentially subordinate the individual to a collective good such as European union). If, alternatively, it is based on the unique nature of the individual, there is a problem of justifying a particular view of those innate qualities. If, finally, it is based on a view about rational choice (the individual knows best) then it is vulnerable too to different views about human nature.[61] In particular it is open to criticism of those who recognize the many weaknesses in human nature.[62] It is the view that it is in the weakness of human behaviour that the origin of social rules should be sought that the prudential approach is rooted.

(b) The moral The underlying justification of a prudential approach to the rules of a political order lies not just in a view of the weaknesses of human nature and behaviour, but also in a view of the relationship between prudential values and the ethical.

First, prudence should not be equated with utility. Prudence is sometimes seen erroneously as a self-regarding virtue rather than about interrelationships, and about immediate advantage rather than the longer term.[63] Prudence is thus seen as closely related if not synonymous with 'utility' and subject to the same deficiencies as an ethical guide.

However, rules of prudence are not the same as rules of utility. Prudence has a more precise meaning and application than 'utility'. In its application to the rules of a political order, prudence gives special attention to the coercive aspects of interrelationships in civil association. Rules that allow for governments to exercise coercion may be useful for achieving certain ends but not prudent. Nor is prudence about short term self-interest. Utility does not have a clear time dimension. Utility satisfaction may reflect either short term or long term interests and short or long term motivations. By contrast, through such concepts as rules that pre-commit, prudence, in its political application, gives weight to the long term.

Second, it is correct to draw a distinction between prudential values and moral values. It may be prudent to act in a particular way (for example, keeping quiet to save one's own skin) but not moral (for example, in standing up to an immoral political regime). If what is morally valued is valued only for prudential reasons then, equally for prudential reasons, that value may be ignored (Kant gave the example that it might not always be prudent to keep a promise). These distinctions are valid and important.

Third, however, it does not follow (as Kant argued) from the premise that rules of prudence can be overridden by moral and ethical concerns, that prudential values cannot serve as regulatory values in a political order.[64] Not all social rules are moral rules. The difference between prudential values and moral values can be seen as an advantage. The difference means that the rules of a political order can always be questioned on ethical grounds. This is as it should be. Someone who defers to authority on customary and prudential grounds must always be able to question their own behaviour, and be able to challenge authority, on ethical grounds. The important question is the relationship between the prudential and the ethical.[65]

(c) Relationships The relationship between prudential values in a political order and moral values is a coordinate one.

Prudential rules serve an ethical purpose analogous to moral rules as guards against weakness in human behaviour in political association, including moral weakness.

It can be seen not just as a prudential but also a moral virtue to accept limits on behaviour.[66]

Prudential rules provide a base line for the behaviour of governments so that, if the limits are overstepped by government, not only are prudential values in society being challenged but ethical judgements may also be triggered.

The prudential principle that choice should not be imposed does not specify a moral end because it allows for the maximum area of moral choice and judgement. This in itself is an ethical virtue. It allows for the richness of moral choice, recognizes that differences in moral valuations within a society may not be reconcilable (particularly through the political order) and recognizes that moral values will change over time.

Rules that guard against choices that are imposed through political processes, recognize that choices imposed by, or through, the political order, break or weaken the connection between the moral actor (whether the individual or the community) and the act. Government is interposed as the agent – an agent over which the actor may often feel to have no choice and no control.

Prudential values recognize that choices that are imposed are choices that are changed (for example, from the morality of giving gifts to the morality of paying taxes) or even voided.[67]

For these reasons, despite the differences between moral and prudential values, the case can be made that rules of prudence may serve as values that are coordinate with ethical judgements in political association. Prudential values that constrain the ability of the political order to impose choice are those most likely to be compatible with an ethical order.

(d) The application of the non-coercion principle The arguments that have been made about the nature of European political union up to this point have been purely theoretical. It has been argued that a constitution for Europe should not be seen in terms of the political ends to be achieved, since these will vary over time and their attainment can never be guaranteed. Instead, the constitution should be seen as bringing about a rule based political union centred on processes. These processes have to be validated by external standards of value. In turn, the acceptance that the rules of a constitution have to be rooted in values opened up a discussion about those potential values. It has been argued that the most important values are those about the processes of political association themselves and that the most important criterion is that choices should not be imposed. The justification of this approach lies in seeing the right processes for a political association as enshrining rules of prudence. Prudential values that constrain government are not the same as ethical values but they are the most compatible with the exercise of moral judgement.

The next stage of the discussion is to move from the theory towards its practical applications. In particular, the general prudential principle that choices should not be imposed has to be shown to offer a practical foundation for a rule based approach to Europe's political order.

Notes

1   Popper's criticisms of 'historicism' apply.
2   This connection is explored by Boulding: 'The value scales of any individual or organisation are perhaps the most important single element determining the effect of the messages it receives on its image of the world'. Boulding, K.E. (1977), *The Image – Knowledge in Life and Society*.
3   See, for example, the discussion by Professor Herbert Simon on the acceptability of Hitler's ideas. 'Reason was not, could not have been, our principal shield against Nazism. Our principal shield was contrary factual beliefs and values'. Simon, H.A.

'Alternative Visions of Rationality', in Arkes, H.R. and Hammond K.R. (eds) (1986), *Judgement and Decision Making: An Interdisciplinary Reader*.

4   Von Humboldt remarked of his treatment, in the Sphere and Duties of Government, of the coercive powers of government, 'The less a man is induced to act otherwise than his wish suggests or his powers permit, the more favourable does his position as a member of a civil community become. If, in view of this truth (around which all the ideas advanced in this essay properly revolve)..'.. von Humboldt, W. (1792), *The Sphere and Duties of Government*.

5   'A supreme principle is what is logically first in some field, in that everything else in the field depends for its justification more or less directly on the principle, whereas the principle in turn is not dependent on or justified by anything else'. Gewirth, A. (1981), *Reason and Morality*.

6   A recent example of a liberal search for a guiding principle is provided by the 'Principle of Generic Consistency' of Prof. Alan Gewirth (ibid). John Rawls also looked for a general regulatory principle in, 'a public conception of justice'. Rawls, J. (1972), *A Theory of Justice*.

7   In distinguishing between civil association and the state, Hegel identified the ethical with the state. 'The state is the actuality of the ethical idea'. Hegel, *Philosophy of Right*.

8   'Just as the pure theory of law eliminates the dualism of law and justice... so it abolishes the dualism of law and state'. Kelsen, H. (1946), *The General Theory of the Law and the State*.

9   'It shows that the State...is, at best, nothing but the personification of the national legal order'. Kelsen, ibid.

10   According to Kelsen the legislator's law is authorized (validated) by the constitution. 'In this authorizing of specific persons to create general norms lies the essential function of a constitution'. Kelsen, H. (1964), 'The Function of a Constitution' in Tur, R. and Twining, W. (eds), *Essays on Kelsen*.

11   For Kelsen the basic norm is 'a norm presupposed in juristic thinking'. 'It represents the ultimate basis of the validity of all the legal norms forming the legal order'. Kelsen, ibid.

12   'Rules of law, if valid, are norms. They are, to be more precise, norms stipulating sanctions'. Kelsen, (1946), op. cit.

13   'A norm the validity of which cannot be derived from a superior norm we call a 'basic' norm'. Kelsen, ibid.

14   'That is the basic norm. This basic norm authorizes the individual or the sum of individuals who laid down the historically first constitution to posit norms that represent the historically first constitution'. Kelsen, (1964), op. cit.

15   'Elected organs, such as a parliament and a chief of State, are, by and large, organs for the creation of general norms', Kelsen, (1946), op. cit.

16   '... a positive legal order represents a system not of coordinate but of superordinate and subordinate norms – that is a hierarchy of norms, whose highest tier is the constitution'. Kelsen, ibid.

17   '... the legal order of a federal State is composed of central norms valid for its entire territory and local norms valid only for portions of this territory'. Kelsen, ibid.

18   '... on the condition that one presupposes the basic norm: one ought to conduct oneself as the constitution prescribes, that is, in conformity with... the commands of the creator of the constitution'. Kelsen, ibid.

19   'What cannot be found in the contents of positive legal norms cannot enter a legal concept'. Kelsen, ibid.

20   'The basic norm is only the necessary presupposition of any positivistic interpretation of the legal material'..'. Its content is determined by facts'. Kelsen, ibid.

21   What is a norm? 'The norm is the expression of the idea that something ought to occur,

especially that an individual ought to behave in a certain way'. Kelsen, ibid.

22   'A norm however is neither true nor false, but valid or invalid'. Kelsen, H. (1973), *Essays in Legal and Moral Philosophy.*

23   '. . . the norm is the import of an act of will' and 'A norm posited by an act of will occurring in the real world is a positive norm'. Kelsen, ibid.

24   'The validity of this first constitution is the. . . final postulate, upon which the validity of all the norms of our legal order depend'. Kelsen, (1946), op. cit.

25   'Since political freedom means agreement between the individual will and the collective will expressed in the social order, it is the principle of simple majority which secures the highest degree of political freedom that is possible within society'. Kelsen, ibid.

26   '. . . the public use of man's reason must always be free, and it alone can bring about enlightenment among men'. An Answer to the question: 'What is Enlightenment' in Reiss H (ed) (1970), *Kant's Political Writings.*

27   '. . . no one can doubt that the convention for the distinction of property, and for the stability of possession, is of all circumstances the most necessary to the establishment of human society, and that after the agreement for the fixing and observing of this rule there remains little or nothing to be done towards settling a perfect harmony and concord'. Hume, D. (1740), *A Treatise of Human Nature.*

28   'One may think of a public conception of justice as constituting the fundamental charter of a well-ordered human association'. Rawls, op. cit.

29   According to Kant, reason cannot will that the wealthy should neglect the struggling, 'A will ordaining such would contradict itself, when, in the course of events, it would willingly avail itself of the compassion and kindness of others, and yet would see itself deprived of these by the harsh law emanating from its own maxim'. Kant, I. (1797), *The Metaphysics of Ethics.*

30   The two principles that the individual would choose according to Rawls are first, 'equality in the assignment of basic rights and duties' and secondly, 'that social and economic inequalities. . . are just only if they result in compensating benefits for everyone'. Rawls, op. cit.

31   Lomanski offers this view in his account of the moral community, 'if the extremes are avoided, neither individualism nor the possibility of harmonious social existence need be forfeited. . . it can. . . connote a relaxed assurance of one's place. . . as a full and equal member of the moral community'. Lomanski, L.E. (1987), *Persons, Rights and the Moral Community.*

32   See, Sen, A. (1973), *On Economic Inequality.*

33   Adam Smith insisted on property rights being seen in a broader context. 'Civil government, so far as it is instituted for the security of property, is in reality instituted for the defence of the rich against the poor, or of those who have some property against those who have none at all'. Smith A. (1776), *An Inquiry into the Nature and Causes of the Wealth of Nations.*

34   Ackerman argues that the Rawls approach legitimizes everything from imposed uniformity to imposed domination and that the Rawls criteria make it too easy to manipulate the chooser and the choice set. Ackerman, B.A. (1980), *Social Justice in the Liberal State.*

35   Gewirth argues, 'the inductive justification assumes that we can differentiate the morally right from the morally wrong in persons' particular moral judgements and hence infer what is the morally right general principle by generalising from the morally right particular judgements'. He asks the question of what happens if particular judgements are disputed. Gewirth, op. cit.

36   Rawls adopts a serial order, 'by ranking the principle of equal liberty prior to the

principle regulating economic and social inequalities'. Rawls, op. cit.

37 Rawls offers only an economic argument based on the assertion that liberty becomes more important as wealth in society increases. This assumption that liberty matters less in a poor society is not tenable. The lack of right to private property or freedom to contract may lie at the root of the poverty.

38 Rawls for example makes the crucial assumption that social relationships can be characterized in terms of cooperation alone. His 'underlying conception' is of, 'a well-ordered society as a scheme of cooperation for reciprocal advantage regulated by principles which persons would choose in an initial situation that is fair'. Rawls, op. cit.

39 Lewis, D.K. (1986), *Convention: A Philosophical Study*.

40 'Agents confronted by a coordination problem may or may not succeed in each acting so that they reach one of the possible coordination equilibria. . . but they are more likely to succeed – if they do – through the agency of a system of suitably concordant mutual expectation'. Lewis, ibid.

41 According to Axelrod in prisoners dilemma, 'the strategy that works best depends directly on what strategy the other player is using and, in particular, on whether this strategy leaves room for the development of mutual cooperation'. Axelrod, R. (1984), *The Evolution of Cooperation*.

42 The importance of interactions in individual valuations has been explored in particular by Becker. '. . . the greater the contribution of his social environment to his social income, the more his welfare is determined by the attitudes and behaviour of others rather than by his own income'. Becker, G.S. (1974), 'A Theory of Social Interactions', *Journal of Political Economy*, 82.

43 Axelrod concludes on the importance of teaching players the 'values, facts and skills that will promote cooperation'. Axelrod, op. cit. The same point is made by Brams. 'In general, it seems, it takes some time for a mutual trust to develop between players that enables them to escape the compulsion to assume the worst and shift to the cooperative strategies that result in the mutually beneficial outcome'. Brams, S.J. (1976), *Game Theory and Politics*.

44 The importance of commitments and of repeated play is set out by Fudenberg and Tirole. 'Commitments can be of value, since by committing himself to a given sequence of actions a player may be able to alter the play of his opponents'. 'Repeated play with patient players not only makes 'cooperation' – meaning efficient pay offs – possible, it also leads to a larger set of other equilibrium outcomes'. 'The reason repeated play introduces new equilibrium outcomes is that players can condition their play on the information they have received in previous games'. Fudenberg, D. and Tirole, J. (1992), *Game Theory*.

45 'Coordination problems. . . are situations of interdependent decision by two or more agents in which coincidence of interest predominates and in which there are two or more proper coordination equilibria'. Lewis, op. cit.

46 The conditions Axelrod proposes for successful decision rules involve the avoidance of unnecessary conflict by cooperating as long as the other player does, but provocability if the other player defects followed by forgiveness after responding to defection. This 'carrot and stick' approach means that rules begin to move away from a pure focus on cooperation even in positive sum settings. Axelrod, op. cit.

47 Schelling gives a more complete guide to the many different settings in which bargaining takes place. Schelling, T. (1984), *Choice and Consequences*.

48 '. . . here then is the origin of civil government and society. Men are not able radically to cure, either in themselves or others, that narrowness of soul which makes them prefer the present to the remote. They cannot change their natures. All they can do is to change their situation. . . these persons, then, are not only induced to observe those rules in

their own conduct, but also to constrain others to a like regularity, and enforce the dictates of equity through the whole society'. Hume, op. cit.

49 Pears explores the many and various sources of weaknesses in connecting individual values and individual actions – ranging from lack of information, incorrect processing of information, Lack of control (akrasia) self deception, emotions, weakness of will, wishful thinking and acting against one's better judgement. His account also allows for the self to be seen as composed of multiple personalities. Pears, D. (1984), *Motivated Irrationality*.

50 The best known account of rules as indirect strategies of pre-commitment is given in Elster, J. (1984), *Ulysses and the Sirens*.

51 A criticism of viewing rules just as devices that thwart, and in favour of viewing them as devices to help transform and manage choice, is given by McClennan in his theory of 'resolute choice'. McClennan, E.F. (1990), *Rationality and Dynamic Choice: Foundational Explorations*.

52 Wicksell, K. (1896), 'A New Principle of Just Taxation' in Musgrave, R.A. and Peacock, A.T. (eds) (1958,) *Classics in the Theory of Public Finance*.

53 'Society is absolutely necessary for the well-being of men'. Hume, op. cit.

54 'All the members of human society stand in need of each others assistance, and are likewise exposed to mutual injuries'. Smith, A. (1778), *The Theory of Moral Sentiments*.

55 'The age of shepherds is that where government properly first commences. And it is at this time too that men become in any considerable degree dependent on others'. Smith A. (1762–64), *Lectures on Jurisprudence*.

56 'It is by society alone that he (man) is able to supply his defects. . . By the conjunction of forces our power is augmented; by the partition of employments our ability increases; and by mutual succour we are less exposed to fortune and accidents'. Hume, op. cit.

57 'It is not power as such. . . that is bad, but only the power to coerce'. Hayek, F.A. (1960), *The Constitution of Liberty*.

58 '. . . the society proceeding from mutual help only, yeelds not that security which they seek for'. Hobbes. T. (1651), *de Cive*.

59 'Coercion occurs when one man's actions are made to serve another man's will, not for his own but for the other's purpose'. Hayek, op. cit.

60 Even Hobbes placed his sovereign under limits. According to Hobbes the sovereign was to rule justly, 'without breach of the naturall lawes and injury against god' and it was the duty of rulers, 'in all things, as much as possibly they can, to yeeld obedience unto right reason, which is the naturall, morall, and divine law'. Hobbes, op. cit.

61 Adam Smith held a rationalist view of human nature. 'Every man is certainly. . . fitter and abler to take care of himself than of any other person. Every man feels his own pleasures and his own pains more sensibly than those of other people'. At the same time however he emphasized the stoic philosophy of self-restraint and self-discipline. Smith, (1778), op. cit.

62 Schelling suggests that the proneness of individuals to err suggests the need for some kind of 'command' theory. 'Decision theory is the science of choosing in accordance with one's existing preferences, maximising the satisfaction of one's values. When the values that govern one's preferences are liable to be displaced by values that one deprecates, we need in addition something that might be called command theory – the theory of self command, or self management'. This is in essence analogous to rules of constraint. Schelling, op. cit.

63 Lomanski defines prudence in the following terms, 'the skill involved in juggling possibilities for action in the light of their opportunity costs and probabilities of future goods and ills is the virtue of prudence'. This is more a definition of a narrow self-interest rather than prudence. Lomanski, op. cit.

64 Kant disposed of prudence as a regulatory principle on the grounds that prudence is not an unqualified good. Kant drew a further distinction between prudence as a 'pragmatic imperative' and the laws of morality which provided moral imperatives. Pragmatic imperatives could suggest a course of action but not command. They are only means to an end not ends in themselves.

65 Pears suggests, 'there are obvious differences between the two. . . When moral and prudential values conflict, it is generally assumed that moral values should carry the day, and from this it is sometimes inferred that the intrinsic effectiveness of moral valuation is greater. The premise of this inference may be conceded. . . but the inference itself should be challenged. It may even be more plausible to suppose that the intrinsic effectiveness of prudential valuation is greater'. Pears, op. cit.

66 'It belongs to our moral faculties,...to determine. . . .when and how far every other principle of our nature ought either to be indulged or restrained'. Smith, (1778), op. cit.

67 'The achievement of self discipline. . . must on any theory of morality be a constituent of a good life. But what is valuable here is voluntary restraint, not submission to coercion, which seems quite empty of moral value'. Hart, H.L.A. (1963), *Law, Liberty and Morality*.

Part II
PROCESSES AND COERCION

4 Value differences in Europe

'The public welfare which demands first consideration lies precisely in that legal constitution which guarantees everyone his freedom within the law, so that each remains free to seek his happiness in whatever way he thinks best, so long as he does not violate the lawful freedom and rights of his fellow subjects at large'. Immanuel Kant, *On the Relationship of Theory to Practice in Political Right*, 1792.

I Principles and practice

European political union will succeed, or fall apart, depending on how well its constitutional processes work in practice in the three areas of the greatest potential difficulty. These three areas are:

- the handling of the diversity of values and interests that exist in Europe. European political union has to be able to turn this diversity to its advantage rather than let it become a source of endless disagreement and weakness. The question is how to structure the rules so as to achieve this reconciliation.
- the redefinition of the role of the nation state. No one wishes to see a return to the nationalism of the 1930s. But there are also dangers in overcentralization. European political union puts in place a larger framework for political association for the peoples of Europe. At the same time it also makes possible the expression of more local and regional interests and diversities. Both developments weaken the traditional state and its institutions. As a result, European political union can be seen simply as a threat to existing institutions. It does not have to be seen in these stark terms. The role of the nation state can be redefined within a system of differentiated jurisdictions so that the inherited and traditional legitimacy of the Member States can underpin rather than challenge the legitimacy of the new European framework. The key question is how to structure a new relationship between jurisdictions.
- the taking of collective policy decisions in Europe at the highest level of

collective decision making, wherever that may be located. The imposition of choice will again lead to the processes of the Union being exposed to constant challenge. Friction and fragmentation will result. Yet, at the same time, there is a need to avoid rules that lead to collective paralysis.

Europe's constitution must have rules which apply specifically to these areas of the greatest difficulty in European political union. These are the areas where political association in Europe can most easily and most badly go wrong.

This chapter and the two following chapters discuss the main constitutional approaches to these three crucial aspects of processes in a European political union. The discussion distinguishes between:

(i) Provisions in a constitution that deal directly with values and value differences

Such provisions establish normative guidelines for political processes. The most familiar guidelines are those to be found in declarations of rights. The aim of these and other forms of such provisions, is to recognize the shortcomings of politics as a means to arrive at collective choices when there are substantial value differences in society. Limits on political processes may be justiciable (for example, certain kinds of declarations of rights). In such cases, the constitution must be clear which are to be justiciable and which are not. In cases where limits are intended to be justiciable, the applicable jurisdiction must also be clear. For example, cases involving individual and civil liberties might be left primarily to the jurisdiction of Member States, or entrusted to a Union court or to a specialized procedure such as that under the European Convention on Human Rights.

The crucial question is how to frame the constitutional guidelines in ways which allow for the expression of diversities and not as a means of imposing uniformities. Relying too much on politics, in areas where political processes are not well suited to the reconciliation of interests, will expose the legitimacy of European political processes to constant question. On the other hand, attempts to impose values through constitutional provisions will lead to similar questioning. The values expressed directly in a constitution have to be framed in such a way as to steer through this dilemma.

(ii) Provisions that focus on the distribution of powers

These are the provisions that will establish relationships between different and potentially competing jurisdictions in Europe. They involve taking a view on 'optimum domain' in Europe – whether most of the important issues of public policy should be assigned for collective decision taking by the Union itself or whether there are advantages in a system of multiple jurisdictions. If there are advantages in multiple jurisdiction, then the relationship between the different jurisdictions has to be defined in the constitution.

(iii) Decision rules

These are the rules for deciding whose preferences shall prevail in collective decision making. They are the rules that have to strike a practical balance between rules that allow for all choices to be made by mutual consent against the risk that such rules could never allow for effective decision making processes.

Although, for discussion purposes, these different areas and the approaches to be taken to them can be distinguished, they are, in practice, closely related. A constitution that expresses normative limits on collective choice through politics with the aim of allowing for the expression of a diversity of values, will find the intent of such provisions undermined if there is not at the same time in place a system of multiple jurisdictions that allows for different preferences to be reflected in different jurisdictions. Getting that relationship right is difficult. For example, declarations of individual rights and civil liberties may perform a useful role in limiting the domain of politics. However, if they are enforced by a 'court of the Union', such declarations become a very powerful means through which a central jurisdiction can extend into areas intended for other jurisdictions. Thus, there has to be clarity as to where normative limits are to be applied and how they are to be enforced. Similarly, if decision making processes allow for minority preferences easily to be overruled, the purpose of setting limits on politics, or on the powers of the collective domain, will equally quickly be eroded. Conversely, if decision taking procedures do not provide for effective collective decision taking, a system of multiple domain and limited politics will come under challenge. There is therefore a need for a consistency check on the approaches to be adopted across these different areas.

The general principle that the processes of the Union should minimize coercion provides a consistency test. It suggests approaching the more specific rules suited to each of these areas by:

- concentrating the normative guidelines for political processes on the weak points of the political method of collective choice (for example, where there are special problems in the way of achieving consistent political choices or in respect of choices that affect the long term). The guidelines should be framed as procedural limits on political choice and not as attempts to predetermine the outcomes of political choice (declarations of social rights are mistaken);
- establishing a system of multiple jurisdictions that would allow for different preferences to be reflected through different jurisdictions, rather than looking for a single focus for collective choice in the Union;
- graduating the decision rules of the Union in ways that would reflect different

sensitivities in different areas of collective choice. Procedures must protect against the risk of choices being imposed in areas that are of the highest importance. They must also balance the interests of the different jurisdictions.

This chapter opens the discussion by considering the role of politics as a means to reconcile the different interests and different values held in Europe. It looks at the case for the rules in Europe's constitution to set normative limits on politics and how such limits should be formulated.

II Approaching value differences

(i) The constitutional perspective

A key function of any constitution for Europe is to set the framework for political processes. The framework must be able to provide for the expression of those values and interests that are shared across Europe. At the same time it must also allow for the expression of those that differ. If political processes fail to capture shared values and shared interests then Europe will fail to reap the benefits of political cooperation. Institutions and procedures will then become vulnerable to the politics of frustration. If, on the other hand, political processes do not allow for the expression of differences in values and interests, the legitimacy of the constitutional structure will be under constant challenge.

A constitution can be a simple document if all values and interests are shared and held equal in importance and equal in esteem in society. Much can then be done by convention without the need for a constitution at all. Where, however, there is potential tension between what is held in common and what is viewed differently, the constitutional task is more difficult. At the same time, the requirement for the constitution to set the framework for the handling of differences becomes vital. Tensions can pull the Union apart. Alternatively, frustration may trigger the intolerance of ideology as a way of imposing a 'solution' on differences rather than trying to sort them out. Ideology offers a short cut to handling differences, to dealing with minorities and to pressuring otherwise passive majorities. Ideology simply seeks to override them. A constitution can provide one line of defence against ideology through the way in which it treats value differences.

(ii) Value differences in Europe

Because differences within a society makes the framing of a political order so much more difficult, there is a temptation in Europe to stress what is held in common and to wish to gloss over the differences. The emphasis on what is shared and held in common is indeed important. The European Union will be built on the common interests of the Member States and their citizens. If there were no mutual gains to be had from pursuing interests together there would be little reason for a Union. Equally there must be a basis of shared values. In the absence of shared values, attempts to build a common approach in areas of mutual interest would constantly founder. In these two respects European political union can reasonably be viewed simply as an exercise in social coordination. Coordination can capture both shared values and achieve mutual gains.

At the same time, it has to be recognized that interests will not always coincide within the European political union as a whole. They will frequently conflict. Equally, values may not always coincide. Even more frequently the weight to be attached to particular values may differ. From this perspective political processes must do more than coordinate – they must be able to handle differences.

Differences in Europe come from a variety of sources. There are important shared elements in Europe's history – for example, the experience of wars in this century – but also there are the differences – for example, between countries that went under foreign occupation and those that did not. There is the shared experience of the Cold War – but again a major difference whether this was experienced from western Europe or within the Russian sphere of domination. There is (to take a less dramatic example) a shared concern about environmental degradation in Europe but a more acute concern from countries at higher income levels in northern Europe than from the lower income countries of southern Europe. Again on domestic policies, there is a shared concern to acknowledge the social dimension to market rules but disagreement on how to recognize it and what weight to attach to the 'social'. In looking to the outside world there is acceptance that whatever order is established in Europe will have to find its place within the larger global order of trading rules and standards of behaviour. But there are differences of view as to how Europe can fit within this larger context. Some see Europe as needing to develop its 'identity' as an increasingly independent and self-contained bloc. Others see the need for European rules and institutions to find their place within the broader multilateral setting. On foreign policy there are different views as to which external relationships are the more important, how far Europe needs to act 'out of area' in support of international rules of behaviour and how far and in what ways to act in concert with others – notably with the United States.

The list of what is shared and what is different can be multiplied many times. Some of the differences revolve around 'domain' – whether Europe provides the right arena for collective choice. These questions will be discussed in the next chapter. But, even after questions of domain have been settled, there will still remain questions of values and value differences within the European domain. In practical terms the questions include whether Europe's constitution should enjoin common social values; how language and religious differences should be treated; whether ethnic ties could be allowed to overrule rights of free movement and rights of residence and whether environmental values deserve and can receive special recognition.

The key question is to what extent values on these and similar questions and value differences can be brought together through the collective choice processes of politics and to what extent, and in what manner, such questions should be addressed directly in the constitution itself.

(iii) The plausibility of politics

The idea that politics in the European Union can be relied upon to build on what is shared and to reconcile those interests and values where they diverge is an attractive one. It rests on the assumption that politics provides a method through which it is possible to bargain between differences in preferences in ways which leave the proponents of different viewpoints still satisfied with the overall outcome of the bargaining process. There are many countries in Europe where this assumption appears valid and that are able to rely on politics for this purpose. Written constitutions play a relatively limited role in restraining the sphere of politics. Law too plays a much less decisive role than it does, for example, in the United States.

The plausibility of the political method for reconciling preferences is increased by the role of the modern party system. Parties can provide a mechanism for bargaining. They purport to represent some kind of summation of opinion, at least for their party supporters. The party platform may also indicate an ordering of preferences. The growth of parties on a pan-European basis is important precisely because it will increase the potential for differences to be settled through the political process. Voting methods are also important. Proportional representation is seen as a way to encourage the reconciliation of different interests through bargaining rather than the sharpening of differences through the practice of adversarial politics.

Nevertheless, it is oversimplifying the setting in Europe to suppose that political practices within Member States can easily be transposed to the European Union. Differences within most Member States are not as pronounced as across Europe as a whole. In those Member States where differences have been pronounced (whether because of income, or generation, or because of the more emotive differences of language or religion) the political method has not always worked well to contain them. Quite apart from these reasons for caution, there are other more fundamental reasons why politics is unlikely to provide the means for reconciling differences in Europe. These reasons concern the inherent shortcomings of politics as a method for arriving at collective choices.

III The shortcomings of politics

The shortcomings of politics as a method to resolve differences in preferences and values can be seen from three different perspectives.

- One viewpoint focuses on the general problem of the aggregation of preferences through politics.
- The second concerns the specific frailties of politics as a method.
- A third perspective looks at the vulnerability of politics to both majorities and minorities.

It is because of weaknesses arising from each of these sources that Europe's constitution needs to place politics within procedural limits. The purpose of the framework is to strengthen politics in areas where it can work well but to establish constraints where it does not.

(i) The problem of aggregation

Politics assumes that some kind of summation or ordering of preferences is possible in society through political methods so that preferences in society can be reflected accurately. Combined with a generally acceptable decision rule (for example, that the majority should prevail or that as many major interests should be represented in decisions as possible) the assumption is that a choice can be made that will command assent. The difficulty with these assumptions is that aggregation, either through summation or through the ordering of preferences, raises very formidable obstacles.

(a) Summation An early attempt to provide a rule for deciding on preferences in a democratic setting and which linked individual preferences to collective choice is associated with the utilitarianism of Bentham.[1] Correct decisions were those that reflected the greatest happiness of the greatest number. This rule attempted to provide a comparative measure of individual preferences (utility), together with a decision rule (the majority should prevail).

It was especially as a criterion by which institutions could be judged that utilitarianism had a radical cutting edge when first formulated. Any institution that appeared to benefit only a few became immediately suspect and the possible target for abolition or reform. Institutions had to make a measurable contribution to social welfare (to public utility). They could be judged by their output. The contribution also had to be in the interest of the majority of people. In addition, by basing the concept of the social good on the good of individuals, rather than a good defined independently of individual desires, it also had a powerful appeal against established authorities (whether of the church or state) that might attempt to define the public good on behalf of the public. Again the radicalism entered by questioning whose interests were being served.

As a rule for deciding between different preferences and values in politics, utilitarianism has long been criticized. It has been criticized primarily because it oversimplified the problem of the aggregation of preferences.[2] It assumed that individual utility could be measured in a meaningful way. It assumed further that summation is possible – that different preferences could simply be added together. It also assumed, without further question, that interpersonal comparisons of utility could be made.[3] Finally, it has been criticized for the simple majoritarianism of the decision rule – that majority preferences should decide.

Utilitarianism remains a powerful test of both institutions and rules in society. This is because the question it asks, as to whose interests an institution or rule is serving, remains a highly pertinent question. It does not however provide a sufficient basis for deciding on the answer to the question – is the rule or institution a good rule or good institution? Nor is it a method which justifies viewing the summation of votes or opinions through political processes as sufficient for determining between differences in preferences.

(b) Comparing orders of preference The centre of attention of most discussion of collective choice in recent years has not been on trying to make interpersonal comparisons of utility but, instead, to compare the way in which individuals rank or order their preferences and then see how the most preferred ranking can be obtained. This has been the focus of much recent welfare economics and social choice theory precisely because the central problem in welfare economics has been seen to be deriving a social maximum from individual preferences. Technically, social choice theory involves the assumption that an individual has a definite ordering of all conceivable social states in terms of their desirability to that individual; it assumes that preferences between different pairs of alternative social states are consistent and it assumes that the relationship between preferences can be ordered. On the basis of these assumptions, a functional relationship can be expressed which states the social ordering of alternative social states correspond-ing to each set of individual orderings of alternative social states. By analogy, politics can also be seen as a way to express and channel such orderings.

The inference that politics can act as a way to express social orderings accu-rately is undermined by Arrow's 'impossibility' theorem.[4] This theorem has shown just how difficult it is to derive a social maximum from a methodology which rejects the possibility of interpersonal comparisons and which relies instead on comparing orders of preferences held by individuals. The theorem imposes five apparently reasonable conditions on the construction of a social welfare function. The conditions are themselves value judgements. The conditions are as follows:

- There is an 'admissible set' of individual ordering relations for which the social welfare function defines a corresponding social ordering (the 'admissible set' defines the available choices).

- There is a positive association between the social ordering and alterations in individual values.
- The choice made by society from a given environment depends only on the orderings of individuals among the alternatives in that environment.
- Individuals are free to choose (choice is not imposed).
- Social choice is non-dictatorial (all choices in all situations are not imposed by one person against the wishes of all others).

From these apparently reasonable conditions, the theorem shows that freedom of individual choice is incompatible with collective rationality. Excluding the possibility of interpersonal comparisons of utility, the only methods of passing from individual tastes to social preferences which do not reflect individual desires negatively and which will be defined for a wide range of sets of individual orderings are either imposed or dictatorial. The theory denies therefore any easy way to aggregate preferences in society.

The difficulty in going from individual choice to collective choice through politics was recognized early on in the exploration of majority voting rules. Condorcet showed at the end of the eighteenth century that a simple majority vote would not necessarily provide a decision where the majority would prevail in a multi-alternative setting. (Condorcet's 'paradox' involves a three person, three alternative setting). Arrow's theory is not technically a generalization of Condorcet's paradox because it involves different conditions.[5] But it is more devastating in its implications. This is first, because it brings together the methodology of choice as used in economics and bargaining theory in a way which appears to have a general applicability to aggregation in politics.[6] Second, it does not assume a single particular decision rule (simple majority voting) but looks to establish any binary collective decision rule that could be generalized to a multi-alternative choice.

How applicable is the impossibility theorem to politics? Does it undermine belief in the ability of politics as a way to achieve social coordination. The two can be seen to be very closely connected. Both centre on questions of 'rational' choice. Political choice involves choice between policy preferences – usually when choices are limited or constrained. Choosing between politicians or between parties is, at least in part, often a choice between policies. The most important function of modern government is to choose between priorities and to set the direction of public policy. If the closeness of the analogy is accepted, the conclusion must be that the aggregations that are achieved through political choice are going to be rather crude approximations of preferences in society. Decision making that relies just on politics will be associated with imposed choices.

The awareness that politics cannot point to a method of aggregation that would suggest, even in theory, that it could provide an accurate reflection of preferences in society is reinforced by other imperfections of politics in practice.

(ii) Politics as a methodology

The further questioning of the political method has also come from other applications of economic methodology to politics. Public choice theory suggests that institutions no less than individuals are motivated by their self-interest which may diverge from any general interest. Theories of 'rent seeking' which view those in positions of political power as able to exploit profitable opportunities also suggest that such behaviour cannot be relied upon to produce outcomes that are in the interest of all. The methodology of economics has more generally pointed to how manipulative behaviour by those in power, particularly in respect of the creation of client relationships through public expenditures, as well as the opposing attempts at rule capture by interest groups, make the outcomes of political processes likely to diverge from real preferences in society.

The voting procedures of a democratic society, or in a representative assembly, do not provide a check against such problems. This is not only because of the voting 'paradoxes' where preference orderings may be divided in such a way that the solution preferred by most does not emerge on top. In a setting where the behaviour of one actor may influence the behaviour of another, game theory suggests it may be rational for an actor to misrepresent their true preferences. It may also be rational to abstain in situations where the individual seems powerless. At best, voting will likely lead political processes to focus on the 'median' voter.[7]

What these perceptions imply are that politics will not only fail to reflect the range of preferences in society in any other than a crude way but that political behaviour can also distort preferences. The implication is that constitutional rules are needed to recognize these weaknesses and to correct for them.

(iii) Tyrannizing majorities or determined minorities

Well before the more recent applications of economics to politics, political processes were thought to be unlikely to express preferences in society accurately. In particular there was the fear that majorities would use political power to impose their preferences on minorities.[8] In fact the problem is more complicated.

The greatest damage to liberty in Europe in the twentieth century has not come from majorities but from determined minorities. The problem of the majority in the democratic state has been its passivity and acquiescence in the face of strongly motivated and ideologically driven minorities. The political method is open therefore to attack from two sides. On the one hand minorities need protection from majorities. On the other hand, rules must offer majorities protection against the capture of institutions and rules by dedicated minorities.

The defeat of fascism and the collapse of communism does not mean that Europe is no longer prone to the politics of dedicated minorities. On the contrary. Proponents of European political union must also avoid the traps open to the dedicated and must look for a political framework that can gain broad public support throughout Europe and that is capable of maintaining support.

IV The implications for the constitution

Whatever the shortfalls of politics as a method of collective choice, and whatever the inherent difficulties in collective choice itself, we are still left with the need for collective choice as well as a need for politics for all those choices that cannot be settled through the market place. The practical issues therefore surround how to set the framework for politics in the light of its shortcomings as a method.

(i) Stressing similarities

The problem of moving from individual preferences to aggregate preferences is very much reduced if preferences in society are similar. In such circumstances the assumed impossibility of interpersonal comparisons becomes much more questionable.[9] The imperfections of politics are thus likely to matter very much less. Gaps between majorities and minorities will not be large. Politics as a coordinating mechanism appears more plausible. Thus one reaction to the difficulties with politics is to stress the interests and values that are shared across Europe and hope that these similarities will outweigh the areas of divergent preferences.

Unfortunately, in the context of Europe's history, the prudent assumption seems to be that differences in preferences and values may be extensive across a wide range of decision taking. In addition, it also seems a safe assumption that differences may be strongly held. If they are strongly held, then the imposition of contrary preferences through attempts at the aggregation of politics may simply be unacceptable. In this case a European constitution that relied exclusively on political processes for settling differences is likely to founder.

(ii) Disputing the analogy

An alternative response is to dispute the relevance of the methodology of economics to politics. In general terms the argument is that a method of economic analysis which begins with individual behaviour is being confused with political individualism.[10] More precisely, there are three different ways in which the relevance of the economic method can be disputed.

First, the concept of 'rationality', as defined in economics, can be questioned as an unreal characterization of individual choice processes.

Second, the concept of 'rationality' as defined in economics can be challenged as an unreal characterization of collective choice.

Third, it can be questioned whether individual behaviour in situations involving collective choice can be characterized in the same way as behaviour in situations only involving individual choice.

(a) The characterization of individual choice Questions about the characterization of individual choice have been raised in respect of whether individuals do weigh all alternative choices as assumed in preference theory or whether they go through a much more limited sequence of decision taking, better characterized, for example, by theories of 'bounded' rationality.[11] The economist's definition of 'rational' choice is much more stringent than simply acting with good reason.[12]

(b) The characterization of collective choice One line of questioning about the nature of collective choice has already been discussed. It centred on the question as to whether collective choice can be properly viewed in terms of 'maximizing' behaviour.[13] In highly important respects, collective choice seems to involve the notion of constrained behaviour.

(c) Differences in behavioural assumptions The idea that differences in behavioural assumptions are warranted in comparing individual behaviour with collective behaviour is summarized by the conventional distinction made between the individual as a consumer and the individual as a citizen. In acting as a consumer the individual is seen to be fulfilling a narrower function than as a citizen. The modes of reasoning are also seen to be different. Even if the mind of the individual is viewed as a 'consumer' there seem to be different roles for it to play.[14] Put in more general terms, the question is whether the idea of an individual having a single mode of 'rational' behaviour is not a gross oversimplification of the individual as a multi-faceted decision taker.[15]

According to the distinction between the individual as citizen and the individual as consumer, choosing between consumer goods in the market place is not seen as the same as making political choice because consumers are seen to be concerned only with their own private interest and choose between courses of action affecting only themselves. There is seen to be no place for altruism, and no place for individual choosers to consider the effect of their choice on another. By contrast, in political choice, interactions are seen to be important. Choosers in politics do not see themselves just as private decision takers. Their choice will affect others. Ethical considerations including altruistic behaviour may be very important. In addition, ethical views may include holistic values (values about the social whole that cannot be reduced to the values of individuals in the social whole). Traditionally, the method of politics has given great weight to discussion and the need to state reasons openly. In contrast again, individual consumers do not have to justify their choices.

The criticism that the citizen should not be confused with the consumer has a powerful resonance – not least when societies are reacting against what are seen to be materialistic values.[16] Non-materialist philosophies continue to play an important role in European politics (most notably in 'green' politics which influences most political parties). It is therefore a strand in Europe that has to be given some weight, as indeed do holistic values. Sometimes criticisms of the materialist assumptions of economics are misguided. As discussed earlier, economics does not enquire into motivation – it only postulates choice. Ethical considerations can lie behind a choice – for example, the purchase of products that are environmentally 'friendly'. Individual choice can also be influenced by the perceived outcomes of collective choice – for example, taking vacations at off peak periods.

Even allowing for misunderstandings about the treatment of choice in economics, the underlying issue is whether reservations about the way in which 'rational' choice is characterized in economics are such as to suggest that the problems of collective choice, as revealed by the 'impossibility' theorem, can be ignored in looking at collective choice in politics. This is difficult to do. Problems of aggregation remain also under different interpretations of 'rationality'. The problems of politics as a method of collective choice do not rest simply on the impossibility theorem. The issue seems to lie in what interpretation should be given to the theorem rather than in challenging the difficulties of aggregation. In this context, it is not always appreciated that the interpretation of the impossibility theorem as offered by the author himself was to put the spotlight back on the normative element in choice.[17]

(iii) Reintroducing the normative

The results of the impossibility theorem themselves point to possible methods of treating the rules governing the political process, so that the rules might help overcome the problems of aggregation and distortions in politics, even under different concepts of 'rationality'. In particular, they suggest looking at values as ways to set the boundaries of politics and as a way of reintroducing the possibility of comparisons between choices. The question is how to encapsulate the normative element.

The value assumptions on which the impossibility theorem is built suggest the lines of inquiry about normative guidelines for politics. Are there ways of narrowing down in advance of political debate what is an admissible set of values to be included in the political bargaining process?[18] Is it possible to increase the likelihood of a positive association between individual values and social orderings by obtaining pre-agreement on at least some orderings where politics has intrinsic difficulties in handling preferences? Is it possible to reduce the tensions from imposed solutions by agreement on certain values in advance? Some values might be held to be untouchable through the political process. Others might be looked to as a means of establishing a certain direction for political bargaining.

These are all questions that can be treated as constitutional questions because they can help define the rules within which politics takes place. They are about the normative boundaries of politics. The difficulty lies in framing the rules in ways which allow for differences rather than imposing uniformities. This difficulty can be overcome if the rules are seen as setting procedural standards and not about pre-determining outcomes.

V Normative limits on politics

The imperfections of politics can be recognized and addressed potentially in four main ways.

The first is by establishing pre-agreement on values that are intended to give a positive 'steer' to politics. Such values aim to set a certain direction to politics or set a floor under political discussion. They are usually expressed in the form of lists of positive rights (for example, social and environmental rights). The difficulty with this approach is that it leads to the imposition of values because it hopes to pre-establish the outcomes of politics.

The second goes in the opposite direction by establishing areas that are not to be dealt with by politics. This class of rule aims to narrow the range of political debate by means of exclusions. For example, they might exclude questions of religion from political discussion.

A third approach is to try to limit the reach of politics. Even if it is accepted that there is a wide range of matters that potentially can be encompassed by politics, there remains a sphere where the collective action of politics is seen as inappropriate. The limits on the reach of politics are established by declarations of individual and civil liberties.

A fourth approach is to try to obtain pre-agreement on how the procedures for political choice should be arranged in areas where it is particularly weak. This approach recognizes the undesirability of trying to predetermine outcomes by pre-agreements. Instead, it sets the different objective of trying to get agreement in advance on the procedures applicable in selected areas where political choice is procedurally flawed. Areas typically identified in this context are in respect of choices affecting the longer term. They lead in the direction of establishing special rules and arrangements for monetary and fiscal decisions.

Each of these approaches reflects an underlying doubt about the ability of politics to handle social preferences and, in particular, conflicting preferences. There is, however, a basic distinction between expressing values as positive rights to be obtained through politics and expressing values in a way to set procedural limits on politics. Declarations of positive rights aim to provide orientation to politics over many of the most important aspects of public policy. They try to predetermine outcomes. As a consequence they become a means of imposing choices through politics. By contrast, the other approaches focus on procedural aspects of political choice. Exclusions that limit the range of politics, or assertions of rights that limit the reach of politics, both try to establish a pre-agreement on what politics should not cover. The idea of achieving a limited pre-agreement on the way to handle public policy choices which affect the longer term aims to limit current choices in order to avoid the pre-emption of future choices.

When the pre-emptive capacity of politics is constrained and when the range and the reach of politics is limited, the effect is to allow for the expression of a greater rather than a lesser variety of preferences in society. The possibility of choices being imposed through the collective processes of politics is reduced. The result of limiting politics is to allow for a greater diversity of values. The way in which these different guidelines on politics can be framed is discussed further below.

(i) Pre-agreement on positive rights

Attempts to get pre-agreements on positive rights typically take the form of declarations of social rights including, for example, rights to education, employment, shelter, health care, as well as environmental rights to clean air and water. As aspirations they may command much support throughout Europe.

The difficulty lies in seeing how pre-agreed values about what political processes are intended to accomplish can protect against the weaknesses of politics. Even if all politics were to be devoted to accomplishing these ends, they tend to ignore that not all social goals lie within the power of political processes (for example, the ability to create jobs) and that when such goals have been the objective of politicians the results have been destructive (communism achieved 'full' employment without achieving a productive economy that could meet other aspirations). Moreover, such declarations tend to ignore resource constraints. They often assume that collective action through politics is the best way to achieve the goals rather than looking to what can be achieved through market choice.

The attempt to predetermine political debate in this way is a mistake. The role of politics is in providing a means to resolve questions of collective choice. An approach to its procedural weaknesses is required. By trying to shape the outcome of political bargaining, the strength of politics as a means to achieve agreement on collective choice is being denied, while its weaknesses – the temptation to claim that all important aspirations can be met by politicians, or are suitable to political choice – are being accentuated.

(ii) Exclusions

The idea that politics is not well suited to handle certain areas of dispute in civil society has traditionally been expressed in the context of trying to define the correct role for government[19]. These areas can be identified through 'exclusion' rules.

The purpose of exclusion rules is to bar certain topics from being decided in the political arena or in the judicial system. They are sometimes referred to as 'gag' rules.[20] They refer to areas of the most extreme sensitivity in a society where different viewpoints are strongly held and unlikely to be resolved in political debate. As a result of such strongly held views, any attempt to decide one way or the other is inviting such dissension that the political and constitutional system itself will be called into question. The treatment of slavery in the early United States provides one example.

At first sight, exclusion rules appear somewhat distant from Europe's constitutional order. However, in practice, the European Union has acted precisely to extend gradually the range of subjects to be dealt with collectively, while postponing those that were likely to be most sensitive. As political union becomes more formalized, the question is whether exclusions should be recognized on a more systematic and more permanent basis. Are there areas of such sensitivity that it would be better to recognize in the constitution that they should be barred from Union processes for a long time to come, if not indefinitely?

The leading claimants for exclusion rules in a European constitution relate to religion, language and, more generally, to the other ties of ethnicity. The underlying issue is how the rules of a civil association, which a European constitution aims to entrench, can coexist with the ties of 'primordial' attachments.[21]

Such 'primordial' attachments in Europe can be associated with contiguity and kin, with religion, with language or dialect and with particular social practices. They are frequently seen as in some sense 'irrational'. They have also been associated with the relics of previous political associations.[22] It would be foolish to deny their continued strong existence in parts of Europe – whether expressed in a local or regional context or at the national level. While degrees of intensity vary, they can in one way or another be regarded as pervasive throughout Europe[23]. The question is whether, and how, to recognize them in Europe's constitution.

One approach is to ignore such ties and hope that the rules of civil association can be accepted and will triumph. The difficulty with this view is that the process of building support for a European political order inevitably inflames these other ties.[24] Unless they are recognized, they can become a major obstacle to the acceptability of political union. The alternative approach is to avoid inflaming them by acknowledging the importance of exclusions in the key areas of language and religion.

This approach is far from problem free. The difficulties lie in defining the scope of exclusions. For example, an exclusion to the effect that religion and language will not be the subject of Union authority will also have an impact in restricting Union activities in education and training. The area of even greater difficulty is framing exclusions in relation to the other ties of attachment – contiguity, kin, and social practices. Such ties are challenged, for example, by rules relating to freedom of movement and the right of residence and non-discrimination on grounds of nationality. Exclusions would qualify these rights or allow for local variations. Non-discrimination on grounds of nationality has long been a cornerstone of economic freedoms in the Economic Community. Its extension or application into areas of ethnic discrimination within a nation has obvious appeal. Yet again it may be prudent for the constitution of the Union to accept limitations on Union involvement when, for example, free movement runs up against ethnic sensibilities.

The kinds of exclusions outlined, may appear to set unnecessarily restrictive limits to the legislative and judicial range of a Union constitution. Their justification lies in accepting that the ties of civil association will take a very long time to entrench in the context of European political union. Their imposition in sensitive areas will not bring about such an association. On the contrary, imposition will likely delay the acceptance of a European political union. The impact of European association is in some cases masked because the focus of some local or regional ties is still on loosening the powers of the Member State. This provides a support for the Union that will quickly pass if the powers of the Union simply replace those of the individual state.

The exclusion of certain types of issue from the collective choice processes of politics does not necessarily mean that the values of civil association cannot be pursued as Union responsibilities through other means – notably through Union law and through alternative justiciable constitutional provisions. Indeed, those declarations of individual and civil liberties that are the hallmarks of civil association and that are intended to limit the reach of politics may well be used to extend civil values through the law. But whether this alternative channel should constitute a Union responsibility depends on how a system of multiple jurisdictions is articulated. It could be that responsibility for the implementation of individual and civil liberties should rest with the Member States and not with the Union. Hence, although exclusions are framed in the negative – what politics is not to touch – it should be recognized that their effect may be to allow, within a system of distributed powers, for the expression and exercise of values that will not be generally acceptable. These might be ethnic or religious values in particular jurisdictions. The expressions in particular jurisdictions of values that are not acceptable within the Union as a whole can be mitigated by the setting of minimum standards of entry for the Union (for example, through the need to accept the rights expressed in the European Convention on Human Rights). However, the consequences of exclusions should be recognized.

The final justification for exclusion rules rests on putting a value on constitutional method itself. Exclusion rules may restrict both Union politics and the Union judiciary from intervening in certain areas in order that Union political and judicial processes can work in others. They mean putting a value on the constitutional method as a whole. They involve a value judgement that exclusions are justified for the sake of obtaining political and judicial processes in other areas.

(iii) Individual rights

Declarations of individual rights are the most common means of declaring an area 'off limits' to politics. They recognize the temptations of political processes to intrude. They can be seen as attempts to establish 'reserved territory' for the individual[25] or to establish individual values that are above collective values.[26] They include such traditional rights as free speech and freedom of association.

Such declarations do not go without challenge. Above all, they may be questioned on the grounds that other values (for example, community values) have equal claim to respect or that the value to be attached to the individual calls for collective action as much as it calls for reserved areas where collective action should not intrude. The case for the special treatment of individual values has therefore to be rooted in the view, not only that the special problem of political processes lies in the imperfection of going from individual preferences to aggregate preferences, but that it is individual preferences that are particularly likely to suffer in the aggregation process and from the weaknesses of the political method.

As mentioned already above, it is a different question as to whether such protected areas should be enforced through the law of the Member States or the law of the Union. The view that the protection should rest with the Member States depends on perceptions of how judicial powers are best distributed within the Union.

(iv) Pre-agreements on orderings

The purpose of achieving pre-agreements on the ordering of certain values is to anticipate where the political process is likely to fail. The area of political choice most vulnerable to failure concerns inconsistencies that arise in the context of time preferences.

The best known area of potential inconsistencies relates to monetary policy.[27] It is legitimate to see price stability as a constitutional issue because large price fluctuations make rational social behaviour very difficult and the penalties fall on those who are least protected. Both effects may encourage political extremism. Unfortunately, politicians are likely to perceive a short term trade-off between full employment and price stability. They may, in general, favour a faster rate of monetary, or real growth, than is consistent with the attainment of price stability.[28] For these and other reasons, there is a case for a body established independent of political processes and charged with exclusive responsibility for maintaining price stability. Such a body may, or may not, help achieve price stability. But the separation of responsibilities should make political choices more transparent and possibly help maintain a longer term perspective on the choices involved. In the case of Europe's constitution, the case for an independent agency to be responsible for maintaining price stability seems to have been won with the Maastricht Treaty.

There is however, a more general problem with time preferences in politics which has to do with the systematic tendency of political processes to place a higher value on the short term rather than the long term. In so far as governments can pre-empt the resources in society, they are prone to claim them for the present generation rather than for future generations. They can do this by spending in the current period through borrowings which will have to be repaid in a future period. There is therefore a strong case for enshrining values which bind governments against this sort of behaviour. The example with the longest history is a stipulation against deficit financing. Deficit financing pre-empts the options of future generations because a significant part of their income may have to be spent on paying for the choices of the previous generation. Prohibitions therefore bind one generation but keep the options of future generations open.[29]

It can be argued that it is a mistake and contradictory to distinguish between one generation and another in this way. Constitutions themselves consist of rules and institutions which are intended to be passed on. Similarly, the institutions of the market are based on property rights and contracts that convey and obligate. If deficit financing arises from education or health spending it may be spending which benefits the next generation. Spending on defence is also of intended benefit to future generations who may be born free as a result.[30] The theoretical case for ordering cannot therefore be based on a simple prohibition against binding future generations. It must rest on the more general claim that politics gives too much weight to the present and that rules have a place in counteracting systematic bias in political choice.

There does seem to be a strong practical case to support this more general claim. The trend over the last fifty years has been for ever growing government expenditures, coupled with an increasing pre-emption of the resources of succeeding generations. From this perspective, a constitution should contain fiscal rules against deficit financing in times of normal economic activity and limits on peacetime government indebtedness. In a system of distributed powers, a particularly effective type of constraint may be to deny the central jurisdiction any independent means to tax. This limits the power of the centre to build the client relationships which tilt those with political power towards making current expenditures and pay-offs at the expense of the future.

Moving outside the area of constitutional rules that relate to monetary and to fiscal policy, there is a similar case for saying that the bias in politics to favour the present generation at the expense of future generations applies to environmental degradation. It would follow that if constitutions are to correct for the short time horizon of politics in relation to public expenditures, one should also attempt, in a consistent manner, to have constitutional provisions that favour environmental protection.

The difficulty lies in framing environmental safeguards in a constitution in a way analogous to say fiscal rules. Declarations of environmental rights which try to predetermine political outcomes are flawed for the reasons discussed earlier – in particular that they presume too much of political choice. Declarations that might be attached to market rules (for example, that the market should respect 'sustainable development') are not clearly related to key market mechanisms (whether the market is looked at as a system of pricing or as a system of property rights). There is, in addition, the problem that provisions that enjoin politicians not to undervalue the future in respect of the degradation of the environment may lead to action that hampers the ability of the market to value the environment through individual valuations (for example, through property and recreational values). One possible avenue lies in a rule relating to balance sheet accounting. Attention to the stock of wealth would counteract an overemphasis on income flows and perhaps provide some discipline against the tendency of politicians to confuse current and capital expenditures and to hide obligations off budget.

VI Normative limits and the diversity of values

There appears, at first sight, to be something paradoxical in setting limits on politics as a means of protecting a diversity of views and practices in society when politics is intended as a means of sorting out diverse preferences and bargaining away differences. But the kinds of normative limits on politics that have been discussed above address very specific areas of weakness in politics as a method of collective choice:

- the exclusions deal with the tensions that can arise between the ties of civil association and other 'organic' ties and that can be exacerbated when a new form of political association is put in place;
- the declarations of 'reserved areas' for individual and civil liberties deal with the inability of politics to reflect all preferences and thus set limits on collective interventions;
- limited pre-agreements on the ordering of priorities through monetary and fiscal rules (including possibly balance sheet conventions) attempt to address the tendency of politics to systematically undervalue the future.

The result of limiting choice through politics in areas where politics is weak as a method of collective choice is to leave a greater area available for community or individual choice in the protected areas. The organic ties of region and locality are respected, individuals are respected and the freedom of choice for future generations is respected. Moreover, the constraints apply to whoever wields power through politics. They constrain majorities with political power. But equally, if power is captured by a dedicated minority in the face of a passive majority they also serve to limit what can be done under the rules by minorities.

Normative boundaries on politics recognize the difficulties in aggregating preferences in society, the imperfections of politics as a system for reflecting preferences and the need to watch against whoever controls the levers of political power – whether representative of majority opinion or representative only of minority views. Such constraints are needed in Europe's constitution because the diversity of values in Europe means that the problems of aggregation and the crudities of politics are particularly pronounced. The temptations for ideologically driven minorities, including those acting in the name of Europe, are high. There will be a long period of coexistence between the new ties of civil association and the old ties of attachment. Normative limits on politics reflect the underlying importance of establishing non-coercive processes in Europe. There is also an underlying consistency with prudential values in having rules that focus on specific areas of weakness in political choice.

An important implication of setting procedural limits on politics is that the constitutional rules establishing those limits may be justiciable. They thus open up the possibilities of a greater use of law in a European political union. However, the greater use of legal channels of redress is not synonymous with a greater use of central law. As already mentioned, in a system of distributed powers, justiciability may sometimes best be located within the Member States (for example, in respect of individual and civil liberties). In addition, certain disputes may be sparked by questions of the interpretation of the rules (for example, over fiscal rules). In these cases, a judicial process for interpretation should not necessarily be assumed. Political processes may thus be reintroduced. However, rules can still serve a useful purpose. They ensure publicity is given to the types of political behaviour that trigger breaches in the rules. In so far as interpretation triggers special procedures, governments may still be held in check.

More generally, rules that constrain the imposition of collective choice through politics need to be supported by consistent constitutional processes in other areas. The rules for taking collective decisions in areas that are within the legitimate territory of politics in a European political union must take account of the diversity of preferences. So too must the rules on the distribution of powers in the Union. In both decision taking and in the arrangements governing the distribution of powers, there have to be safeguards against different ways in which coercion can be applied. The question of how to arrange the distribution of powers in a European political union is discussed next.

Notes

1   'With respect to actions in general, there is no property in them that is calculated so readily to engage, and so firmly to fix the attention of an observer, as the tendency they may have to. . . that which may be styled the common end of all of them. The end I mean is happiness: and this tendency in any act is what we style its utility'. Bentham, J. (1776), *The Fragment on Government.*

2   'Principles founded on observation and experience never can become the groundwork of any law; for, to invent one capable of reducing to harmony all the appetites and

by-ends of mankind, and at the same time founded on them, is altogether impossible'. Kant, I. (1797), *The Metaphysics of Ethics. Bk II.*

3   Bentham's suggested method was as follows: 'Sum up all the values of all the pleasures on the one side, and those of all the pains on the other. The balance, if it be on the side of pleasure, will give the good tendency of the act upon the whole, with respect to the interests of the individual person; if on the side of pain, the bad tendency of it upon the whole. Take an account of the number of persons whose interests appear to be concerned; and repeat the above process with respect to each. Sum up the numbers expressive of the degrees of good tendency, which the act has, with respect to each individual, in regard to whom the tendency of it is good upon the whole: do this again with respect to each individual, in regard to whom the tendency of it is bad upon the whole. Take the balance; which, if on the side of pleasure, will give the general good tendency of the act, with respect to the total number or community of individuals concerned; if on the side of pain, the general evil tendency, with respect to the same community'. Bentham, J. (1789), *An Introduction to the Principles of Morals and Legislation,* (eds) (1970) Burns, J.M. and Hart, H.L.A.

4   Arrow, K. J. (1951), *Social Choice and Individual Values.*

5   'Arrow's Paradox, although more general than the classical voting Paradox in one respect, actually is less general in another'. Schwartz, T. (1981), *The Logic of Collective Choice.*

6   'It generalizes the economist's concept of a demand function as well as the set theorist's concept of a choice function'. Schwartz, ibid.

7   Most of these points flow from 'public choice' literature of which the classic text is Buchanan, J.M. and Tullock G. *The Calculus of Consent.*

8   'The people. . . may desire to oppress a part of their number; and precautions are as much needed against this as against any other abuse of power'. Mill, J.S. (1859), *Utilitarianism, On Liberty and Representative Government.*

9   'Mathematically, at least, it is possible to construct suitable social welfare functions if we feel entitled to say in advance that the tastes of individuals fall within certain prescribed realms of similarity'. Arrow, op. cit.

10   See Blaug for a discussion of the relationship between the methodological individualism of economics and political individualism. Blaug, M. (1980), *The Methodology of Economics.*

11   See Simon, H.A. (1955), 'A Behavioural Model of Rational Choice', *Quarterly Journal of Economics. 69.* A brief summary of the development of theories of rationality is provided in March, J.G. (1977), 'Bounded Rationality, Ambiguity, and the Engineering of Choice' in Bell D.E., Raiffa H. and Tversky A. (eds) (1988), *Decision Making.* As March notes, 'We do not have a single, widely accepted, precise behavioural theory of choice'. This still appears to be the case. See also Simon, H.A. (1985), 'Rationality in Psychology and Economics', in Hogarth, R.M. and Reder, M.W. (eds) (1987) *Rational Choice.*

12   'For the economist. . . rationality means choosing in accordance with a preference ordering that is complete and transitive, subject to perfect and costlessly acquired information; where there is uncertainty about future outcomes, rationality means maximising expected utility, that is, the utility of an outcome multiplied by the probability of its occurrence'. Blaug, op. cit.

13   'The choosers in question choose as though they were maximising something – something or other, not necessarily anything in particular, not necessarily preference satisfaction in any antecedently understood sense of preference'. Schwartz, op. cit.

14   '. . . we have at least two distinct roles for our minds to play, that of the information processing and reasoning machine by which we choose what to consume out of the array of things that our resources can be exchanged for, and that of the pleasure

machine or consuming organ, the generator of direct consumer satisfaction'. Schelling, T.S. (1988), 'The Mind as a Consuming Organ' in Bell, Raiffa, Tversky, op. cit.

15   'Each of us seems to be split between a private and a public self. The 'economic man' within us strives for personal hedonistic satisfaction. He regards other people as so many means to his own selfish ends – or as constraints and obstacles to his pursuit of happiness. The 'social man', by contrast, is governed by moral and social norms. . . The problem is to understand the relation between these two homunculi'. Elster, J. (ed) (1986), *Introduction in, The Multiple Self.*

16   The relation between the private consumer and the public citizen has been explored by Hirschman, A.O. (1982), *Shifting Involvements. Private Interests and Public Action.*

17   'It is the ordering according to values which takes into account all the desires of the individual, including the highly important socializing desires, and which is primarily relevant for the achievement of a social maximum'. 'We must look at the entire system of values, including values about values, in seeking for a truly general theory of social welfare'. Arrow, op. cit.

18   'Identifying the feasible set is an important, interesting, neglected part of the total choice process'. Schwartz, op. cit.

19   For example, in his discussion of the role of government, Humboldt excluded both education and religion from the activities of the state. 'National education seems to me to lie wholly beyond the limits within which political agency should properly be confined'. 'All which concerns religion lies beyond the sphere of the State's activity'. von Humboldt, W. (1791), *The Sphere and Duties of Government.*

20   Holmes, S. (1988), 'Gag Rules or the Politics of Omission' in Elster, J. and Slagstad, R. (eds) *Constitutionalism and Democracy.*

21   See Geertz for a discussion of the conflict between civil and primordial sentiments. Geertz, C. (1973), *The Interpretation of Culture.*

22   Weber, M. (1978) in Roth, G. and Wittich, C. (eds) *Economy and Society.*

23   'For virtually every person, in every society, at almost all times, some attachments seem to flow more from a sense of natural – some would say spiritual – affinity than from social interaction'. Geertz, op. cit.

24   'The reduction of primordial sentiments to civil order is rendered more difficult, however, by the fact that political modernization tends initially not to quiet such sentiments but to quicken them'. Geertz, ibid.

25   The concept of 'reserved territory' is associated with J.S. Mill. 'that there is, or ought to be, some space in human existence thus entrenched around, and sacred from authoritative intrusion, no one who professes the smallest regard to human freedom or dignity will call in question: the point to be determined is, where the limit should be placed; how large a province of human life this reserved territory should include'. Mill, J.S. (1854), *Essays on Politics and Society.*

26   'Individual rights are political trumps held by individuals. Individuals have rights when, for some reason, a collective good is not a sufficient justification for damaging what they wish, as individuals, to have or to do, or not a sufficient justification for imposing some loss or injury upon them'. Dworkin, R. (1977), *Taking Rights Seriously.*

27   Dynamic inconsistencies are defined by Cukierman as occurring, 'When the best policy planned currently for some future period is no longer best when that period arrives'. For a discussion in the context of monetary policy see, Cukierman, A. (1992), *Central Bank Strategy, Credibility and Independence.*

28   This perception of time inconsistencies does not rely on accepting the assumptions of some monetarists that whatever the short run effects of monetary policy on prices and output, economic expectations will adjust so that monetary policy has little effect on output in the long term.

29   For an extended discussion of monetary and fiscal rules and the discount rate of politicians see Brennan, G. and Buchanan, J.M. (1985), *The Reason of Rules*.
30   Holmes, S. (1988) in Elster, J. and Slagstad, R. (eds), op. cit.

5 Powers and their distribution

'The governments of commonwealths must be diversified according to the diversities of their situations'. Jean Bodin, *The Six Books of a Commonwealth*, 1576.

I Redefining the nation state

There are three sources of initial difficulty in analyzing systems of distributed power in Europe. The first arises out of the apparently simple problem of nomenclature for a system of distributed powers in Europe. The second is the passion that can still be evoked by the nation state and those who oppose any redefinition of its role. The third is the equally passionate advocacy by some of a European Union where all significant powers are vested in the Union.

(i) Nomenclature

Terminology appears a trivial source of difficulty. In practice it is a far from trivial cause of confusion. A word such as 'federal' is associated with central powers in the minds of some and decentralized powers in others. A word such as 'union' is benign for some and associated with foreign domination by others.

The label most frequently employed to describe a system of distributed powers in Europe is 'federalism'. There are two decisive disadvantages with the term. First, it is imprecise as a description. There are many variations of distributed powers that are called 'federal'. It therefore does not serve to characterize in a clear way the relationship between jurisdictions. Second, it is a term that does not convey the quality of the resulting political association. Historically, there has been no connection between the use of the term and its relationship with a free society. On the one hand, the term is applied to the United States which is a free society. On the other hand, it has equally been applied to the former Soviet Union or the former Yugoslavia which were not. These are critical drawbacks. European political union must be based on a clear characterization of the relationship between jurisdictions in the Union – between the Union, the Member States and between regional and local structures. In turn, the relationship between jurisdictions must reflect a view as to how it relates to the maintenance of a free society in Europe. It is a system of distributed powers consistent with a free society which Europe needs. The discussion that follows thus avoids the use of the term 'federal'.

(ii) Redefining the nation state

The nation state, in Europe's recent history the central focus for the exercise of political power, is being eroded from two different directions. There is a desire for more power to be wielded closer to people at the local and regional levels. At the same time the power of independent action by the nation has been lost because key objectives (such as defence) require nations to act together. States can still be defined by territory. But territory is no longer synonymous either with control or with scope for independent action.

Uncertainty about the role of the nation state arouses two apparently contradictory emotions. The nation still retains a powerful appeal as a focus of loyalty and identity. At the same time, there is considerable popular disenchantment with national governments. Alongside the disenchantment with governments goes disrespect, some merited and some not, with the institutions of government. Some localities and regions see the larger association of the European Union as benign because it weakens the grip of their traditional and immediate higher authority (the national government). This attitude needs to be interpreted with caution. It is unlikely to survive for long if the Union itself becomes a centralized and even more distant authority.

A disrespect for government is a healthy antidote to expecting too much from government. It is preferable to Europe's long tradition of undue deference to authority. A questioning of existing structures is a necessary prelude to a new political settlement in Europe. Nevertheless, the malaise can be destructive. There is an urgency to settling the question of how powers are to be distributed within the Union and how powers are to be exercised collectively. The answer to these questions inevitably involves a redefinition of the role of the nation state.

(iii) The vesting of powers in the Union

Europe starts on the search for the right form of distribution of powers at a considerable disadvantage. A number of the Member States, including both France and the United Kingdom, have a long history of centralization and inexperience with systems of distributed powers. There are other European nations where the democratic tradition is recent and yet others where the habits of civil association are still being built or rebuilt.

Analysis of how political powers are best distributed within a European political union involves three distinct questions.

The first is whether there is a general principle that can be used to determine the necessary powers of the Union. Attempts to establish such a general principle centre on the concept of 'market failure'. The generalization is that the Union must be vested with the powers needed to deal with the key dimensions of 'market failure'. This approach hence attempts to establish a direct link between the different aspects of market failure and the powers of the Union.

The discussion below suggests that concepts of market failure do not provide a direct link to the necessary powers of the Union. In the absence of such a general principle, the second question is how to match particular areas of political choice to particular jurisdictions. This involves criteria for establishing 'optimum domain' (what is best done where).

Theories of 'optimum domain' suggest, on balance, that not everything should be done by Europe acting collectively but that instead there are advantages in having a system of multiple jurisdictions. This gives rise to the third question – how should different political jurisdictions relate to each other? The relationship can be expressed as 'hierarchy' – with powers flowing down to other jurisdictions from the Union. Conversely, the relationship can be expressed as 'delegation up' – where the powers exercised collectively are, in selected areas, explicitly delegated by the different jurisdictions composing the Union. Alternatively, the relationship between the Union and the jurisdictions within the Union can be expressed as independent and coordinate.

These different questions are often conflated. Those who wish to see more done by the European Union may stress the advantages of political choice rather than market choice by emphasizing the powers needed to deal with market failures. Having established a case for choice through the political mechanism, the same proponents of European political union may make the further assumption that collective choice is best exercised by the Union rather than considering other potential jurisdictions. This in turn leads to an oversimplification of how to characterize relationships between different jurisdictions.

The result of confusing these distinct questions is the danger that advocacy of European political union comes to reflect systematic bias – bias in favour of collective choice and against market choice; bias in favour of the Union as the best jurisdiction to settle all major issues of public policy, and, a bias in favour of a hierarchical distribution of powers as a way of minimizing the rivalries of alternate jurisdictions. Such advocacy polarizes the debate about the right form of distributed powers in Europe. The debate is presented as a choice between the Union and the existing domain of the Member States. Such polarization makes it difficult for the Union to gather support other than in response to crisis or by appeals against the nation state. Neither provides a desirable basis for political union in Europe. Responses to transient crises do not always reflect rational long term responses. Appeals against the nation state aggravate frictions between the new form of civil and political association in Europe and the ties of attachment and sentiment to the old. If political union in Europe is to succeed, it must be based on a much more discriminating, and much less polarized approach to defining political relationships.

II   General guidelines for defining Union powers?

The idea that there is a general rule to help establish the necessary powers of the European Union starts from the proposition that those powers traditionally associated with government rather than the market (such as external relations and defence) should rest with the Union. To these traditional areas of non-market choice should be added the economic powers to establish and maintain the rules of the market and, in addition, the powers necessary to deal with market failure. The general rule therefore creates a presumption that the Union should be able to exercise powers in all areas other than those that can be left to market choice.

Leaving aside traditional areas of government, such as external relations and defence (which will be mentioned later), the content of this proposed rule depends very heavily on the concept of market failure. It tries to establish a direct link between the powers of the Union and the different aspects of market failure. The argument runs that since the market is subject to failures and the framework of the market is set for the Union as a whole, so too must the general principle of market failure be recognized in the rules of the Union. This means vesting in the Union the powers of collective action in areas perceived as likely to be prone to market failure. Depending on how the concept of market failure is defined, this general approach would establish the powers of the Union in many areas of domestic policy. Together with those areas such as foreign policy, security and defence which traditionally belong to political and not market choice, the Union would be equipped with potential powers to act on most important matters of public policy.

Three sorts of market failures are commonly held to provide a guide to the division between market choice and political choice. They are the failures associated with the provision of public goods, the handling of externalities, and the recognition of the social dimension of the market. The discussion below examines whether these aspects of market failure, taken together, can establish a direct basis for defining the necessary powers of the Union.

(i) Public goods

Public goods are those goods that, once provided, can be enjoyed by all without detracting from the benefits derived by others. Private goods are those suited for individual consumption. The market allocates them efficiently. Public goods cannot be divided. Once made available, they are available to all (non-excludability) and the consumption by one user does not detract from consumption by another user (non-rivalry of benefits). They are seen as goods that the market will underprovide or fail to provide.[1] Public goods are commonly thought of as physical goods such as roads and airports. They can also be services such as the armed forces, the judiciary and the police.

The existence of 'public goods' has long been recognized. Earlier definitions saw them as goods that should be produced but individual investors lacked incentives to do so.[2] This lack of incentives could be linked, among other characteristics, to an inability of investors to charge the users of the public good. This way of looking at public goods remains valid for certain purposes.[3]

In practice, there are very few 'pure' public goods. For example, at a certain point, additional users of roads or airports will impinge on other users through congestion or wear and tear. However, there are many more goods that have public good characteristics. The implication of the existence of such goods and services is alleged to be that their provision needs public sector involvement. Many have European dimensions (such as the putting in place of European infrastructure networks and interconnections). Thus, a prima facie case is established for the Union to gain the powers to provide such goods with public characteristics.

There is however no straightforward connection between public goods and the powers of the European Union.

First, the connection between public goods and public provision has become tenuous. Modern technologies for charging, combined with modern techniques of capital markets that distinguish between different types of risk and allocate them to different classes of investor, mean that there are many goods and services conventionally thought of as 'public' that can in practice be provided by the private sector.[4] Infrastructure and utility investments are the clearest examples. But private provision has also extended into other areas traditionally thought of as 'public' (including, for example, policing and security) and mixed private and public provision could become increasingly common in other services such as health care. Thus, the equation between public goods and public provision is often one of habit and convention. In the real world, as market practices develop, the boundaries will be constantly changing. The rationale for public provision is often a reflection of the market in history rather than a reflection of the contemporary market.[5]

Second, the key role of government is as a provider of the policy setting.[6] Public policies can themselves be seen as a form of public good – a Union wide policy of free movement of capital is a policy of which all can avail. Similarly, the benefits of stable expectations which flow from a credible commitment to low inflation are benefits that accrue to all. Even in respect of physical goods and services the key role of government is increasingly defined in setting the regulatory or policy framework within which private investors can accept risk. The question therefore becomes one of where the policy setting is best established. In this connection there can be no automatic presumption that Europe is the right location for determining most public policies. The case that the Union is the appropriate setting depends very heavily on arguments about 'externalities'.

(ii) Externalities

An external diseconomy is said to exist when a transaction results in a disadvantage to another person who is not a party to the terms of that transaction. Thus a policy being pursued by one European state that has potentially adverse 'spillover' effects for another offers potential economies if all the parties concerned have a say in the terms of the policy. The best known examples are air and water borne pollution. Other examples include immigration policy. The justification of handling external trade policy as an area of public policy best handled collectively rests, in part, on the fact that the policy of one Member State will impinge on another.

Since many policies will have wider effects outside national boundaries, theories of externalities provide a case for bringing most areas of public policy into Union jurisdiction. If the handling of policies within a national context is seen to be associated with the prevalence of a large number of externalities, then this in turn leads to the view that most public policies should be handled by Union wide structures so as to 'internalize' the externalities.

A more precise look at externalities does not however support any straightforward link with the powers of the Union.

First, externalities exist where markets do not exist. They exist where it is impossible or too costly to define or enforce property rights, or where it is too costly or difficult to organize a market. The initial and best response therefore may be to enquire into the reasons for the absence of a market and to explore whether a market can be stimulated or simulated. Administrative responses may aggravate a problem. Administrative responses to overfishing around Europe have so far aggravated problems of a diminishing fish stock while a market oriented response might be more effective. Administrative responses to airport congestion may be less effective than allowing a market to grow in landing rights. If there is a role for the Union it is in helping establish property rights or organizing the market framework.

Second, whether the market response needs to be organized on a European Union wide basis depends on how extensively the externalities spread. There are many external effects that extend beyond a national jurisdiction but do not extend Europe wide. In such instances, bringing in other Member States that do not have a direct interest in the matter may be helpful, but equally may not. The implications are that some areas of overlapping public policy concern are best handled by the coalition of jurisdictions with that concern and not necessarily by the Union as a whole.

Third, and most important, there can be no presumption that the external effects of policies will be disadvantageous. On the contrary spill-over effects may stimulate better practice in other jurisdictions. The mere existence of policy externalities between Member States does not establish a case for Union jurisdiction. A common external trade policy which impedes market access through various non-tariff barriers will be more damaging to the interests of the citizens of the Union than restrictive policies attempted by a few of the Member States which will be undermined by freer policies elsewhere. In this example, externalities will be positive rather than negative. Thus, the mere citing of externalities says nothing about the necessary powers of the Union. There has to be a much more searching examination as to whether the external effects of public policies in different jurisdictions are likely to be positive or negative.

The case that the Union needs to be vested with the powers to deal with market failures in the provision of public goods and in the recognition of externalities is bolstered finally by the claim that the Union must be equipped to deal with the third aspect of market failure – the social dimension.

(iii) The social dimension

As discussed earlier, a market system will be associated with unequal outcomes and there will be those who will not be able to flourish in a market system. If the rules of a market system are to be acceptable and not imposed, there is a case for recognizing this social dimension – including in the definition of Union powers.

Again, however, there is no clear connection between recognizing the limits of the market and defining the powers of the Union. There is no agreement in European countries as to where precisely on welfare grounds to draw the boundary between choices best left to market processes and choices best exercised collectively through political processes. While there has come to be an acceptance that the state should not be involved in the production of goods, there is no consensus on the role of the state in the provision of services (for example, postal services). In addition, perceptions of the role of the state in the provision of education and health are changing as the demand for health services outstrips the limits of government budgets and as concern for Europe's commercial competitiveness forces questions to be asked about the quality of state provided education. Moreover, the role of the state in welfare provision is also becoming the subject of rethinking as negative incentive and dependency effects are recognized. As long as such questions remain a matter of political debate within Member States in Europe and, as long as there is so much to be learnt from the emulation of best practice, it is difficult to see how such questions can be expressed as a constitutional presumption in favour of Union powers in these areas.

Concepts such as public goods, externalities and the social dimension all reflect different ways in which markets can be said to fail. They therefore appear to lead towards a definition of powers for the Union which can be centred on the general phenomenon of market failure. On closer examination, none of these concepts leads to any clear general conclusion that justifies extensive Union powers.

Moreover, the general attempt to base the necessary powers of the Union on a direct link with market failure is a mistaken one.

Theories of market failure cannot lead to clear conclusions about the role of European government when government itself is also prone to failure. Even if a market solution is an imperfect one, it does not follow that a European system of government can do better.

The boundary between market choice and political choice is likely to be constantly shifting. The role of a constitution is to underpin the institutions of the market and the institutions of government. A constitution cannot however demarcate a fixed sphere of operation for either the market or the government without quickly being overtaken by events.

The attempt to link market failure directly with the powers of the Union essentially treats Europe as a unitary state. The dimensions of market failure have to be treated in a much more discriminating fashion in order to provide guidelines as to where powers are best exercised in a system of distributed powers.

For these reasons, concepts of market failure do not provide, and cannot provide, a direct basis for establishing the powers of the European Union. Instead, the powers of the Union must be determined in relation to the advantages and disadvantages of having the same powers exercised elsewhere. Union powers need to be approached through an assessment of the relative efficiency and appeal of different political domains. This is the approach taken in theories of 'optimum domain'.

III Optimum domain

Theories of optimum domain try to establish why a particular jurisdiction is the appropriate jurisdiction for political choice and why it may be better than an alternative.

Theories of optimum domain are closely related, but three different perspectives can be distinguished:

- theories stressing allocative efficiency which suggest the importance of matching the boundaries of a jurisdiction to the boundaries of the task;
- theories stressing cost efficiency which suggest that setting the boundaries of different political domains must also take into account transactions costs in different domains;
- theories stressing the importance of preference distinctions (differences in preferences will affect both allocative efficiency and transactions costs).

(i) Allocative efficiency

Theories of allocative efficiency define optimum political domain as being achieved when the boundaries of a domain providing public goods is matched with the beneficiary group. The theory looks for 'equivalence' or a 'correspondence' between the boundary of the public good and the boundary of the political domain.[7] The implication is that there will be multiple domains corresponding to the different scope of the public goods provided and that there will be inefficiencies in the absence of such a matching. For example, there will be diseconomies if a wide domain cannot reflect (in the public good it provides) the different preferences in a smaller domain and a case therefore for smaller domains. Conversely, there will be a case for a wider domain if a small domain cannot reach all those who would benefit from a particular public good. Public goods which provide benefits across several jurisdictions are more efficiently provided jointly.

If this general approach is applied to Europe, it means trying to identify those public goods or public policies whose optimum boundaries coincide with those of the Union, compared with those policies where the boundaries are closer to those of the nation state or region on the one hand, or an international jurisdiction wider than the Union on the other hand. It means looking at each area of public policy separately.

In practical terms this approach suggests that the powers of the Union should be limited. The Union is too small a domain for handling key areas of external relations. Conversely, the Union is too large a domain for handling many areas of internal policy.

In external policy, for example, the rules of international trade and capital movements are best set at the global level. A different example concerns defence. Europe's defence has long rested for its credibility on the United States. Although the US can expect Europe to take up a much larger share of the burden, international rule enforcement is in the interest both of the US and Europe and it makes sense to continue to use joint instruments such as NATO. Civil war in the Balkans has exposed deep frictions in rebalancing the relationship between the interests of European members of NATO and the United States. The frictions do not alter the fact that the defence and security interests of Europe and the United States are best met through continued alliance.

In respect of the internal policies of the Union, both the micro-economic changes needed to maintain the competitiveness of European goods and service industries, and the welfare reforms needed to reshape welfare programmes, are arguably better achieved by Member States pursuing their own approaches and learning by doing so. The role of the Union would simply be to encourage best practices. The membership as a whole has more to gain from emulation than from common policies.

It remains possible to argue that the Union can function well as the 'second best' domain in many areas. Economists are used to exploring second best solutions. It may seem unappealing politically to gather support for the powers of the Union on the grounds that the Union is a second best domain. Nevertheless, there are two important ways in which the Union may be attractive from this perspective. The first is as an intermediary between the Member State and the global domain. The second is as a 'fall back' domain when alternative jurisdictions find themselves unable to solve questions of political choice. Both factors are relevant in Europe. When the institutions of individual Member States are not functioning well in settling questions of public policy it is tempting to look to the Union as an alternative domain. In practice, in a number of European countries the attraction of European political union is, in part, a reflection of negative perceptions of institutional shortcomings in the Member State concerned. Nevertheless, if the Union is to gather support for positive reasons and to maintain that support, it remains important to distinguish between those activities inherently better to be carried out by the Union and those that remain inherently better suited to other jurisdictions. If there are problems within alternative jurisdictions they need to be sorted out within those jurisdictions themselves. Treating Europe as a fall back domain is thus unsatisfactory as a means of justifying Union powers.

However, the idea that the Union needs the powers to be able to act as an intermediary raises different questions. They revolve around the transactions costs and savings associated with locating powers in different domains. These are considered next.

(ii) Transactions costs

Cost based approaches to optimum domain establish the optimum size of the collective unit by comparing the costs to a jurisdiction arising from the spill-over effects of excluded jurisdictions to the additional costs of decision taking when excluded jurisdictions are brought within the group.[8] If the additional costs of decision taking in a larger domain are outweighed by reductions in spill-over costs then a wider domain is preferable to the smaller domain. It is an approach based on institutional economics.[9] Such arguments were earlier expressed, and continue to be expressed, in terms of 'convenience'.[10]

In looking at the transactions costs and savings associated with different domains and different institutional arrangements, it is important to distinguish between two very different ways of viewing transactions costs.

One approach is to look at political structures as organizers and coordinators of non-market choices.[11] This perspective tends to emphasize the cost savings from the coordination of policies. It is thus a perspective that stresses the advantages of organization utilizing Union powers and structures.

The other looks at government as the supplier of policies. This second perspective stresses the advantages of competitive supply rather than monopolistic government. It is a perspective inclined to lean against Union powers.

(a) Organizational costs The organizational costs of political choice parallel those of market choice. They comprise:

- information costs. These are costs associated with giving and receiving signals about policy. In politics these are associated with the way in which voters inform themselves, the ways in which institutions inform themselves and the ways in which governments exchange information.[12] In a large European Union with an extensive electorate and many Member States, information costs will be high unless measures can be taken to simplify communication.
- negotiating costs. In Europe these are associated with aligning preferences of Member States within the Union and with the costs attached to negotiating common policies within the membership. These can be high given the number of participating Member States and if alliances or voting coalitions between the Member States are unstable. They can be reduced, either through reducing the number of alternative jurisdictions, or through having decision taking based on the simplest method (for example, simple majority voting) or by according central institutions (such as the Commission) independent powers to bring about common positions. Negotiating costs are also associated with dealing with external parties as well as in respect of forging common positions on internal Union policies. There seem obvious cost savings to be gained from the Union dealing with external parties, rather than Member States acting individually.
- there are the costs of dealing with uncertainty, particularly how others party to or affected by a policy decision will react. Uncertainty affects individuals, other economic agents, such as businesses, and governments.[13] Uncertainty can be high in a large and complex European Union. It would appear that uncertainty costs could be dramatically reduced if responsibility for major public policies were to be clearly located with the Union.

Organizational cost criteria can be applied to different areas of public policy and to different actors. The general case is that there will be organizational savings in each of the three areas identified above through having important areas of public policy vested with the Union. A particular illustration can be given in respect of monetary union. Multiple currencies in the Union increase the information costs to users in order for businesses and individual investors to make a rational currency choice. At the same time a single currency will reduce the uncertainties attached to different monetary regimes. In addition, having a single agent in charge of price stability (the European Central Bank) will enhance the credibility of monetary rules and thus provide a form of negotiating saving compared with different monetary authorities coordinating their actions.

A different example of negotiation savings arises in the area of external policy. If the Union speaks 'with one voice' on foreign policy or external trade matters, negotiating costs with external parties are reduced, the uncertainties of counterparties to the transactions are diminished and again the bargaining power and credibility of the Union is increased.

The general tendency to associate organizational savings with larger rather than smaller political domains has been challenged however in the context of club theory. The relevance of club theory to the distribution of powers in the Union is limited. In the context of group size, however, club theory suggests the disadvantages of large groups.[14] In practical terms, this type of argument is echoed in suggestions that political union in Europe is best pioneered by a small core of only a few countries.

The theoretical disadvantages of large membership are associated in particular with the declining return from membership for any one member of an expanding group, and the reduced benefits from any club good that is in finite supply. For example, the inclusion of central European agricultural producers into the European Union will diminish the benefits of the Common Agricultural Policy to existing members as well as reduce financial transfers from a fixed Union budget for other poorer Member States. If the enlargement of the Union to include all European countries is taken as given, the implication is that some Union policies will no longer confer benefits that outweigh the costs and that certain powers are better repatriated.

There is however a further, and much more fundamental, reason why savings do not necessarily accrue from assigning powers to the Union. It is because the immediately apparent savings on organizational costs may be outweighed by longer term supply side considerations.

(b) Supply costs An emphasis on the supply costs of government draws on the parallel between the government as a producer of public goods and private producers of private goods in the market. If there is only one provider of public goods or policies there is no check on the costs of collective action. By contrast, the existence of several political domains is likely to reduce costs because competition between jurisdictions is introduced.

The implication of this argument is that general claims about the organizational advantages of having larger domains cannot be substantiated – it all depends on the nature of the policy that ensues. More specific claims that larger domains will reduce 'externalities', or the spill-over effects of policies between jurisdictions, have to be substantiated by strong evidence that the spill-over is indeed of a negative nature. In many areas of public policy there will be reasons to associate greater benefits with having more than one source of supply of public policies. There are the advantages of decentralized information, a greater variety of discovery procedures, a greater chance of achieving best practice through successive approximations and adjustments in the different jurisdictions, the benefits of competitive entrepreneurship in government and the likelihood of greater adaptability.[15] The existence of spill-over effects between neighbouring jurisdictions draws out these benefits because they provide a test of policies and help make transparent the costs associated with them. They test whether public policies are founded on full information and the degree to which they reflect preferences. Competition between jurisdictions will also test the robustness of public policies. Those that withstand the test will have enhanced credibility. Credibility should not automatically be associated with larger rather than smaller domains.

Transactions cost theories are thus ambiguous at best. There are organizational savings associated with larger units, both because bargaining power is greater for a large unit rather than a small, and because one actor avoids the coordination costs associated with several. But there are supply costs in having a single source of public policy.

Supply cost considerations create a presumption that public policy should be produced under a single jurisdiction only in two cases. The first is where the public policy is truly indivisible.[16] The second is where preferences are uniform. In cases where there are no variations in preferences, different jurisdictions would simply produce the same public policy mix. This is not the situation of Europe. The case where preferences differ is considered next.

(iii) Preference distinctions

Theories that focus on preferences approach optimum domain as that domain which most accurately and efficiently reflects preferences.[17] The task is to get a correspondence between jurisdiction and preferences.

Again there is a parallel with providers in the market. Different jurisdictions supply different mixes of goods (public policies) at different costs (tax levels). With a mobile population, people can 'shop around' and choose the product mix which best suits themselves. The root of the theory however lies in a proposition about public goods – that equilibrium will fall short of optimum supply because, in the case of public goods, individuals have incentives not to reveal their true preferences.[18] The opportunities for dissembling may increase in large jurisdictions. Multiple jurisdictions provide a way in which true preferences can be expressed.

There are many practical objections that can be made to this way of viewing political domain. People may not be mobile (particularly in Europe where there are language barriers and housing market rigidities). The link between public policy mixes and the tax costs of the policies concerned may be difficult to perceive. Fiscal transfers between jurisdictions may blur distinctions even further. The extent to which product mixes and preferences can be divided up will be limited by spill-over effects. Nevertheless, the ability of any large political association to reflect true preferences is highly questionable.

In combination, these three different perspectives on optimum domain suggest that Union powers should be defined sparingly. At first sight, organizational savings suggest there are advantages in having most areas of public policy decided by the Union. This is because a reduction in the number of jurisdictions promises to reduce coordination costs within the Union and increase the credibility and clout of public policy. Uncertainties will be reduced. However, the force of this argument is greatly weakened by the other considerations. Widely differing natural boundaries to public goods or public policies will make a single jurisdiction a costly supplier of policies. The diversity of preferences in Europe also means that a large jurisdiction is unlikely to be able to respond to different preferences. The monopoly role of a single supplier of public policy means that there is an inadequate means of checking against erroneous or costly policies or adjusting policies to situations where preferences are not uniform.

How is the balance to be drawn? Theoretical analogies with the market suggest the importance of having alternative policy 'products' on offer to meet different preferences and to discover best practice. An examination of particular areas of public policy also suggests there are advantages in recognizing the relative efficiency of different domains, except in the rare instances where a public policy is indivisible. Thus, on balance, theories of optimum domain establish a case for a system of 'multiple jurisdiction', or 'multiple domain' in Europe:

- as a way of achieving an efficient matching of public policy with available jurisdictions;
- as a way of arriving at the true costs of public policies;
- as a way of revealing true preferences for public policies.

IV Relationships between jurisdictions

Theories of optimum domain establish a persuasive case for multiple domain in Europe. They do not, however, characterize the relationship between jurisdictions. A higher level jurisdiction could, in theory, contract lower level jurisdictions to deliver public goods that are differentiated according to the lower level jurisdiction or to preferences in it.[19] Conversely, lower level jurisdictions could band together to provide public goods that are common to all of them. The question of how to orchestrate relationships between the different jurisdictions is thus left open.

There are three principal ways in which, in theory, relationships between jurisdictions can be arranged in Europe.

The first is hierarchical. All powers would be vested in the Union. Other jurisdictions (the Member States and their regions) would be subordinate and exercise powers delegated by the centre.

The second involves independent and coordinate powers. The powers of the Union and the powers of Member States (and their regions) would be independently derived. Each would have authority in specified areas or, for example, the powers of the centre could be defined and the powers of other jurisdictions defined in part as residual powers.

The third is for powers to be delegated up. All powers would be vested with the associating Member States (other than those which may rest with their regional or local authorities). The powers of the Union would be those expressly delegated by the Member States. The Union would have no independent authority of its own.

These different ways of distributing powers can all be gathered together under the label 'federal'. But, as mentioned earlier, this either involves using the same word to describe fundamentally different relationships between jurisdictions, or alternatively, it involves creating sub categories of 'federalism' where there is even less agreement on terminology.[20] It seems therefore less confusing to look at underlying structures, except in the case of specific references to the central (federal) government of the United States.

The discussion about the distribution of powers is sometimes further confused by terms such as 'subsidiarity' and related references to areas of 'exclusive competence' of the existing European Union. Subsidiarity can be interpreted, either in the sense of powers that flow down, or, as powers that are delegated up. An area of 'exclusive competence' can be seen either as an area of independent authority of the Union or as an area where the Member States have agreed to act collectively and delegated authority accordingly. Both terms therefore can be used to mask, rather than make transparent, what is really involved. Obfuscation can be useful politically. But, if the European Union is to rest on popular support and understanding, the relationships must be clear.

Within Europe there is a long tradition of thinking in terms of a distribution of powers that is hierarchical. It is a habit that reflects the legacy of monarchical forms of government and associated theories of kingship and church organization.[21] The idea of independent powers for the Union and the states was that adopted by the founding fathers of the United States – in part in reaction against European habits. At the other end of Europe's political traditions runs the view that political association starts with the individual.[22] This tradition led, in part, towards a consideration of the role of contract as an organizing principle of government and, more radically, to a consideration of ways in which powers could be delegated upwards. Each of these three alternative ways of defining relationships between jurisdictions has a claim to provide the right structure for a European political union. Only one can be adopted. They lead to fundamentally different arrangements of powers and institutions. The constitution must be clear as to which is chosen.

(i) The hierarchy

Under a hierarchical ordering of jurisdictions, powers will be vested in the highest level and cascade down to the lower levels. The powers exercised at the lower levels may be considerable – but they will be powers delegated down from the most senior level of government – the Union. Residual powers would be retained by the central authority. Lower level jurisdictions will be accountable for the powers they exercise not only to local electorates but also to the higher level authority that has delegated powers to them. The relationship will be a dependent relationship.

It may be thought that establishing a settled constitutional framework for Europe would inevitably establish European institutions at the apex of a hierarchical system, in part because the constitution would itself represent the most important rules of the political association and (in cases where the rules are justiciable) superior law. It is important, however, to distinguish between the ordering of legal instruments (including the constitution itself) and the ordering of powers and forms of organization. A constitutional law might be ranked higher than an ordinary law but a constitution can establish any ordering of powers. Even constitutional law might be made from the bottom up (by referendum, for example, or through the case law of ordinary courts) and does not necessarily imply a top down organization of legal authority.

(a) Advantages The great advantage of a hierarchical ordering of powers is that certain types of transaction costs in the Union can be greatly reduced. The main preferences in the political association are expressed simply at one level – the Union level. In institutional terms this would mean that the most important means of expressing political choice would be through elections to the European Parliament and, for example, through an elected President of the Union (possibly the President of the Commission). National and regional institutions would become subordinate to Union authorities. Elections to these lower level bodies would reflect choices on those who would exercise powers delegated by the Union.

(b) Disadvantages The great disadvantage is in supposing, in an area as diverse as Europe, that preferences can be easily simplified at the Union level. The more varied the preferences in the Union, the less likely it is that the Union will match, or achieve correspondence between, the powers it delegates and the national and regional policies desired. The greater will be the costs imposed on any subordinate jurisdiction where preferences diverge from median preferences in the Union as a whole. Moreover, higher level authorities are unlikely to wish to see different preferences expressed at lower levels and would likely acquire, over time, the financial resources in order to gain oversight and control over subordinate jurisdictions. The relationship between jurisdictions becomes one of bargaining about delegated powers and resources and not an ability to test alternative policies or put alternative preferences into practice.

The attempt to express preferences at one main level will reduce the quality of political expression at subordinate levels for other reasons. Local and sectional interests will focus their efforts to influence policy on the main level. Not only will subordinate jurisdictions be bypassed but an institution such as the European Parliament would, far from expressing Union concerns, or the preferences of the average voter, become the voice of local and sectional interest groups. In this respect it would acquire the characteristics of the Congress of the United States where, as a result of the gradual centralization of powers at the Union level, local and sectional concerns now generally prevail.

An equally fundamental objection to viewing European political union as hierarchy is that it concentrates the democratic process on powers exercised at the centre. In a democratic system of government the virtues of participation and expression that are sought must permeate the system at all levels.[23] It was in the vigour of local democracy at the municipal level that de Toqueville found the basis of political freedoms in the early United States.[24] It was the great achievement of the founding fathers of the American system to break away from the hierarchical examples of Europe in the distribution of powers. They tried to ensure that the central (federal) government would rest dependent on the people by expressing the powers of the states and the powers of the Union as independent and coordinate.

(ii) Independent and coordinate powers

In the American system of government, the central (federal) government is formally independent of the states. Equally, the states formally derive their powers independently of the central government. It has been called a 'compound republic' allowing for concurrent and autonomous jurisdictions.[25] These formal characteristics can still be seen in the American system. Each American citizen may claim rights under two governments (the federal or the state), each is subject to two laws (state and federal) and each pays two sets of taxes.[26] The approach appeared to solve the problem of coordinating multiple jurisdictions. The citizen could participate in the central jurisdiction for their shared interests and participate in the state and local jurisdictions in respect of their local and special preferences.

(a) Advantages The American system of government has enormous virtues – not least in the way that it has been consistent with nation building in the face of an expanding number of states entering the Union and the need to absorb continuing waves of immigration. This ability to knit together very diverse populations within a democratic framework underlies the appeal of emulation – the creation of a 'United States of Europe'. However, before rapidly concluding that such a system has immediate applicability to Europe, there are reasons for caution – quite apart from the evident sociological differences and the fact that the ability to absorb immigration has probably owed more to local and municipal government in the United States than to the division of powers between the centre and the states.

(b) Disadvantages One simple historical reason for caution is that the way in which state and federal powers were framed did not succeed in preventing a civil war. Europe does not have to wrest with slavery. It does, however, have to take into account deeply felt divisions of other kinds. The reason for caution of a more contemporary nature lies in the fact that, despite the formally independent authority of federal and state government, the central (federal) government has come to dominate the system. The construct of the founding fathers has not worked to prevent the emergence of a centralized form of government.[27] In many respects the states have, in practice, become dependent on the federal government. Political processes have in practice become focused on the federal level.[28]

The question of whether this evolution is a 'good' or a 'bad' development is not at issue. The issue instead is that a constitutional settlement is intended to bring about a stable distribution of powers (except for changes agreed through the processes of amendment).[29] The American constitution has not achieved this stability in basic relationships.

At first sight, it is tempting to ascribe this evolution to the enormous changes in the functions of government since the times of the founding fathers. But this does not explain why these powers accrued to the central rather than to state governments. There were other factors at work in the institutional arrangements themselves.

These factors seem to have included the following:

- The independence of the central government meant that the states had no effective means of their own to control central decisions. Constitutional amendment procedures have been too cumbersome to use other than on rare occasions. Even as a threat of last resort, the states possessed no right of secession as a means to check encroachments, or to dissuade, or deter, central policy making.
- The unconstrained power to tax gave the centre superior resources to use to bid for voter support and to establish client and dependent relationships – including the states themselves. Tax resources and spending programmes are now dominated by the centre. Revenue sharing by the centre only serves to disguise dependencies and has the further disadvantage of blurring responsibilities.[30]
- The institutional connections between the states and the centre that were intended to enable the states to hold the central institutions as a whole in check proved ineffectual.[31] The election of members of the US Senate by state legislatures was abolished by the end of the nineteenth century (in response to machine politics) and the electoral college for selecting the President (based on the number of representatives and senators from each state) has, in practice, been superseded by direct election. The last remaining trace of state presence in the federal arrangements is the overrepresentation of small states in the Senate. The system of checks and balances between the different branches of the American federal government does not stop their ability collectively to take on

more powers at the expense of the states.

* The reliance on a federal body (the Supreme Court) and on judicial processes of constitutional interpretation and change has led to an enormous extension of federal powers. The implications of the Court for the distribution of powers between centre and states were not fully foreseen by the makers of the constitution who saw the Court as the 'least dangerous branch' compared with the risks they saw of the Congress and the President trying to expand their powers.[32]

Europe may be attracted by the model of the United States in giving the centre constitutionally independent powers at the same time as giving Member State powers with constitutional protection. But the centralization that has occurred under the arrangements in the United States, as well as the very different social setting, suggest great caution. Moreover, any similarly modelled independence of powers for the European Union and for the Member States would have to reexamine those aspects of the arrangements in America which have contributed to the growing dominance of the centre – the collapse of the institutional connections between states and the centre, the role of central taxation and the role of the Supreme Court. There is moreover an alternative model – a system in which the powers of the centre are delegated by the Member States.

(iii) Delegation upwards

In a system where powers are distributed upwards, the powers of the centre are those expressly delegated by the members of the Union. The centre does not wield independent power. The institutions of the members will continue to play a role in the institutional arrangements of the Union. Resources for the centre will also come through the members of the Union rather than from an independent power of the centre to tax. Just as powers can be delegated, they can also be withdrawn – for example, if a collective policy is not working.

(a) *Advantages* The advantage of such a system is first that it is the one most compatible with retaining the advantages of multiple domain. Members will be careful not to drift too far from reflecting the preferences in their own domain. Members will also have a self-interest in retaining the possibility of different approaches to questions of public policy. It is the one most likely to be conducive to best practice in public policy by allowing for experimentation and by exposing the true costs and benefits of different approaches. Second, it may provide for a more stable long term relationship in the distribution of powers. The ability of the centre to bid for electoral support and to build client relationships through its own resources will be limited. Members can decide what to do collectively on a periodic basis and withdraw powers if collective action is not proving effective. The rules for withdrawing powers that are not working can be made easier to exercise than those that delegate new collective powers to the centre. There is thus less likely to be a one way dynamic. In addition, the ways in which members choose to act together can also vary without having to conform to one institutional mode in all areas of their collective activity. Third, the great practical advantage of such a system for Europe is that the existing structures of the Member States can continue to play a significant role in the Union. Thus, the inherited legitimacy of the existing political order can underpin the new arrangements, rather than being seen to be in conflict. The existing habits of civil association can be incorporated into the new association without the same degree of challenge to traditional ties of contiguity and feeling. Finally, it is the system most likely to be compatible with maintaining the civic virtues of participation and expression at all levels of political activity.

It is important to distinguish between a system where powers rest with the Member States to be delegated upwards and a simple club.[33] Some of the key behavioural features of the present European Union are analogous to theoretical models of club behaviour. Like a club, it can be seen as a voluntary association brought together by the perception of mutual benefits; some of the benefits can be kept within the group of members rather than accruing to outsiders, notably a say in the setting of the rules, and there are organizational savings in acting together.

However, the club analogy has important drawbacks as a model for the European Union. First, clubs tend to be formed just on the basis of a shared interest in particular outcomes. This may characterize the strength of the present Union. But it also characterizes its weakness – the subordination of rules and processes to intended outcomes. Second, club theory offers no insights into the internal arrangements of power within the club. Thus the club analogy does not offer a path for the further development of the Union as a rule based political association. On the contrary, the club analogy illustrates some of the fears associated with the present structure of the Union – the fear that the Union's effectiveness will diminish as it extends the purposes of association; the fear that it will become less effective as it enlarges, and, the fear that inadequate attention to processes will either undermine support for the Union, or, result in the ignoring of the most important values in political association in Europe. A system which provides for the Member States to delegate powers to the centre for express purposes, and which has a clear structure for its main procedures and institutional relationships, goes well beyond viewing the Union as a mere club.

(b) Disadvantages One disadvantage of a system of powers delegated to the centre is that members may fail to exploit commonalities. A second disadvantage is that the costs of bringing together many different jurisdictions are high. These disadvantages centre around two points.

- The first is institutional – the apparent complexity of organizing the relationships between the institutions of the Member States and the institutions of the Union.

- The second is the difficulty of arriving at decision procedures in a system where Member States remain pivotal in policy making. The decision rules must allow both for commonalities to be exploited where they exist but, at the same time, provide for different preferences and different approaches to be reflected where such differences exist and can be accommodated.

The difficulties attached to defining the relationships between the institutions of the Member States and the institutions of the Union should not be underestimated. Neither should they be a deterrent to trying to articulate a non-hierarchical relationship between jurisdictions in European political union. The clarifying of relationships between the institutions of the Member States and the institutions of the Union is one that needs to be undertaken, not only in the case where the powers of the Union are those delegated up by the Member States, but also, as American experience suggests, where the powers of the Union and the powers of Member States rest on independent and coordinate bases. Only if powers are distributed in Europe on a hierarchical basis can relationships be simplified through a straightforward system of subordination. But hierarchy is the least desirable way of distributing powers in Europe and the one likely to encounter the greatest resistance.

Particularly important in this context, as American experience also shows, is how to frame relationships between the law of the Member States and the law of the Union. If the law of the Union develops as superior law in all, or most areas, then the idea of independent powers of the Member States, or the idea of powers delegated up by the Member States, is nullified. A single jurisdiction is created through superior law. The implication of any non-hierarchical way of distributing powers is that two systems of law (state and Union law) as well as international law must continue to coexist. This means that considerable caution must be shown in regard to the legal powers of the centre. For example, declarations of individual and civil liberties, if entrusted to the centre, may become instruments for intrusion over a range of policies originally intended to be within the jurisdiction of the associating state. In the case of Europe, this particular problem can be avoided by leaving the enforcement of individual rights and civil liberties with the Member State, subject to appeal to the specialized Court of the European Convention on Human Rights, which is not associated with other aspects of Union jurisdiction. But it still leaves the more general problem of relations between legal systems needing to be addressed.

The further implication of the coexistence of the law of the Member State and the law of the Union (and international law where relevant) is that methods have to be found for handling potential conflicts between legal systems. Moreover, such conflicts will frequently involve reference to the way in which the distribution of powers is defined in the constitution. Settlement could therefore, on crucial occasions, depend on constitutional interpretation. If that interpretation rests in the hands of a Union court (say the European Court of Justice) that court would be ruling on a matter of its own powers and where it itself was an interested party. The question of maintaining a system of multiple jurisdictions (either in a system of independent Member State and Union powers, or where Union powers are delegated by the Member State) involves therefore finding the right judicial arrangements for conflict resolution as well as the right arrangements for constitutional interpretation.

The question of how to structure institutional arrangements (including those relating to constitutional interpretation) in a manner consistent with a system of powers delegated to the centre, is explored more fully in later chapters. However, before that further discussion, the question of decision procedures in a system of multiple domain must first be addressed.

Notes

1   See Cornes, R. and Sandler, T. (1986), *The Theory of Externalities, Public Goods and Club Goods*.
2   Adam Smith described them in this way.
3   Tiebout followed this definition in his 'Pure Theory of Local Expenditure'. Tiebout, C.M. (1956), 'A Pure Theory of Local Expenditures', *Journal of Political Economy*, 64.
4   See Demsetz, H. (1970), 'The Private Production of Public Goods', *Journal of Law and Economics*, 13.
5   The best illustration of this point is provided by the discussion by Coase of the lighthouse in economics which, despite his analysis, is still today casually included among the types of goods that 'must' be provided by the public sector. 'The lighthouse is simply plucked out of the air to serve as an illustration. . . such generalisations are not likely to be helpful unless they are derived from studies of how such activities are actually carried out within different institutional frameworks. . . the early history shows that, contrary to the belief of many economists, a lighthouse service can be provided by private enterprise'. Coase, R.H. 'The Lighthouse in Economics', *Journal of Law and Economics*, 17. A more up to date example is provided by air traffic control which, because of its historical connection with air defence, is commonly thought of as a public good. It too could be provided by the private sector.
6   'The true outputs of governments are policies and. . . these are the relevant objects on which to focus attention in formulating a theory of the public sector'. Breton A. (1974), *The Economic Theory of Representative Government*.
7   'There is a need for a separate government institution for every collective good with a unique boundary, so that there can be a match between those who receive the benefits of a collective good and those who pay for it'. Olson, M. (1969), 'The Principle of Fiscal Equivalence: The Division of Responsibilities Among Different Levels of Government', *American Economic Review*, 59. See also Oates, W.E. (1972), *Fiscal Federalism*.
8   'The group should be extended as long as the expected costs of the spillover effects from excluded jurisdictions exceed the expected incremental costs of decision-making resulting from adding the excluded jurisdictions'. Buchanan, J.M. and Tullock, G. (1962), *The Calculus of Consent*.
9   A focus on transaction costs stems from the attention given by Coase to the costs attached to using the pricing mechanism. 'Their existence implies that methods of coordination alternative to the market, which are themselves costly and in various

ways imperfect, may nonetheless be preferable to relying on the pricing mechanism'. Coase, R.H. (1992), *The Institutional Structure of Production*. See also, Coase, R,H. (1937), The Nature of the Firm, *Economica*, 4.

10 In a not dissimilar way J.S. Mill noted the role of government as a convenience. 'There is a multitude of cases in which governments, with general approbation, assume powers and execute functions for which no reason can be assigned except the simple one, that they conduce to general convenience'. (He gave as an example the coining of money). Mill, J.S. (1848), *Principles of Political Economy*.

11 This is the approach taken by Breton, A. and Scott, A. (1978) in *The Economic Constitution of Federal States* who view organizational costs as the key to the distribution of powers. 'We conclude that, in a world of zero organizational costs, the search for a theory of the structure of the public sector or of federalism is fruitless. The basic question of such a theory – that of the assignment of functions – does not even arise!. . . the essential nature of a structure for the public sector is to be found in the presence of positive organizational resource costs, not in public goods or externalities'.

12 See Downs, A. (1957), *An Economic Theory of Democracy*.

13 See North, D.C. (1990), *Institutions, Institutional Change and Economic Performance*.

14 The disadvantages of size are explored in Olson, M. (1971), *The Logic of Collective Action*.

15 Hayek has stressed the advantages of decentralized information; Popper the advantages of better discovery procedures; Polanyi the benefits from successive approximations and mutual adjustments in policy; Breton the benefits of competitive entrepreneurship in government and North the greater adaptability of decentralized governance.

16 See Chamberlin, J. (1974), 'Provision of Collective Goods as a Function of Group Size', *American Political Science Review*, 68.

17 'The greater the number of communities and the greater the variance among them, the closer the consumer wiil come to fully realizing his preference position'. Tiebout, op. cit.

18 See Cornes and Sandler, op. cit.

19 The shortcomings of theories of optimum domain in treating relationships between domains is admitted by Brennan and Buchanan: 'The 'economic theory' of federalism is no different from standard normative economics in its implicit assumptions about politics. The normative advice proffered by the theory is presumably directed toward the benevolent despotism that will implement the efficiency criteria'. Brennan, G. and Buchanan, J.M. (1980), *The Power to Tax: Analytic Foundations of a Fiscal Constitution*.

20 Riker offers the following sub-categories of federalism. 'We can distinguish two major types of federalism: one in which federal decisions are made exclusively through the machinery of the central government (this type we can describe as centrally directed or centralised), and the other in which federal decisions are made, partially at least, through the machinery of local governments (this type we can describe as peripherally directed or peripheralised)'. There is however no agreement on such terms. See Riker, W.H. (1987), *The Development of American Federalism*.

21 Bodin gave an early example of a hierarchical distribution of powers related to kingship: 'There are in fact six degrees of dependence below the status of an absolute prince who holds of none and is dependent on none'. Bodin, J. (1576), *The Six Books of a Commonwealth*.

22 Rousseau represents this line: 'No man has a natural authority over his fellow'. Rousseau, J.J. (1762), *The Social Contract*.

23 Mill voiced strong objection to the idea that democracy can reside only in a central government: 'A democratic constitution, not supported by democratic institutions in detail, but confined to the central government, not only is not political freedom, but

often creates a spirit precisely the reverse, carrying down to the lowest grade in society the desire and ambition of political domination'. Mill, J.S. (1848), op. cit.

24   'Local assemblies of citizens constitute the strength of free nations. . . A nation may establish a system of free government, but without the spirit of municipal institutions it cannot have the spirit of liberty'. De Toqueville, A. (1835), *Democracy in America.*

25   'This new concept allowed for a limited national government to be formed and to exist concurrently with independent and limited state government'. Ostrom, V. (1987), *The Political Theory of a Compound Republic.*

26   'Subject to the few express and implied restrictions, each State retains its sovereign power to govern. The federal government also has all the characteristics of a unitary government within its functionally limited sphere. The result is that within any territorial unit (any State) there are always two governments – State and federal – operating side by side but each sovereign and independent within its functional sphere. Each of us (unless an alien) has dual citizenship; he is a citizen of the United States and of the State in which he resides'. Cox, A. (1976), *The Role of the Supreme Court in American Government.*

27   'As Americans approach the end of the second century in their experiments with constitutional choice, those experiments manifest patterns of increasing dominance by the national government over all aspects of life'. Ostrom, op. cit.

28   De Toqueville's judgement that, 'The Federal Government is,. . . the exception; the Government of the States is the rule' would hardly apply today. De Toqueville, op. cit.

29   The Federalist papers argued that 'The powers delegated by the proposed Constitution to the federal government are few and defined. Those which are to remain in the State governments are numerous and indefinite'. Nobody would argue that this reflects the present balance. See *Federalist Paper*, No. XLV. (Madison J.).

30   'Revenue sharing is undesirable, because it subverts the primary purpose of federalism, which is to create competition between jurisdictions. Each jurisdiction must have responsibility for raising its own revenue and should be precluded from entering into explicit agreements with other jurisdictions on the determination of uniform rates'. Brennan and Buchanan, op. cit.

31   Madison had argued that because of the institutional connections, 'Each of the principal branches of the federal government will owe its existence more or less to the favour of the State governments'. *Federalist Paper*, No. XLV.

32   De Toqueville was concerned about the fact that the Supreme Court would be judge in its own cause in cases involving the conflict of federal and state laws but concluded (erroneously), 'The Federal judges are conscious of the relative weakness of the power in whose name they act, and are more inclined to abandon a right of jurisdiction in cases where it is justly their own, than to assert a privilege to which they have no legal claim'. De Toqueville, op. cit.

33   'A club is a voluntary group deriving mutual benefit from sharing one or more of the following: production costs, the members' characteristics, or a good characterized by excludable benefits'. Cornes and Sandler, op. cit.

6 Rules for taking decisions in the Union

'There is but one law which, from its nature, needs unanimous consent. This is the social compact; for civil association is the most voluntary of all acts'. Jean Jacques Rousseau, *The Social Contract*, 1762.

I The quality of choices

Decision rules in the European Union deal with the question of how precisely to frame the rules of assent and dissent on matters of collective policy. They deal with the need for decision takers to be able to take positive actions and also to be able to block actions.

The power to take positive actions and the power to block can be seen mathematically as simple mirror images – the majority required to take a positive decision also defines the minority required to block. But the weight given to assent or to dissent and the way in which dissent is to be treated can differ in extremely important ways. Some rules give greater prominence to the power to block. Others might give equal treatment to the power to take positive action and the power to block. Neither do rules necessarily have to treat dissent in the same way. In some cases, those in dissent will have the preferences of others imposed on them. In other cases, the affirmative decision may only apply to those assenting while those in dissent can opt out or opt in.

In the framing of the decision rules for European political union, there appears to be an inherent conflict between what is practical and what may be 'best' in terms of the quality of procedures and decisions. An emphasis on practicality looks to the speed and ease of methods of decision taking. Voting thresholds and the necessary majorities thus should not be set too high. By contrast, an emphasis on the quality of decision taking puts the stress on trying to arrive at the 'right' decisions, the ones which most accurately reflect preferences in the Union and those that command the widest assent. Decision thresholds should therefore be set high. Hence there appears to be an unavoidable tension between the costs of inaction and the costs of wrong actions.

A similar dilemma centres around the treatment of dissent. At first sight it seems clear that effective decision taking requires those who are outvoted to accept in all circumstances the decisions of those in the decisive majority. Measures to respect the preferences of those in dissent seem in inevitable conflict.

Again there is a tension between effective decision taking rules and rules that reflect the diversity of preferences.

The dilemma is not new.[1] But it is vital that it is resolved. If the quality of decisions taken in the Union fails to reflect preferences or to command assent, then the worth and the legitimacy of the Union will itself come under question. There will be an equal questioning of the Union if its procedures do not allow it to take timely and effective decisions.

An unconsidered emphasis on the speed and ease of decision taking leads in the direction of having as many decisions as possible in as few hands as possible. It is an argument in favour, for example, of concentrating decisions with a body such as the Commission or with the votes of the largest Member States. Even the briefest pause for thought suggests that such 'solutions' raise as many questions as they solve.

Decision taking can be viewed from two different angles:

- The first approach is to look at the choosers – does there need to be a simple majority in favour, or unanimity, or a threshold in between? Are those who make the choice to be treated as equal?
- The second approach is to look at the subject matter of choice – should choices on matters of great importance or of great sensitivity to opinion be treated as equal to other choices?

These two different perspectives on decision rules do not necessarily lead to contradictory conclusions. There is a traditional case for combining elements of each approach in the final rules.[2] There is the more recent suggestion that a unifying method of analysis can be found by looking at both choosers and the subject matter of choice from the perspective of the costs of collective action.[3] Whether it is the choosers or the choices that are looked at, there are indeed common concerns. Both perspectives have to take into account sheer practicalities – methods of decisions have to be found. Both approaches are concerned with questions of equality. Should each participant be treated as equal? Should the subject matter of choice be treated as equal?

The analysis which follows suggests that, in the circumstances of European political union, neither the choosers nor the choices can be treated as equal. In any system that maintains the Member State as a participant in the direction of public policy for the Union, the disparities between Member States have in some way to be recognized. Equally, it is valid to recognize that some choices will be seen as more important than others. Moreover, in a Union where preferences are not always held in common and where sensitivities are not always felt equally across Europe, it will be prudent to have a variety of ways of accommodating dissent. The analysis suggests therefore that:

- inequalities between the Member States are best recognized through the development of a system of concurrent majorities in which the number of states and their size differences are recognized alongside their proportionate shares in votes based on population;
- differences in the relative importance of different areas of collective choice are best recognized by graduating majorities around qualified majority voting in a way that makes it more difficult to overrule minority preferences in areas of greater importance;
- dissent needs to be treated flexibly even in the case of concurrent majorities and graduated voting. The balance of advantage lies, not in insisting that dissenters are forced to accept a common position where interests or preferences conflict, but in allowing for majorities that have the necessary 'critical mass' to pursue their preferences, while accepting that dissenters should have the option as to whether to 'opt in' or 'opt out'. 'Critical mass' is more relevant than 'common action' in areas where there are strong differences of opinion on important issues.

II Choosers

The numbers and characteristics of those making key choices in the Union give rise to two key issues for decision procedures in the Union. First, there are the different implications of different voting thresholds – those majorities necessary to make a decision – for the number of participants in the decision. In a decision group of thirty members it may make a great deal of difference whether a simple majority of participants can take a decision (in which case fourteen participants can be overridden) or whether an eighty per cent majority is required in which case only six participants can be overridden). Second, there is the question of how to treat inequalities among participants in the decision group. Any system for the Union that builds the Member States into its decision taking procedures has to be able to deal with inequalities among the participants. In a European Union of thirty Member States, the two most populous Member States will have a combined population equivalent, approximately, to the combined population of over twenty of the smallest Member States. If each Member State has a single vote, it would be technically possible to arrive at a simple majority while representing less than fifteen per cent of the population of the Union. Conversely, if votes are weighted according to population, it would be possible for the four largest countries to achieve a simple majority even if the other twenty six Member States were opposed.

(i) Thresholds

There are two important benchmarks for taking decisions – the simple majority (where a half of the decision taking group plus one are needed) and unanimity (where all votes must be in favour of the choice). A choice in favour of either of these two rules has the advantage of simplicity. Each is easily understood. Between these two benchmarks are various levels of qualified majority. A choice of qualified majorities for decisions reflects a choice for more complex rules.

(a) Majority voting Simple majority voting is traditionally justified on one of three grounds.

First, it allows for equality between voters. Each vote counts the same as another. If a minority is allowed to determine a choice then their votes count for more. Simple majority voting is the one decision rule which precludes the possibility that more people will be outvoted by less. With a higher threshold, a minority can block. With a lower threshold, a minority can prevail.

Second, it is fair. It can be shown that in a system of voting between equals and, when an equal weight is given to the need to act as against a desire to be able to block, majority rule voting is as good as any alternative rule for achieving a correspondence between individual values and collective choice.[4]

Third, it is practical. Higher thresholds will be more difficult to attain. Simple majority voting economizes on the information required to make the decision.[5]

(b) Unanimity Unanimity has the unique characteristic that no decision can be imposed on any participant. Participants in a minority may come under pressure to join a consensus but, in any single decision, a strongly held position cannot be overruled. It is a voting rule which is likely to favour the expression of true preferences. This is because it ensures that a decision cannot be taken unless each participant perceives for themselves that the decision will improve their own position.

Where a decision is not an isolated one, but is part of a sequence of decisions, the behaviour of a participant in one context may have a spill-over effect into other decisions. The result could be that behaviour under the unanimity rule may be closer to that under majority voting because the blocking possibilities will not be used or will be traded. Nevertheless, absolute protection to a single dissentient remains. If an 'optimal' choice is defined in terms of decisions that make at least one person 'better off', without making any other person 'worse off', then unanimity provides the one method by which each participant can judge for themselves whether they feel better or worse off. In any other decision method, participants may find themselves outside the decisive group and thus have choice imposed upon them. Unanimity is hence the decision rule typically associated with the ideal that choices should not be imposed and that decision taking procedures should not coerce.[6]

In making comparisons between the claim of majority voting to be as good as any other rule for reflecting preferences and the claim of unanimity to best reflect preferences, it is important to recognize the asymmetry of the unanimity rule. Its emphasis is on the blocking of collective choices that are not wanted by those in dissent. By contrast, the simple majority rule gives an equal weight to the desire to achieve a decision as compared with the desire to block a decision.

The asymmetry of the unanimity rule can be justified either on the general principle that, other things being equal, the participants in a political union will prefer to make decisions for themselves as the best way of ensuring the realization of their own preferences. Collective action thus requires extra justification. Or, alternatively, the asymmetry can be justified on the basis that a bias towards the status quo is justified so as to help ensure that a system of multiple jurisdictions does not get overwhelmed by a general tendency of decision making to gravitate towards the centre. Both these justifications can be seen as constitutional justifications. Thus, unanimity is usually considered as a method for deciding on constitutional rules, rather than as a method for making political choices within a constitution.

The difficulty with unanimity as a rule for policy choice is that it is impractical.[7] Unanimity is difficult to achieve except in small like-minded groups. By contrast, European political union brings together large groupings where often there will be a diversity of opinion on any subject. A generalized requirement for unanimity in political choice is likely to bring paralysis to decisions in bodies that employ it. This will not necessarily bring decision taking in the Union to a halt. The more likely effect is to divert the centre of decision taking to bodies with less burdensome requirements, or to procedures outside political processes (such as the law). If such diversions are not intentional, then the purpose of rule based procedures is undermined.

(c) Qualified majorities The use of qualified majorities can be seen as a way to try to overcome the inadequacies of either unanimity or simple majority voting. First, qualified majorities acknowledge as a practical matter the desirability of a rule that is less stringent than the unanimity rule but which is also less permissive than simple majority rule.[8] Second, they respond to situations where participants in a decision are not equal. Third, they allow for settings where the decisions themselves are in some sense 'unequal'- for example, some more important than others. When inequalities arise, simple voting rules break down.[9]

The practicality of different voting thresholds can be viewed simply as a question of the costs involved in bargaining. A simple majority in favour of a decision should be the easiest and least costly to reach. Unanimity will be the most difficult and the most costly to achieve.[10] Qualified majorities raise the costs of decision procedures compared with a simple majority rule, but lower them compared with the costs of obtaining unanimity. Thus, if voting rules are regarded as essentially ways of reducing decision costs, then lower bargaining costs provide a rationale for moving from a unanimity requirement towards simple majorities.

However, the concept of bargaining costs involves not just the question of the ease or difficulty of reaching agreements but also the costs to those not in agreement with the decision of having the preferences of others imposed on them. The defence provided by the unanimity rule against imposed choice minimizes this kind of potential cost of collective action to any individual participant.[11] This perspective again raises questions about the homogeneity of the group and the homogeneity of the choice. Like-minded groups can accept less restrictive rules. Their members will find it relatively easy to reach accommodation and will not be too concerned about the potential costs if the preferences of others in the group come to prevail. By contrast, sharply differentiated groups will have both high bargaining costs and heightened fears from any other than restrictive rules. In addition, the perception by participants of the costs of imposed choices would likely differ in different areas of choice.

From this perspective, decision rules have to be looked at, not just in terms of whether they make it easy and relatively less costly to achieve choice, but also as to whether they offer protection against the perceived costs of imposed choices. If the fears of imposed costs are high – either because the group is diverse in its preferences, or because the different areas of choice are perceived to carry very different potential costs, then rules will be tilted towards restrictions on choice and away from simple majorities. Whether the net effect of more restrictive decision rules will be to increase the overall costs of decision-making is less clear. If Member States feel themselves to be well protected by the formal rules of voting against any fears of being overruled on subject matters of importance to them, the dynamics may be conducive to generally easier decision taking in practice. In a well working political union it should become increasingly possible to dispense in practice with the formalities of voting and rely increasingly on consensus.

A possible guide to the ways in which complex decision rules can be specified is provided by differences between the subject matter of choice. This is because the fears of imposed costs are likely to vary according to the type of decision at issue. The prospect of being overruled on a matter, say of part time employment conditions, may be costly, but not as costly as, for example, the implications of being overruled on a security and defence policy issue involving the possible commitment of armed forces. However, before discussing this possible way of framing complex decision rules, there are other approaches to inequalities among choosers that first need consideration.

(ii) Inequalities between choosers

The treatment of inequalities among choosers is a troublesome one. In voting settings where the electorate as a whole participates, each participant is counted as equal to another. There are no longer disqualifications on the grounds, for example, of gender or lack of education. Neither are there pre-qualifications on grounds of property. Member States in a European political union however are clearly not equal. There are enormous disparities in size of population, great differences in wealth and equally great differences in the way in which policies undertaken in the jurisdiction of one Member State will affect others. Therefore any system of decision taking in the Union that involves Member States has to address the problem of inequalities.

As a practical matter there is much to be said in favour of avoiding overcomplicated decision rules. Complicated rules make decision taking itself more difficult. They also make it more difficult to explain to public opinion how decisions have been arrived at. A first question therefore is whether there are other constitutional methods of recognizing inequalities which can help keep the decision rules themselves as simple as possible. A second question is whether the complexities could be reduced by prior adjustments to the voting weights of participants.

(a) Constitutional alternatives There are two main alternatives that might replace the complex decision taking procedures that accompany qualified majority voting systems.

One approach is to bypass the source of the cost and complexities – the Member State. It means looking at ways in which preferences can be expressed directly, without involving the intermediation of Member States in taking public policy decisions. This means looking to the Commission and the Parliament as the key decision taking bodies.

The second approach is to allow for the preferences of Member States to be expressed within a bicameral system. One chamber of the European Parliament would be directly elected. The other could represent the Member States. A bicameral system can be articulated to produce results equivalent to complex voting rules.[12]

As discussed in the previous chapter, the first of these alternatives is not compatible with a system where powers exercised collectively are those delegated up from the Member State. In a system where the centre exercises only those powers expressly delegated by the members of the Union, the Member State, its representatives and its institutions, will need to remain involved in collective decision taking at the centre. The same is likely to be the case in a system where the powers of the Union and the powers of the Member States rest on independent foundations. American experience suggests that a strong institutional connection between the states and the Union is needed as one important component to help prevent the dominance of the centre. The removal of the Member State from public policy decision taking by the Union is compatible only with a hierarchy of powers in the Union in which all main decisions are taken on one level – the Union level – and where at the same time alternative bodies (not involving the Member State) exist for decision taking. This arrangement of powers is the least consistent with the advantages of multiple jurisdictions.

The second alternative, of a bicameral arrangement, makes an assumption about the functions of the Member State in a system of distributed powers. It suggests that Member States do not have a role in the public policy setting role of government, but rather that they have a role in the functions of representative assemblies. Representative assemblies can perform a number of useful functions, but their role in giving direction to public policy is usually rather limited. Such an assumption about the proper place for the Member State therefore cannot rest on the basis of the complexities of decision taking alone. As long as the Member State is seen as a possible participant in the governmental function of deciding on the direction of public policy in the Union, there is no constitutional alternative to trying to settle on decision rules that reflect inequalities among those involved in public policy choices.

(b) Voting weights The assignment of votes to each Member State according to the share of that Member State in the population of the Union is the only system consistent with the principle that each person's vote in the Union should count the same as another. In practice, the recognition of the role of participating states in a Union tends traditionally to be associated with the less populous states receiving more votes than their share of population would justify. Inequalities are reduced by a weighting that favours the small participants.

The limitations of this approach in Europe arise from the disparities in population size between the largest and the smallest Member States. In a Union of thirty Member States in which voting was to be determined by shares in population, the half comprising the smallest Member States would need to receive a voting weighting four times their population share in order to block a decision requiring a simple majority and almost three times their population weight in order even to be able to block a decision for which a two thirds majority was required. Yet more than a modest degree of distortion is difficult to justify in theory and unlikely to be acceptable in practice. Weighting according to a criterion other than population (for example, by GNP) might be applicable in particular circumstances – such as decision taking on the budget where (at present) contributions are GNP linked – but is difficult to justify as a general rule.

(c) Concurrent majorities In the absence of generally applicable weighting adjustments to reduce inequalities between Member States, the focus of decision rules that reflect both the Member State as well as population size in decision taking, turns towards systems of concurrent majorities. Under such a system the majority required to pass a collective decision requires not only the reaching of a certain proportion of votes cast (weighted broadly by population) but requires also a certain number of Member States to be in favour, or at least not opposed. For example, a concurrent majority might comprise half the number of Member States (plus one) and affirmative votes from states that account for half of the population. By insisting that a certain number of states as well as a certain share in population

are both necessary for a decision, a system of concurrent majorities lowers the number of members that can be overridden in any decision. In the absence of such a rule, in a Union of thirty members, the six largest members accounting for around seventy per cent of the votes and the four largest accounting for over one half, would dominate.

Concurrent majorities can be framed not just to take account of two measures (the number of states and their share of population) but also to take into account a third measure if needed. Such a need arises when there is not an even distribution in the population measure and when there are extreme values at either end of the scale. This is the case with the population distribution in Europe. The third measure might look at the size categories of countries so that not more than a stipulated number of small Member States could be overruled in certain decisions and not more than a certain number of large states.

In the absence of such a third measure, size disparities in Europe mean that public opinion may perceive a 'large country problem' as well as a 'small country problem'. In a Union of thirty Member States it would, for example, be possible for four of the largest six Member States to be overruled in a decision requiring a simple majority on each of the two scales while three of the six largest Member States (for example, France, Italy and Spain together) could be overruled even on a matter requiring a two thirds majority vote. Such results may not always be acceptable to public opinion and might also weaken the credibility of the majority decision.

In the practical world of coalitions and alliances, such awkward and possibly destructive results would rarely happen. But alliances and coalitions within a union also trigger their own tensions – particularly where they become semi-formalized as a way of avoiding unwanted outcomes. In order to avoid the semi-formalization of coalitions and alliances, a system of concurrent majorities using three measures is probably necessary.

This discussion of inequalities between the Member States of the European Union suggests that decision taking that continues to reflect the Member State will develop as a form of concurrent majorities. Nevertheless the question still remains as to how a system of concurrent majorities can be arranged to be practical and intelligible. It is in this context that, as mentioned above, differences between the subject matter for choice can provide a guide.

III The choices

Within national political systems, decision rules do not necessarily discriminate in obvious ways between different areas of choice. In some European countries, the requirement for certain important decisions to be taken by special majorities may be expressed as a constitutional requirement. In others, such distinctions are not made. For example, in the British system, a government with a bare majority in the

House of Commons can, in theory, go to war as easily as it can legislate on the licensing of dogs (technically this could be done under the prerogative powers of the Crown without parliamentary approval). The absence of formal distinctions in some Member States however does not necessarily mean that such distinctions can be avoided in a European political union. In individual Member States there will often exist more of a consensus on different issues (including the most important) than can be expected in Europe as a whole. Moreover, whatever the outward appearance of the use of simple majorities in the national context, in practice, the rules of procedure and the use of conventions often work to set different thresholds of consent for different types of decision.[13]

Distinctions between different areas of political choice can be seen from three different perspectives. Each involves different ways of trying to discriminate between categories of choice. Potentially, they thus provide a guide to how the necessary concurrent majorities can be graduated according to the relative importance of the subject matter.

A first approach is that of cost. Different areas of choice have different costs attached. These differences could be recognized in the rules so as to make it more difficult to impose costs in the areas where imposed costs are potentially the greatest.

A second approach is to look at the setting of the decision. Is it a setting where all participants stand to benefit or could the benefit of some participants be at the expense of others? If such a distinction can be made then the rules could make it more difficult to impose choices where conflicts of interest are involved.

A third approach is to look at qualitative differences between preferences and in particular whether normative or ethical differences between different subjects of choice can readily be established.

(i) Cost based differentiation

It is tempting to avoid enquiring into why participants have different fears about different areas of decision taking or why preferences may be felt more strongly in some areas than others. The differences may appear subjective and a common ordering may be difficult to find through rational discussion. One way to avoid this problem is to try to express differences simply in terms of 'cost'. Collective decisions in some areas, for whatever reason, will simply be seen as more costly than others. In these 'costly' areas, decision rules will lean towards high majorities and towards the power to block. The cost in this context does not reflect a monetary cost (although it may do). It stands as a proxy for any reason why imposed choices may be seen as more objectionable in some areas than others.

This is a useful way of viewing collective choice for some purposes. It brings certain features of political choice into a unified theory – for example, the treatment of logrolling (vote trading) and side payments. It helps focus the questions that such behaviour evokes. What does such behaviour imply about the rules themselves – are the rules inefficient and suboptimal or does such behaviour represent market smoothing and arbitrage mechanisms that should be expected even within a well articulated system of decision rules?[14]

The generality of the cost approach is also a weakness. In practice, in the actual framing of rules, the proposed rules do have to be applied to particular areas. A justification can be demanded of the proposed relationship. This does mean looking at actual areas of choice, and the motivations and reasons given for perceptions of 'costs'.

(ii) The setting

One dimension which helps identify not only a reason why differences between decision rules might arise, but which also helps identify what class of decision rule might accompany what class of choice, is the setting itself. Participants may be more inclined to agree on a rule such as simple concurrent majorities in settings where the nature of the choice is such that all will benefit (in positive sum settings). Conversely, settings where the gains of one participant are more likely to involve a loss for another participant (zero sum settings) could be associated with more complicated decision rules. In areas of choice where all participants will suffer costs (non-zero negative settings) such as a decision to mount a peace making action, a very high threshold might be required.

The strength of this approach is that it focuses the rationale for rules directly on the self-interest of participants in collective choices. It is not inconsistent with a cost based approach but has the added advantage of pointing to areas where costs are likely to be perceived as different. It leads to trying to classify different choices according to the setting. For example, decisions which promote free and open markets represent a setting where there will be mutual gains. Hence decisions which deregulate markets could be seen as suited to simple majority voting. Decisions on the other hand which increase regulatory costs (for example, decisions which add to environmental regulations) might require higher concurrent majorities. Foreign policy decisions could be seen as more likely to involve decisions which are positive for some but negative for others. Peace making and peace keeping decisions could impose costs on all participants.[15] The implication would be that foreign policy choices should involve a high qualified majority (for example, an eighty per cent vote in favour) while triple concurrency and near unanimity might be required for collective action on security and defence matters.

Another advantage of this approach is that it attempts to reduce the rigidities associated with complex decision rules and high thresholds. In cases where decisions are difficult to take, they are also difficult to unwind. If it is made easier to take positive sum decisions (for example, to deregulate) and more difficult to take negative sum decisions (for example, to impose trade restrictions) then some of the inertia in complex decision rules is countered.

One limitation of trying to distinguish between the settings is that, even within these categories, the distribution of costs and benefits and losses and gains will fall unequally. For example, the mutual costs of a peace keeping operation may not be shared equally or in equal proportions. Even in situations of general mutual gain, such as the removal of external trade barriers, a cost may still be imposed on a particular sector or particular Member State.

It could be argued that it is because of these differences that vote trading, or other means of arbitraging, will always arise even within a rational general ordering of rules. But another limitation of this approach is that preferences do not just reflect self-interest but also reflect purely normative factors. Some areas will be seen to be intrinsically more important than others and raise stronger feelings than others.

(iii) Normative distinctions between preferences

Normative distinctions between different areas of collective choice go back to traditional attempts to define the essential roles of government. Traditionally, for example, the 'most important' function of the state was seen to be the preservation of territory (foreign policy, security and defence) and domestic observance of the law. These functions could be seen as 'more important' because they represented, on most definitions of the role of the state, the indispensable core functions of minimum government and thus those functions that should be placed above others.

The conclusion that is invited from this kind of traditional ranking of the functions of government is that, in a system of distributed powers, it is in these core areas that the participating states in a European political union are going to be most reluctant to agree to collective decision taking. Hence, decision rules in these areas should require very high majorities to avoid the views of the Member States from being overridden. Probably, in addition, Member States would preserve the right of unilateral action in these areas.

The difficulty is to establish any automatic correlation between such traditional rankings of the intrinsic order of importance of different areas of public policy and the graduation of the rules concerning collective decisions. The decision rules appear to rest on historical and geographical circumstances rather than any intrinsic normative ordering. For example, it was precisely in the area of external security and defence that, in the case of the United States, the Union was granted powers and the states forbidden to keep their own armed forces or enter into treaties or agreements with other states or foreign powers. In postwar Europe, collective arrangements for security and defence have also been the norm – albeit based on consensus and without NATO having the power to enforce its decisions (for example, those on minimum spending levels) or members losing the possibility, in theory, of taking independent action. Part of the difficulty is that traditional orderings associated the state with territory. Public policy boundaries in the modern world no longer correspond to territorial boundaries.

Normative distinctions are important but it seems that, unless they are brought together with other factors, they cannot by themselves provide a clear guide to the graduation of collective decision rules. Normative differences, cost differences and differing perceptions of self-interest all seem relevant to arranging decision rules but do not by themselves lead to a clear guide as to how to graduate decision rules to perceptions that some choices are more important than others.

(iv) Minimizing the areas of maximum risk

One way to bring together these different considerations is to approach collective decision rules in terms of the way that participants see the risks of collective action to themselves. The principle would be that decision rules should be graduated to minimize the risk to participants of the most highly adverse possible outcome of collective decision taking (this type of rule can be referred to as a 'minmax' rule). Risk can include each of the factors already discussed. The risks of collective action will be seen as greater in some areas because of potential economic costs, in others because of potential clashes of self-interest and yet in others again because of the normative importance a participant might attach to certain areas of policy.

The reason why risk is applicable to the choice of decision rules in European political union is that the rules have to be agreed against the background of uncertainty. There is uncertainty as to what precise policy choices might come up in some fields; uncertainty about the true preferences of participants; uncertainty about the possibility of coalitions of interest; uncertainty as to how far Member States will vote for strategic reasons rather than for their straightforward preferences, and uncertainty about how far the interests or sensitivities of a Member State may be engaged.[16] Within a settled and long established political association where preferences are well known, attitudes predictable and not too diverse and where the range of issues is also well established, decision taking rules can be simpler.

Risk has an advantage as a unifying concept because it ties into other procedural standards for political choice. In areas where the risks of 'getting it wrong' are perceived to be high, there will be a particular need to ascertain the true preferences of each participant in the collective decision as well as to ascertain the state of public opinion.[17] The bias against action, inherent in special majorities, would be justified until preferences have been properly established. The implication is that the concurrent majorities needed for a collective decision would be graduated to become steeper as the risks of a damaging decision become higher. In practice, the perception of risks is likely, at least initially, to correspond to conventional ideas of the normative ordering of political choices (for example, decisions about security and defence choices being seen as much more important than decisions about health warnings on cigarette packages).

IV   Dissent and decision rules

Even where there is an attempt to recognize the inequalities between the Member States through a system of concurrent majorities, and even where decision rules are graduated to minimize the risks to participants of wrong decisions in the most sensitive areas, there still remains the question of how to treat dissent in any system of decision taking that does not require unanimity.

One fruitful way of looking at dissent is to view it in terms of 'voice' or 'exit'.[18] The market place allows individuals to express dissatisfaction by changing to alternative suppliers or alternative purchasers. It thus allows for 'exit'. Political choice often involves a monopoly source of supply of policy (a unified government) and preferences must usually be expressed through 'voice'. Exit instruments such as emigration are no longer readily available in a crowded world. Even movement between different jurisdictions in a decentralized union is costly. The question is whether the decision rules themselves should allow for 'exit' for those members of the Union that find themselves in dissent with the decisive majority.

When a Member State finds itself consistently in dissent, the balance of interest may well have swung against membership. Exit therefore means the right to secede from the Union. For members where the balance of advantage rests with continuing membership, the question of exit arises in connection with the possibility to opt in, or to opt out, of particular areas of policy where they find themselves in dissent.

(i) Opting in or out

There are two main objections to provisions which allow for those dissenting from a majority to opt in or opt out. The first is the view that the members of a union have to make a basic decision as to whether the balance of advantage lies in membership or not. If the balance does lie in membership, then the participant should be expected to accept the majority decision on occasions, or in areas, where it may be in dissent. This is a 'fair' return for the benefits perceived to accrue in other areas, or on other decisions, where other dissentients go along with the majority. The second objection is the view that provisions that allow for opting out will inevitably weaken the impact of collective decision making and thus undermine the purposes of the union. The objections are thus about 'equity' and 'effectiveness'.

(a) The virtues of accepting the majority The view that decisions should be seen in

terms of the balance of advantage over the full range of collective decision taking in a union, rather than a calculation of advantage in each area, has much to commend it. It makes for easier and faster decision taking. It allows for fewer distinctions between rules covering the different areas of policy making. It reflects the reality of any group activity that a member may not always be at one with the decisive majority. It allows for reciprocity. A member may go along, possibly reluctantly, with a decision in one area but can look for support in another. When minorities go along with majorities despite differences, and when decision rules do not have to be too fragmented, the union can be seen as strong and cohesive.

These advantages are not in dispute. There is however another perspective. This is simply the desirability of having decision rules that, as far as possible, reflect and accommodate the different preferences of participants. If there are such differences it would, in principle, be desirable to allow the collective decision to reflect them – rather than have imposed a choice that is not wanted by some. If decision rules can avoid the imposition of unwanted choices then the more fundamental choice of a participant having to evaluate the balance of advantage of membership, and possibly having to decide to leave, will be an unlikely occurrence. The union will be strong because there will be less reason to question the legitimacy and representativeness of collective decisions.

Questions of dissent therefore cannot be treated simply as questions of fairness in a union. They centre instead on the representativeness of decision taking and the representativeness of the union. In a representative political system the burden lies in demonstrating that decision procedures that allow for dissentients to 'exit' from a collective decision, or from a particular area of collective decision taking, would severely damage the possibility of collective choice. This involves showing that, despite different preferences, collective choice requires common action by all participants in order to be effective, even if the particular preferences of some participants must be overruled as a result.

(b) Common action or critical mass The question of whether collective choice should involve common action essentially revolves around 'free riders'. Unless collective decisions involve common action, those who remain outside the decision will be able to 'free ride' on those who take collective action. They will not incur the costs of collective action, but they may derive benefits from those who do. If free riders are allowed, the incentives to participate in collective action will generally be weakened. This is both because the impact of a collective choice will be reduced by those who stay out and because the costs and benefits of collective choice will be unfairly distributed.

The free rider problem can be analyzed not as one problem but as three distinct problems:[19]

- There is the need to ensure that participants carry the costs of a public policy choice (or pay for the optimum quantity of a public good such as a common defence).

- There is the need for participants to reveal their true preferences on matters of public policy.
- There is a problem of large groups which lessen the ability of any single member to affect collective choices and reduce the perception of any need to contribute to the costs of a collective policy. Both reduce the motivation to participate in common action.

Each of these three considerations can be held to apply to European political union. The case for defining collective action as common action rests on the view that unless each participant knows that they will have to carry the costs of collective choice proportionately, there will be an incentive to underprovide (for those who expect to have to pay or carry the costs). There will also be an incentive to misrepresent true preferences (both for those who expect to pay and for those who expect to be carried).[20] In addition, the large group problem applies to a European political union because any individual Member State and a large number of small countries may not see their contribution or their preferences as counting for much. Common action ensures that all will be carrying their share of the costs of a collective choice; it means that there is no incentive not to reveal a participant's true preference and it counteracts the tendency of any country to feel that their absence will not be noticed.

The difficulty with this general argument is that it does not overcome the problem that, even if true preferences are revealed, some participants may still not agree with the decisive majority on the collective choice. Not only will some true preferences be overruled, but the collective choice will not be able to be put to the test through a comparison with the choices that reflect different preferences. If participants are allowed to opt out, then the preferences of participants do not have to be overruled, and the collective policy benefits from comparisons with alternative approaches. If the collective policy proves its worth, those who initially opt out will no doubt be persuaded of the advantages of the collective policy and join later. If, on the other hand, those who opt out adopt a more successful alternative policy, then collective policy can subsequently be modified. All will have benefited from the alternative established.

The debate therefore comes down to the question as to whether common action is so completely essential that the collective policy at issue would become impossible in the presence of less than full participation. There may be such cases. But the crucial test is one of 'critical mass'. What is the minimum number needed to test or carry out collective policy? In what circumstances is the minimum number the same as full participation?

The case that the minimum number needed for a collective policy is the full number, and that it is therefore necessary to override any preferences for an alternative and to forego the advantages of policy comparisons, is a difficult one to make. NATO has been a successful alliance despite free riders outside the alliance, and despite members carrying less than their proportionate share of the burden within the alliance. In a quite different example, the fact that all commercial banks could not be coerced into following the same approach to collecting the commercial banking debts of developing countries was beneficial in ensuring that a menu of alternative approaches was developed in the global debt crisis of the 1980s. There may indeed be some areas where a common policy is generally regarded as essential – for example, in the case of sanctions, but these will be rare cases. In normal circumstances critical mass is a more relevant concept for collective action than common participation. Opting in and opting out seem not only possible but also desirable.

If certain members of a union find that they are always, and in almost all circumstances, not participants in the collective decision, then indeed the point is reached where the benefits of membership must themselves be in question – both for that member concerned and for the others. This raises the question of secession.

(ii) Secession and constitutional choice

Secession is usually treated as a matter of the fundamental rules of the constitution rather than a question of the rules for decision taking within a constitution.[21]

The reason for making a distinction between constitutional choices and other choices is that it is the constitutional setting that provides the basis for all means of collective action. It is the constitution that sets the rules – including decision rules. The most fundamental choices thus relate to the constitution itself. On the basis of this distinction it can be argued that the highest voting threshold should be established for constitutional choices. If the constitutional framework is to rest on the maximum possible assent, constitutional choice and decisions about changes in the constitution should thus be based on unanimity.[22] In situations where any member feels that the balance of advantage of belonging to the union has swung against membership, they should be allowed to secede so that the constitutional framework reflects not just historically inherited assent, but a living and continuous assent.

While the right of secession must be the hallmark of a voluntary political union, the idea that there is a very sharp distinction between the rules of constitutional choice and the rules governing collective choices within a union does not necessarily follow. The case that there is such a sharp break can be expressed more formally in terms of seeing constitutional agreement as an agreement to reduce the costs of collective choice.[23]

The view that a sharp distinction between constitutional rules and the rules of policy choice can be based on the higher costs of collective choice in the absence of constitutional agreement seems an oversimplification. First, for the reasons discussed above, rules for political choice should themselves be seen as likely to be graduated in their stringency between simple majorities and near unanimity. There is a spectrum of decision rules rather than a sharp break. Second, while it is the case that in a political union that commands voluntary assent, the rules must always have the backing of each member, it does not necessarily follow that an individual member should be able to block rule changes desired by others. What follows is that the rule changes cannot be imposed on those members not in accord.[24] Depending on the nature of the rule change, the options in the case where, for example, eighty per cent of the membership desire to see a rule change, could run from not applying the rule to members in dissent, to renegotiating the proposed rule change, to negotiating an accommodation between different rules, to secession where the differences are fundamental and unbridgeable.

In favour of the unanimity rule applying to questions of constitutional choice, it can also be argued that the purpose of a constitution is to provide stability to the rules of political association. A constitutional order cannot reflect passing political fashions but must reflect enduring principles. Thus there should be a presumption against change. Rules about altering the constitution itself should therefore favour the status quo. A strong bias in favour of the status quo is accomplished by the unanimity rule.

This again appears an oversimplified approach. A unanimity requirement may simply lead to constitutional change taking place in other ways. The question as to how to balance change and stability in a constitutional setting is an issue which goes well beyond a unanimity rule. In short, the right of secession seems absolutely fundamental in a constitutional order based on voluntary acceptance of the participants. However, in other respects, a unanimity requirement may not provide a coherent rule for decisions about constitutional change.

V The consistency of key processes

At the start of the discussion of key processes in a European political union it was suggested that the most sensitive areas involve the ways in which differences in the Union are to be handled, the ways in which powers are to be distributed and the ways in which collective decisions are to be taken. These areas are interrelated and the approach across each has to be consistent.

The first step is to recognize the limitations of politics itself as a means to achieve collective choice in Europe. Normative limits are the means to establish procedural bounds on politics. This means establishing exclusion zones and may involve derogations where the rational ties of civil association conflict with the irrational. It means avoiding any attempt to establish lists of social rights that try to predetermine the outcome of political bargaining. It means entrenching individual and civil liberties and entrusting them to the Member States. It means establishing monetary and fiscal constraints that recognize the likely areas of inconsistent and short term political choice. A rule would be justified that recognizes that political choice does not handle longer term environmental considerations well, if such a rule could be formulated in constitutional terms.

The second step is to recognize the importance of distributing powers so that Europe can benefit from a system of multiple domain. The relationship between domains should not be expressed as hierarchy. Neither should the union have independent powers and authority. Instead, Europe needs a system of powers delegated by the different domains to the Union. This involves establishing the right relationships between the institutions of the Member States and the institutions of the Union. It also involves having decision rules for the Union that allow for effective collective decision taking but which also accommodate different preferences.

The third step is to recognize, in cases where collective public policy choice in the Union is appropriate, that a system for making decisions based on simple majorities is not the appropriate model, even though it may be the model most familiar in national contexts. Instead, inequalities between choosers and choices must be recognized. This can be achieved through a system of concurrent majorities where thresholds are graduated to offer superior protection in respect of those classes of choices where the risks of damage to the interests or the normative principles of participants are greatest. In almost all cases the relevant criterion for effective decisions will be one of 'critical mass' rather than 'common action'.

The combination of procedural limits on politics, a distribution of powers that limits the jurisdiction of the Union to those areas specifically delegated by the Member States, and, decision rules that reflect the concept of 'critical mass', will allow the Union to continue to benefit from the diversity of preferences and interests in Europe and enable the peoples of Europe to feel that political association rests on their voluntary consent.

At the same time, it must be recognized that, along with the benefits, will come certain less pleasant aspects of diversity in Europe – the choice by some jurisdictions to reflect preferences or to pursue public policies in their domain that are unwelcome and possibly distasteful to others. This downside is the counterpoint to any attempt to impose uniform choices and uniform values across Europe through political or judicial means. It is a cost. But there will always be other values to point to. If all choices are collectivized in Europe, whether through politics or the law, the errors of collective choice will be very much more difficult to perceive and costly to correct.

Finally, this discussion of key procedures suggested that there is not a sharp distinction to be drawn between constitutional choice and collective choice on matters of public policy. Making constitutional rule changes too easy will defeat the purpose of a stable rule based political order. But a presumption against rule changes cannot be carried to the point that change is not possible. In order to start the discussion of the core institutions of the Union and their relationship to the institutions of the Member States, the issue of how to maintain the rules of a constitutional order, and how to handle change, is discussed in the next chapter.

Notes

1   Rousseau pointed to 'two general rules. . . the more grave and important the questions discussed, the nearer should the opinion that is to prevail approach unanimity. . . the more the matter in hand calls for speed, the smaller the prescribed difference in the number of votes may be allowed to become'. Rousseau, J.J. (1762), *The Social Contract*.

2   'There are two general rules that may serve to regulate this relation. First, the more grave and important the questions discussed, the nearer should the opinion that is to prevail approach unanimity. Secondly, the more the matter in hand calls for speed, the smaller the prescribed difference in the number of votes may be allowed to become. . . In any case, it is the combination of them that gives the best proportions for determining the majority necessary'. Rousseau, ibid.

3   Buchanan J.M. and Tullock G. (1962), *The Calculus of Consent*.

4   Rae, D.W. (1969), 'Decision Rules and Individual Values in Constitutional Choice', *American Political Science Review*, 63.

5   'Simple Majority Rule is the one and only two-alternative collective choice process that is sensitive to available voting information but reflects no other information'. Schwartz, T. (1981), *The Logic of Collective Choice*.

6   'In this idealization of political order, 'government possesses no genuinely coercive power. . . no individual can be coerced in such a setting, either by some entity called the 'government' or by some coalition of other individuals in the electorate'. Brennan, G. and Buchanan, J.M. (1980), *The Power to Tax: Analytic Foundations of a Fiscal Constitution*.

7   Wicksell himself acknowledged this in his original formulation of the unanimity principle.

8   The asymmetry of qualified or special majorities should be noted. 'So-called special-majority (as opposed to Simple Majority) rules always give an advantage to 'negative' or status quo alternatives'. Schwartz, op. cit.

9   See Rae, op. cit.

10 'With a generally applicable rule of unanimity, there would be relative overinvestment in decision-making'. Buchanan, J.M. and Tullock, G., op. cit.

11 Buchanan and Tullock, ibid.

12 Buchanan and Tullock note that a two-house system raises costs of decision taking. 'Unless the bases for representation are significantly different in the two houses, there would seem to be little excuse for the two-house system'. They also note that it is not possible to make comparisons readily between a more inclusive single house rule and a two-house system. Buchanan and Tullock, ibid.

13 See, for example, Eggerton for a discussion of some of the relevant literature.

14 'In a very real sense, the introduction of full side payments serves to create a marketable property right in the individual's political vote, his power of collective decision. If this power is marketable. . . some element of scarcity must be present'. Buchanan and Tullock, op. cit.

15 Schelling, T. (1984), *Choice and Consequence*.

16 See Farquharson for a discussion of 'straightforwardness'. Farquharson, R. (1969), *Theory of Voting*.

17 Decision rules are sometimes viewed as information systems. See Schotter, A. (1981), *The Economic Theory of Social Institutions*.

18 This well known distinction comes from Hirschman, A.O. (1970), *Exit, Voice and Loyalty*.

19 See McMillan, J. (1979), 'The Free Rider Problem: A Survey', *Economic Record*, 55.

20 The difficulty of discovering true preferences in large groups should not be underestimated. 'Before we can judge the performance of any proposed institution or voting procedure, we must assess the impact of strategic misrepresentation'. Ordeshook, P.C.

(1986), *Game Theory and Political Theory*.

21 The distinction between the rules relating to constitutional choice and rules for political choice within a constitution is associated with the writings of Professor Buchanan.

22 Rousseau's rule of constitutional contract.

23 'The recognition, at the time of constitutional choice, of the costs that will be involved in securing the consent of the whole membership of the group on any single issue or set of issues is the only reason why the utility-maximising individual will agree to place any activity in the collective sector, and, for activities placed there, will agree that operational decisions shall be made on anything less than consensus. Constitutional choices as to what activities to collectivise and what decision rules to adopt for these activities must depend on an assessment of the expected relative costs of decision-making on the one hand and of the operation of the activity on the other'. Buchanan and Tullock, op. cit.

24 'If then there are opponents when the social compact is made, their opposition does not invalidate the contract, but merely prevents them from being included in it'. Rousseau, op. cit.

Part III
INSTITUTIONS AND PROCESSES

7 Responsibility for the rules

'For all the power the government has, being only for the good of society,. . . so it ought to be exercised by established and promulgated laws, that.. . . the rulers too, (be) kept within their due bounds'. John Locke, *Second Treatise of Civil Government*, 1690.

I Consistency between institutions and rules

Many different institutional arrangements are compatible with democratic societies. On average in Europe, the habits and traditions of democratic practices are thin. Most countries in Europe are democracies but the length of time that democratic rule has been established varies considerably. If the end of World War II is taken as the benchmark for measuring established democracies, only thirteen countries in Europe can be regarded as having established democracies.[1] The form of democracy is generally that of representative democracy where political power is exercised by elected representatives rather than by people directly. Only Switzerland practices a form of direct democracy. Beneath this level of generality there is, however, a considerable diversity of practice. The underlying issue for a European political union is to establish democratic institutions that are consistent with the processes of a rule based constitution and consistent in particular with a system of multiple jurisdictions.

(i) The absence of free standing choices

Decisions about how to structure institutions and their powers in a European political union cannot be treated as free standing choices. Institutions have their own interests and their own motivations. They interact with the rules of a constitution, with rule based processes and with each other. These interactions can be harnessed to help preserve constitutional rules and processes, to help maintain healthy institutions and to help ensure that institutions perform the functions intended. But the interactions can also be perverse. They can work to upset rules, processes and the intentions of institutional design.

The dynamics of institutional behaviour have long been recognized. The ancient doctrine of the separation of powers was developed in part in recognition that the interplay between institutions can be helpful in keeping each within their defined bounds. Recent political theory gives even greater weight to interactions. This is in part because analysis of the ways in which representative democracies actually work has eroded belief that the people themselves will be able effectively to control governments simply through the power of the ballot box. As mentioned earlier in the discussion of the imperfections of politics as a method of collective choice, those in positions of power can be seen both as more strongly motivated to expand their powers as well as more able to manipulate choice.

The increase in attention given to the interactions between institutions and processes has arisen also in response to the growth of government. On the one hand, the growth of government reflects a genuine change in perceptions of the proper functions of government. On the other hand, it also suggests an ineffectiveness in the traditional checks and balances designed to hold systems of government within their proper limits.

Particular examples of the way in which institutions may interact with other rules have already been cited: those placed to make political decisions may wish to extend the scope of their policy making and legislative powers so that they can more easily trade support on one issue for support on another; those able to shape the size of a budget may wish to increase it so that there is greater scope for side payments that will make other decisions easier to negotiate. The competition for the attention of voters provides a more general incentive to offer new programmes and new spending by those with influence over budgets.

The end result of such behaviour is that interactions can distort the intentions of a rule based constitution. Rules that try to ensure space in society for market choice as well as political choice may be diluted. Rules that try to protect a decentralized distribution of powers may be overcome. Rules intended to set limits on the powers of an institution may be evaded.

Institutions are not the only influence on the processes and rules of government. Views or ideologies about the role of government are a powerful influence. So too are the actual demands of events on governments, notably wars and economic emergencies. Institutions however can be the subject of design while events usually are not. Institutions are important because office holders exercise power directly. Moreover, institutions can be seen as the transmission mechanism in change. In acting as the conveyer of change there is a particular danger that they may act as a ratcheting mechanism.[2] This means that while views about the proper functions of government may ebb and flow and while views about the appropriate responsibilities of different jurisdictions may also change over time, the institutions of government accept accretions to their powers but are loathe to relinquish functions. The result is gradual erosion of the limits on government and gradual erosion too of the benefits of multiple jurisdictions.

One reaction to such stresses is to point to the limitations of rule based constitutions as such.[3] These limitations must be acknowledged. But, the view that the evolution of political society reflects only the underlying social and economic forces at work seems an exaggeration in an opposite direction. Institutional design has a role to play. At this early stage in European political union greater attention to institutional design and the relationship with processes seems fully justified.

A second form of response is to look to fortify traditional systems of constitutional checks and balances with newer constitutional arrangements which specifically address the likely behaviour of those with political power. Examples of such arrangements have already been mentioned. Placing the control of money supply in the hands of an independent central bank and out of the hands of politicians is one such device. Setting a limit on public expenditure in the constitution is another. Such limits restrain the extent to which politicians can bid for electoral votes or offer side payments to others with political power. Rules such as these can be important. The earlier discussion of the limits on politics suggested that they should be contained in Europe's constitution. However, they are intended to supplement other arrangements. They do not invite the conclusion that other aspects of institutional arrangements can be downplayed.

The third form of response is in respect of the institutions themselves. Institutional responsibilities must be located and defined to take full account of the anticipated interplay with processes. Within an existing system of government this kind of fundamental review is difficult unless there are well functioning procedures for constitutional review and amendment. In the case of Europe's embryonic system of government, judgements about how institutions may interact with rules that underpin key processes are not only possible but essential.

(ii) The absence of short cuts

It is nevertheless tempting at this point in the evolution of European political union to look for ways of avoiding any detailed discussion of institutions and their roles. Discussions could become extremely divisive – particularly when they involve any attempt to define the relationship between the institutions of the Member State and the institutions of the Union. Two short cuts to avoid any full discussion appear to be available. The first is to point to the existing institutional base of the Union. The second is to look for some easily understood model which reflects the common denominator in the variety of national practices in Europe. Neither serve the purpose.

(a) The existing base There is already an institutional base for the current Union including notably the European Council, the Council of Ministers, the

Commission, the European Parliament, the Court of Justice and the Court of Auditors. There is much to be said for developing this existing framework, together with the less well known but important bodies such as the Council Secretariat and the Permanent Representatives of the Member States (COREPER).

However the development of this existing framework does not provide a means for avoiding fundamental issues about the institutions, their powers and their relationships. These institutional arrangements date back to a time when the membership was small and association had limited economic objectives. The powers originally given are not necessarily appropriate for a political union. Moreover, relationships between the institutions are poorly defined. In addition, relationships between the European institutions and national institutions have barely been addressed. Above all, neither powers nor relationships have been considered in a constitutional framework where the processes of political association are of key importance and where institutional arrangements must be consistent with maintaining good process. Continuing to try to work with the existing distribution of functions and relationships in the entirely different setting of a political union may lead Europe away from durable constitutional arrangements.

(b) Transposition A second temptation, particularly for politicians accustomed to their national settings, is to assume that the practices most familiar from national settings can simply be transposed. Even if no politician would wish to put forward their own state's particular model, there is nevertheless a more general temptation to think that, within the democratic practices of the different Member States, there are enough similarities that a generalized model can be distilled and transposed to the Union.

It would be a mistake to follow this particular path. It leads to false analogies.[4] Lying forgotten behind the formal arrangements of institutions in any Member State there may exist a web of informal practice and convention that may be of equal or even greater significance in the way in which the arrangements actually work. Most importantly, it is not feasible to evade the possibility that a system of government suited to Europe as a whole will necessarily differ profoundly from that of any particular Member State or amalgam of practices across the Member States. To take just one example, the closeness that exists between the governments and the representative assemblies in most European countries is not necessarily the model that is sensible for the Union as a whole. General answers to the question of where to locate responsibilities in Europe's system of government do not spring straight from the practices of the Member States. Nor too do answers to particular questions about particular institutions such as the proper role of a representative assembly in Europe.

There are no shortcuts to finding the right institutional arrangements for European political union. On the contrary, there is a need to approach the question of institutional powers and relationships in Europe from a basis of first principles.

This provides a way of distinguishing in the diversity of practices in Europe what is important and what is not. It helps bring the tacit assumptions behind the different styles of government in Europe into the open. Public support is more likely to be obtained where the institutional arrangements proposed for political union rest on clearly identified principles. It is the only way to ensure that the institutional arrangements will be framed in ways that are consistent with the processes that are most important in the Union.

II Organizing principles

The organizing principles for European political union must achieve consistency between institutions and processes in three key respects:

- In the allocation of core functions in the Union; for example, in decisions on who is to provide the government of Europe.
- In the definition of key institutional relationships in the Union; for example between the governmental body and the representative assembly or assemblies.
- In the arrangements determining how essential processes in the constitution are to be maintained and institutions kept within the rules.

There are two classical approaches to organizing these core functions and key relationships. One is centred on the doctrine of the separation of powers. The other is centred on the tradition of mixed government. Jeremy Bentham criticized both as representing respectively a 'mechanical' and 'chemical' view of government.[5] He leant towards a third possible approach, as a way of measuring the greatest happiness of the greatest number – that of trying to get as close as possible towards a direct reflection of public opinion. Today, in Europe, only Switzerland practices a form of direct democracy. The main legacy of theories of direct democracy is in the perception of parliamentary assemblies as 'intermediaries' between government and the people. The role of direct democracy is therefore considered in the discussion that follows, not as a general model, but in particular applications. The other traditions remain in the mainstream of democratic practice.

Theories of the separation of powers and of mixed government share common objectives.[6] Both aim to enable government to be carried out effectively and both aim to provide inbuilt checks against overmighty government. They differ in how to achieve these ends.

The separation of powers emphasizes the desirability of specialization between those who carry out the different functions of government; mixed government suggests that policy will be carried out more effectively if it has the support of most key interests in society.

The separation of powers aims to check government by establishing a mutual rivalry between the different branches of government so that each will act to keep the other in its place. Doctrines of mixed government see power sharing as the way to avoid any one part of government becoming too strong.

It has been fashionable to deride the doctrine of the separation of powers. Doubts arise because it seems more often honoured in the breach than in observance and because the efficacy of the doctrine is questioned.[7] Moreover, it is the development of mixed government in the form of the 'fusion' of powers that is usually cited as characteristic of parliamentary government in Europe. However, more recent theories of 'consensus' government seek to combine both traditions. Therefore each is considered below.

(i) Separation of powers

Before becoming a theory about how to organize government as a system of checks and balances, the separation of powers was seen as a theory about how to organize government effectively. The separation of powers as an enabling theory of government dates back at least as far as Bodin.[8] He stressed that the different functions of government could be carried out more effectively if carried out separately. Moreover, incursions by those wielding power into the other branches of government would erode that power. Within the framework of Bodin's discussion of kingship he also emphasized (in his discussion of the six varieties of liege relationships) the importance of clearly defined relationships within what would later come to be called the executive branch.

The view that there are gains to be made from separating out the different functions of government remains an enduring aspect of the doctrine of the separation of powers. It underlies belief in the desirability of a professional civil service and in the view that justice is better administered if judicial functions are kept clearly separate from the political. The separation of powers entails that the core functions of systems of government are clearly identified and distinguished.

What has been subject to greater question has been the later development of the theory of the separation of powers as a theory about how to place limits on the powers of government. The idea that by separating powers, the power of government could and should be held in check, was a development associated with Locke and Montesquieu.[9] As is well known, it was in the form of Locke's view of the separation of powers as a defence against the human frailty of those in power, and of Montesquieu's view of the separation of powers as a defence against the autocratic tendencies of the executive, that the theory had a profound influence on the founding fathers of the American constitution.[10]

(ii) Mixed powers

Theories of mixed government also go back to theories of late kingship and the view that the powers of the king should be shared with other powerful interests in society. It is as a theory of representative government that mixed government has developed. In modern form it states that democratic assemblies should represent as many interests as possible and it puts an emphasis on power sharing in government. It looks to 'fusion' between the powers of the government and the powers of the assembly as best capturing the nature of shared and representative government.

At first sight, the power sharing model of government appears much closer to modern realities, particularly in Europe where governments are closely connected with their parliaments. Even in America, the separation of powers was adopted by the founding fathers with considerable qualifications. In practice, within the American system there is considerable connection between the different branches of government. Moreover, the original importance attached to the separation of powers as a means of checking government appears exaggerated.[11] For these reasons, the separation of powers is sometimes seen as of historical importance only and of little relevance to Europe today.

(iii) Consensus democracy

More recently there has been an attempt, in theories of 'consensus' government, to look at systems of government in ways that combine both theories of mixed government and the separation of powers.[12] Such theories are relevant to Europe because, along with the related theories of 'consociational' democracy, they are held to be particularly appropriate forms of government for diversified societies such as the European Union.[13] Consensus theories of government make a major distinction between 'Westminster style' or 'majoritarian' democracy and consensus style democracy. The former is characterized by government by the one party with the majority of seats in parliament, while the latter is typified by coalition style politics, where the government reflects a more representative cross section of parties. Prominent among the characteristics of consensus democracy is the separation of powers. Separation of powers in this context is to be interpreted as a balanced relationship between legislature and executive. This is held up in contrast to a situation where, either the executive dominates the legislature, or the legislative body dominates the executive.[14]

The importance of the distinction in Europe between majoritarian democracy and consensus democracy can be exaggerated. The theory underestimates the extent to which the major British parties are themselves coalitions. It also overestimates the extent to which the practice of coalition government can automatically be assumed to be more representative – instead coalition government may just give minorities or 'back room' managers exaggerated influence. Nevertheless, in a plural society such as Europe, it is clearly vital to judge whether the system of government is sufficiently expressive of the variety of interests.

The distinction between majoritarian democracy and consensus democracy has also brought back onto centre stage the importance of focusing on relationships between institutions. In systems of government that lean away from decisions by simple majorities, the separation of powers is once again seen to be important.[15] The doctrine is being viewed once more in the way that it had been interpreted by Madison. Madison himself was at pains to point out that Montesquieu was not, in his view, advocating a complete separation of powers.[16] Madison viewed it primarily as a theory about achieving the proper allocation of powers. After having decided on a proper allocation, the theory was also intended, in Madison's interpretation, to make sure that no other branch could exercise 'an overruling' influence. Madison's reinterpretation is not inconsistent with modern theories of consensus democracy. His criteria argue in favour of clarity as to whether power is to be shared within a branch of government, or between branches of government, and in favour of clarity as to how far power sharing is desirable. In Madison's view, power sharing should not be extended so far as to confusè core responsibilities.

As Europe approaches the making of institutional choices that are consistent with right processes, the separation of powers remains a key guiding principle for the following reasons:

- as an admonition to define accurately the core functions in a system of government and to decide on their placement;
- as a caution to define clearly the relationships between the bodies that carry out the core functions;
- as a warning, in cases where powers are shared, against one body having an 'overruling' influence in the exercise of a core function by another.

III Core functions: key relationships

(i) Terminology

Discussions of the core functions of government, and the key relationships between the different bodies, are often confused by the use of the traditional terminology associated with the doctrine of the separation of powers. Even though the concept of the separation of powers remains crucial, the traditional terminology no longer corresponds to functions actually performed in modern systems of government. Discussion of core responsibilities in a European political union suffers badly from this confusion. For example, there are references to the

Commission as 'executive' without being clear what is intended by the term. There are also references to the Council of Ministers as a part of the 'legislature' made on the grounds simply that the Council is involved in legislation. The source of confusion is that terms such as the 'executive', and the 'legislature' no longer carry the clarity that they once possessed for the purposes of distinguishing between the different activities of contemporary government.[17]

(a) The executive Historical definitions of the executive have changed over time – for example, the judicial branch was considered at one time as part of the executive but is now generally treated as independent. Within this century there has been an enormous growth in bureaucracy as the executive arm of government – sometimes in a clear agency relationship with the government but sometimes not – so that administrative bodies and the civil service now need to be treated virtually as a separate branch of government.

The significant distinction, for contemporary systems of government, seems to be between the public policy making role of the executive, and the administration role, now carried out by the bureaucracy and specialized agencies. Equally important, the executive function can no longer be perceived mainly as the task of executing the laws made elsewhere (by the legislature). On the contrary, major legislative initiatives will tend to come from the executive whether the US President or a European government.[18] At the same time, there has been an enormous growth in the policy making functions of the executive which do not require legislation. Locke had termed this the 'federative' function – those areas such as defence which called for speed and decisiveness which a deliberative body such as a congress or parliament could not provide. These federative functions of the executive have extended to external policy generally, including trade policy, and notably also to most areas of economic policy making.

As a result of all these changes, the use of the term executive can be seriously misleading. The function performed in Europe usually by prime ministers and ministerial colleagues, in a loose system of collective responsibility, is best termed a governmental function rather than an executive function. The functions of a modern government in Europe include the policy making role in domestic and external policy, the role of the initiation, preparation and passage of any legislation required, and, the decision making role in many areas not requiring legislation. The executive role is best confined to describing the administrative and agency role carried out by the civil service and specialized bodies involved in the execution of public policy.

(b) The legislature In the same way as the term executive is misleading, if a clear distinction is not made between the functions of a modern government (or US Presidency) and civil service and agency functions, so too can the term legislature give a misleading impression of the functions of a modern representative assembly. Governments no longer mainly execute the laws and legislatures no longer

mainly legislate.[19] Legislatures perform a variety of scrutiny and review and other functions and may influence public policy, including legislation. But on the whole in Europe it is the government which initiates, prepares and carries the passage of legislation. The basic reason for this is that representative assemblies are not well suited to legislate.[20] The thought that, because the Council of Ministers is involved in the preparation of European legislation, it is therefore somehow a part of the legislative branch is hence simply mistaken. In the discussion that follows, the term 'assembly' is used instead of legislature so as not to prejudge the particular functions of elected assemblies.[21] In looking for a definition of the role of a modern representative assembly, the key concept appears to be that of 'legitimization'. In performing their various functions, representative assemblies help legitimize a system of government, or indeed, challenge its legitimacy.

(c) The judiciary In a system of distributed powers, the role of the central judiciary may include two very different functions. One is the possible role in the interpretation of the rules of the system of government (the constitutional interpretation role). The other is its role in the implementation and enforcement of Union laws (the old executive role). These are two different functions. In the United States, the Supreme Court carries out both functions. However, the American constitution explicitly refers only to the legal adjudication role (in articles III and VI). Authority to rule on acts of the legislative and executive branches was an authority taken by the Court (in the landmark case of Marbury v Madison 1803).

The separation of powers makes it possible for the judiciary to extend the scope of judicial review to cover the constitutionality of the acts of the other branches of government, and over the acts of the states participating in the Union, but it does not necessarily entail it.[22] There is no question that Europe's constitution needs to provide for arrangements suited to the uniform application of Union law and that this core function must rest with the judiciary. What is a quite different matter is whether oversight and interpretation of Europe's constitutional rules should rest (as in the United States) with the same judicial body responsible for the uniform application of Union law, or with the judiciary at all.[23]

As discussed earlier, the rules of a constitution are not law in any conventional sense. They establish the parameters of the political system. Some of the rules may be intended to be justiciable, others may not. Where the law is to be involved, the rules may specify which jurisdiction is responsible. Whether these rules should be under 'judicial control' is another question.

It is therefore crucially important to define the precise functions to be carried out by the different bodies in a European political union. It is not possible to rely either on historical labels, or on historical practice.

(ii) Core functions

Against this background the most important questions about the core functions of government in any European system of government are as follows:

Which body is to provide the 'government' of Europe – that is set the direction and propel collective policy making on matters of European public policy? Should it be the Commission or the European Council\Council of Ministers?

How are representative assemblies in Europe's system of government to perform their legitimizing functions? Can the representative assembly of the Union by itself confer legitimacy on the system of government in the Union?

How are the constitutional rules governing the institutions and processes of the European Union to be maintained? Should this function be carried out by a central judicial body, such as the European Court of Justice, or are alternative approaches desirable?

(iii) Key relationships

It is tempting to see the core functions outlined above as in some sense 'shared' functions and thus ones where the definition of precise relationships is of secondary importance. However, the sharing of functions may not always be appropriate. Even where a function is shared, the precise relationships still need to be defined. Moreover, running across all the questions of how to define institutional relationships is the question of the relationship of the Member States and their institutions – governments, assemblies and courts – to the institutions of the Union. In the case of the United States it has already been mentioned that the relationships initially provided in the constitution (in respect of the Senate and the Presidency) did not establish themselves in practice. Europe will therefore have to define a clearer role for the Member States if enduring institutional relationships are to be sought.

The three areas where key relationships must be defined are:

- in the arrangement for the representative assemblies. If the national parliaments are to have a continuing representative role to play in Union matters and in the legitimization of Europe's system of government, how are their relationships to be defined with the Union assembly?
- between the Government of Europe and the assemblies. Is the Government to be fused with representative bodies, closely connected or substantially separated?
- in the methods chosen for constitutional oversight. Are the contracting parties to any constitution for Europe, the Member States and their peoples, to play a continuing role in constitutional oversight and if so, how?

In the discussion which follows, the first of the core functional responsibilities to be considered is that of maintaining the rules and processes within which the institutions must work. This is taken up before other functions because it is crucial for determining the relationship between the institutions of Member States and the institutions of the Union. Subsequent chapters look at the responsibility for the Government of Europe and the role of the assemblies.

IV   The nature and methods of constitutional oversight

The methods chosen for constitutional oversight, and the responsibilities attributed, are among the most critical and difficult questions to be decided in the drawing up of a constitution for Europe. There are two fundamental issues involved:

- The first is whether constitutional oversight should be entrusted principally to judicial processes;
- The second is whether, and how, the Member States as the contracting parties to the constitution should remain involved in constitutional oversight.

The connection between these two questions is one of 'representativeness'. Judicial procedures for oversight are not representative. At best they can point to 'after the judgement' consent of the people and the likelihood that judges will not be immune to changes in public opinion. Moreover, they can operate to exclude the contracting parties from a further oversight role. If the contracting parties are to have a continuing role in overseeing the constitution they have established then, in one form or another, a representative style of oversight will be involved – through the governments of the Member States or through their assemblies or through their peoples directly (for example, through referenda). The fact that judicial oversight of constitutional rules in a rule based political order is not representative, does not necessarily invalidate the judicial method.[24] However, it is sufficient to suggest that there can be no automatic assumption that the judicial method is right and proper.

(i) The nature of constitutional oversight

A constitution is intended to provide a stable framework for political association. Nevertheless, as practical experience accumulates with any system of government, changes in the framework may be desired. External circumstances also change. With the passage of time there will be questions of government arising that never were, and never could have been, envisaged by the makers of the constitution. The role of constitutional oversight is therefore not one of opposing all change. Instead the function of constitutional oversight has two sides. It must prevent unintended changes to the rules of the system. Where, however, change in the rules does become necessary or desired, it must provide a procedure for considered change. These are two very different aspects of overseeing the rules of political association. They have different implications for the way in which constitutional oversight is approached and different implications for defining institutional responsibilities.

(a) Preventing unintended change The reasons to look for stability in a constitution go to the heart of the original rationale for a constitution. Constitutions are intended to reduce uncertainty as to what form of government is to be applied. In order to give this assurance, the constitution must give a definitive shape to the key aspects of a system of government and also offer some reassurance about their intended permanence. Where, as in Europe, the history of systems of government has been severely flawed, citizens may look in particular to receive long-lasting reassurances about the processes of government. Moreover, basic questions about the form of political association cannot forever remain in dispute and a constitution is also intended to put at least some questions to rest. Where, again as in Europe, hitherto separate political entities are newly coming together for common purposes, it is necessary to set out the ground rules for the new association. If it is accepted that this new association should embrace the concept of multiple jurisdictions then, in turn, the relationships between jurisdictions must be defined and methods for settling any disputes between jurisdictions must be agreed in advance.

If constitutions are viewed as means of guarding against unintended changes to the rules of political association then it becomes important to try to identify in advance the most likely source of challenge to the rules. This, in turn, has implications for the institutional responsibility for guarding the rules. There is no point in entrusting guardianship to the body that is seen as a likely threat to stability. This would be tantamount to expecting the body to bind itself against challenging the rules. There are long-standing arguments against contracts with oneself. One of the key sources of difference over which body should be responsible for keeping the rules of political association in Europe arises precisely from different views as to where the challenge to the rules is most likely to come from. The founders of the Treaty of Rome were concerned primarily about challenges from the Member States. As Europe enters on political union the opposite fear seems equally relevant – the fear that the benefits of a system of multiple jurisdictions will be vulnerable to challenges from the central institutions of the Union.

The more that the participants in a political association feel the need for assurances against unintended changes, the more likely it is that the constitution itself will be seen as needing to offer permanence and stability in its arrangements. The terms of the constitution itself will make change difficult. Traditionally this has led to a distinction between 'rigid' and 'flexible' constitutions. In particular, the process of federation was seen as likely to lead to the need for a 'rigid' constitution.[25] This is because the constitution is seen as needing to contain firm assurances that the divisions of powers between jurisdictions could not easily be overturned.

There is an inherent tension between giving assurances of stability in the rules of political association and the need for the rules to be able to be adapted to change. The first requirement argues in favour of making changes difficult. The second argues for procedures that make change possible. This tension is sometimes used to argue against the concept of written constitutions. However, in Europe there is no escaping a written text – whether it be called a treaty or a constitution. There is also no escape from the need to be able to accommodate change. The defence should be against unintended changes; the accommodation should be to considered changes.

(b) Accommodating considered change A stable constitution does not mean that the society which lives with it will be a stagnant one. On the contrary, if the rules of the constitution give full play to market processes, operate within a multilateral system of international trading rules and allow for a system of multiple jurisdictions, a rule based system can be consistent with vitality and experimentation. Nevertheless, this same vitality will mean that situations will soon arise that had not been foreseen at the time of the original constitutional settlement.[26]

Pragmatic considerations which give notice of likely change have been traditionally reinforced by arguments that it is improper for one generation to attempt to bind a succeeding generation. This is an argument that rests essentially on parallels with the law relating to contracts. While contracts can be, and often are, valid between generations (for example, in relation to property rights) there is also a long standing tradition that argues against contracts that bind in perpetuity.[27] In a political context this debate was historically echoed in arguments about the extent to which a monarch could bind his successor. It surfaced in a guise that has more contemporary resonance at the time of the debates about the American constitution. Jefferson took the view that one generation could not foreclose the options of the next on constitutional matters. He thus favoured (in theory) a constitutional review every twenty years.

One important practical way in which constitutional rules can provide both for stability and for flexibility is for the provisions of a constitution to be confined as much as possible to general statements of principle. The more details it contains, the more quickly it may date, and the more divisive it is likely to be. The other side of this coin is that generality provides for interpretative licence under the rules and thus throws a greater responsibility on those responsible for their oversight.

(ii) Methods of oversight

There are two ways of combating unintended changes to a constitution. One is to try to prevent measures which might transgress the rules at a formative stage before their enactment. The other is react after the event and to nullify or to strike down measures that have transgressed the rules (the term 'nullification' is not used in further discussion so as to avoid confusion with the nullification debate in America which had a specific context of state rights). Similarly, as mentioned above, there are two main ways to accommodate change – either through amendment or interpretation. These differences in method are important because of their implications for the institutional responsibility for constitutional oversight.

(a) Prevention or voiding An emphasis on preventing measures that transgress the rules of a constitution is likely to involve the representative assembly at the point when it considers draft proposals for the ratification of legislation, or other acts of the government that come before it for approval. Alternatively, the people can be involved directly, if there is provision for referenda to be called either to sanction or protest against a proposed measure. Once measures are taken or passed into law, then a challenge to their constitutionality will involve procedures to void the act. This can take the form of a judicial procedure – a challenge in the courts that the act is unconstitutional. Or again the challenge can take the form of a political procedure to strike down the measure and possibly to amend or clarify that part of the constitution on which the measure had been brought forward.

The advantage usually cited in favour of judicial review after the event is that a judgement about the constitutionality of an act can be better assessed against the background of actual experience of its application.[28] This is an advantage that applies only to certain types of acts. Moreover, judicial review after the event has the disadvantage of denying a voice to the people or their representatives which is possible under the other methods.

(b) Amendment or interpretation Amendment involves deleting, clarifying, or adding to the rules of a constitution. Interpretation means leaving the rules intact (superficially at least) but clarifying, adding or subtracting from their meaning by striking down, validating or letting stand, particular acts under the rules.

The process of amendment as a method of introducing considered change to a constitution, usually involves both testing formal requirements and high thresholds for acceptance of change. For example, amendment in the United States requires a two thirds majority in both houses of congress and ratification by three quarters of the states. In Switzerland, a majority of cantons must approve change as well as a majority of the voters. As discussed earlier, the reason for this is that changes in the rules of political association are seen as the most fundamental changes to which a society can agree. There is thus a case for the requirements to favour stability and to make it easy for minorities to block change.

As mentioned earlier, the formal difficulties of making changes in written constitutions led to an early distinction between 'rigid' constitutions and 'flexible' constitutions. Flexible constitutions were those where change could take place under the ordinary case laws of the Common Law or under the normal system of majority voting in a parliament.[29] With the passage of time this distinction has lost much of its force. The much more important result of making the formal process of amendment difficult is that changes in constitutional practice and in the rules are likely to come about through a process of interpretation of the rules rather than through a process of changing the rules themselves.[30]

An emphasis on interpretation rather than rule changes has two critical implications. First, it appears to tilt the balance decisively towards judicial procedures for oversight. Second, if the role of the contracting parties in oversight has been linked to the amendment method, the contracting parties will find themselves removed, for all practical purposes, from oversight procedures. This is because they may not have a role in judicial oversight. In addition, they will find amendment extremely difficult to make work because of the high thresholds needed to make changes in the rules. These implications apply to the European Union. As membership in the Union grows, it will become increasingly difficult for Member States to agree on rule changes if unanimity, or a high special majority, is required. In the absence of different decision rules on constitutional matters, or other methods to make their influence felt, Member States will find themselves excluded from a continuing role in oversight.

The different methods of oversight are significant therefore because if there is a choice in favour of after-the-event rule keeping and a choice in favour of change to be brought about through interpretation rather than amendment, then the reasons for assigning institutional responsibilities for constitutional oversight to the judiciary begin to appear persuasive. Legal procedures can readily be invoked after the event. Legal methods seem particularly appropriate when questions of interpretation are involved. That this is the right path for Europe to take seems also to follow from the American example.

V The judicial model

American practice suggests that there is only one place for constitutional oversight in Europe – in the hands of a court akin to the US Supreme Court. This implies the European Court of Justice should be developed as the arbiter of Europe's constitution. As with other institutional questions, simple transpositions cannot be accepted without the justification needed to demonstrate that it fits the possibly different circumstances of European political union. As mentioned already, there is nothing inevitable about entrusting constitutional oversight to a court. Even if judicial oversight is appropriate, the judicial authority need not necessarily be a Union body, let alone the same Union court responsible for applying Union laws.

(i) The uniform application of Union law

In a system of distributed powers, the general function of constitutional oversight (wherever in the constitution it is located) involves the power to strike down, validate or let stand, the legislation or the executive acts of either the Union or the Member States, or a legal ruling of a state or Union court, on the grounds of the express or implied provisions of the constitution. This role can be entrusted to a Court and to the procedures of judicial review. It is, however, a quite separate function from the different task of ensuring, in a system of distributed powers, that Union laws are uniformly applied in those areas designated as lying within the powers of the Union.

It is a basic principle of the rule of law that laws should be consistently and uniformly applied. In theory, laws of the European Union could be applied by the courts of the Member States without any system of Union courts. In practice this would lead to widely varying application of the law. Thus there is a need for a Union judicial body, or system of Union courts, and there are a number of different ways in which such a system can be organized. However, in any such system where one set of courts is involved in the adjudication of one set of laws and another on a different set, conflicts become possible. Such conflicts can arise, either when dissimilar rulings are given in similar circumstances, or when there is a clash as to which law applies. In the latter circumstances the Union courts appear to be drawn inevitably into the constitutional adjudication role as to which law should apply.[31] However, there is nothing inevitable about this. On the contrary, there is a strong case against. If conflicts over which law to apply are to be decided by the Union court, it is placed in the position of deciding on the limits to apply to itself. Its rulings are likely to favour the application of Union law. This could defeat the purpose of having Union law operative within the limits defined in the constitution. The alternatives are either to let the judicial systems compete (for which there is historical precedent) or, alternatively, there is precedent in German practice for having a special court for dealing with such conflicts or, yet again, such questions might be seen as 'political' and referred to non-judicial procedures.

The distinction between the constitutional oversight function and the issues involved in ensuring the uniform application of Union law, means that there is no necessary connection between the arrangements for the one being handled in the same way as the other. In the case of the United States these functions are combined in the Supreme Court. But there is a strong historical reason against such a combination in Europe – that is the historical tendency in Europe to see law as the instrument of government. It can lead to constitutional adjudication being viewed as a way of implementing the purposes of the Union government, instead of being viewed about rules that are intended to keep governments in check and to preserve the different jurisdictions. Thus the American example needs to be examined rather more closely before deciding that the transposition of practices is desirable.

(ii) The example of the US Supreme Court

The idea that it should be a Supreme Court that is responsible for the oversight of a constitution appears to flow directly from the view that the constitution embodies a 'higher' or 'paramount' law.[32] The legal skills of distilling the essence of a dispute from a complicated set of facts or circumstances appear vital. Legal skills of textual exegesis also seem particularly apposite when a written constitution is involved. The Bench is frequently seen as a neutral arbiter in matters which are disputed. A representative assembly may be seen as a more likely body to breach the rules and inherently more dangerous if given power over their interpretation.[33] Judges are also seen as inherently less likely than other branches of government to take powers into their own hands.[34] The case method of the law seems an appropriate way to handle change, because alterations are likely to be incremental and in response to specific concerns. In the final analysis, it seems unlikely that a Supreme Court could prevail for long against the established views of public opinion.

Each of these grounds for resting constitutional oversight in Europe with a body analogous to the US Supreme Court is, however, open to challenge.

(a) Higher law The idea that the constitution provides the basic law of a country, or some kind of higher law, does not lead straight to the conclusion that its content is law in the conventional sense. The constitution provides a general framework of rules within which political processes can be contained, constitutional and civic values reflected and the law maintained. It is a higher, or basic law, in the sense of providing a framework of rules.[35] This framework includes defining the limits of the jurisdiction of the Union. In cases of doubt, the rules must be interpreted somewhere by somebody. Whether that 'somebody' is the people themselves, the contracting parties to the constitution (the Member States), representative assemblies or the judiciary, remains an open question and not a foregone conclusion in favour of the judiciary.

(b) The essential nature of disputes In key respects the rules embodied in a constitution are about values – values that are to be reserved from intrusion, that are intended to protect jurisdictions or otherwise to reflect right processes. Even though judicial skills to arrive at the essence of a case appear important, nevertheless it is not at all clear that judges are well qualified to make judgements about disputed values.

This general reservation appears to lose much of its force where the constitution stresses explicit process values. Furthermore, it has been suggested that when confronted with value questions, the judges can interpret the cases in ways that are themselves process oriented ('representation reinforcing' is one suggestion).[36] In particular, those values that are related to defining the limits on political processes would seem well fitted to be protected by a court rather than a political body that might be inclined to bend the rules.

This defence of judges as the guardians of process values does not however lead to the conclusion that a Supreme Court is the right body for adjudication. Process values in Europe have to focus on the articulation of a system of multiple jurisdictions and the protection of value diversities. As mentioned above, a Supreme Court is unlikely to be neutral as between jurisdictions. Moreover, its regular task in ensuring the uniform application of law may not predispose it towards the protection of diversities.

(c) Textual exegesis The advantages of the legal method and textual exegesis become much less persuasive when the issue is one on which the constitution is silent and judges have to appeal either to the spirit of the constitution or step outside its framework.[37] At this point the link is broken between the idea that the purposes of the constitution can be found, expressed or implied, in the text and the expertise of judges in textual interpretation.[38] In the debates about the role of the Supreme Court in the interpretation of the US constitution, it is common ground that complete inference is unlikely to be in the constitution. It has also been argued persuasively that 'clause bound' interpretation (where provisions can be approached as self-contained units and interpreted on the basis of their language) is impossible.[39]

(d) Neutrality It is also open to challenge as to whether a court can be regarded always as a 'neutral' arbiter. As mentioned above, the underlying point in the context of European history is about the risk of confusion between the court as the instrument of government (the old executive role) and the court as the upholder of the rules which set the framework for the system of government. In addition, the European Court of Justice is no different from other institutions in having its own interests at stake. In particular, as mentioned above, it is an open question as to whether a court, such as the European Court of Justice whose interest is bound up with the extension of the scope of activities of the Union and the reach of its own jurisdiction, can be regarded as a neutral arbiter in matters involving disputes between jurisdictions, or between the power of the Union or Union institutions, and the powers of Member States.

(e) Risks The idea that a court presents less risks to a rule based constitution than a legislature and thus provides a safer pair of hands for entrusting the rules, raises the critical issue as to where the rules are seen to be most vulnerable and where challenges are most likely to occur. The founding fathers of the American constitution were particularly concerned about how Congress might abuse its position.[40] In the case of Europe, one of the most vulnerable areas will be the maintenance of multiple jurisdictions. The European Parliament will be predisposed to wish to extend the reach of central powers. As such it cannot be looked on as a likely guardian of a system of diversified jurisdictions. Unfortunately, in this context, a

court such as the European Court of Justice, with its own interest in extending central jurisdiction, is also likely to be a part of the problem and not necessarily part of the cure.

Judicial processes are sometimes seen to present less risks, as well as a guard against dramatic change, because the case method is more likely in general to result in change by increments. However, there are many examples from the United States, as well as some from the much more limited history of the European Court of Justice, to reveal the fundamental and far reaching impact of some particular judgements.

Incrementalism also requires oversight. The key advantage of incrementalism, both in respect of changes in public policy and in respect of the rules of a political system, is that gradual rather than abrupt change is likely to be better suited to large and complex political associations such as a European political union. The disadvantage is that the general tendencies of a succession of adjudications may bring about a substantive alteration in constitutional practices and processes by imperceptible accretions over a period of time. The rules of a constitution can be overturned by slow accretion just as surely as by dramatic action. The process may be more insidious by being less dramatic and less liable to raise concerns that should be voiced. There can be no presumption that the general oversight of the accumulated impact of incremental changes is best left to a judicial body.

(f) The case method The advantages claimed for the case method as an approach to constitutional change are not just those linked to incremental change. The case method means that when change does occur it will not be for abstract reasons but in response to specific situations. The case method will, it is claimed, help keep down the temperature of constitutional debate by focusing on the concrete application of the constitution rather than by encouraging abstract debate. The force of this argument is however weakened in considering the circumstances in which such cases actually arise. They arise precisely when there are doubts about the rules and how to interpret them. The advantage claimed for the case method thus must rest on the view that judges are better able to arrive at the right opinions in cases of doubt about the rules. This is not a self-evident truth. Moreover, the effect of relying on judicial interpretation rather than any other means of resolving doubt is to foreclose any more representative means of bringing about constitutional change. A court is divorced from the people and can, in only a highly limited sense through the appointment system, claim to be a representative body. If interpretation is to be the primary route for constitutional change, there is a problem in having it so far removed from the ultimate source of the rules – the people themselves acting directly or through their governments or assemblies. This reintroduces the question of the continuing role of the contracting parties to the constitution – the Member States, their peoples and their institutions.

VI The involvement of the contracting parties

(i) Interpositioning

The realization that the contracting parties to a constitution could quickly find themselves frozen out of any continuing role in the process of constitutional oversight arose very early in the United States, even before the Supreme Court asserted its right of judicial review.[41] The debate centred around 'interpositioning' or 'nullification' (the right of a state to strike down an act of the federal government). The debate eventually became tainted because of its subsequent association with slavery. Before then it very much occupied Madison in his final years.

The issue of interpositioning concerned the right of an individual state to reject a federal law on the grounds of unconstitutionality. It is difficult to defend such a position for an individual state (other than on a political subject where a constitution specifically allows for opt out procedures). But the debate was significant because it involved the more general issue of the way in which the states could oppose acts of the federal government that they felt to be unconstitutional.

At the time they could be enumerated as follows:[42]

- the right of protest;
- the influence exercised on the President through the electoral college and (in extremis) through the impeachment process;
- the influence exercised in Congress through those elected by state legislatures to the Senate;
- the possibility of mobilizing enough states to call a constitutional convention or to pass amendments to the constitution;
- the right to secede (rejected by Madison but contemplated as an option by Jefferson);
- the right to take 'extraconstitutional' action (the revolutionary past of the United States made the justification of overturning a constitution easier to contemplate for Madison and his age).[43]

What was significant about Madison's position is that, while denying the right of a single state to annul a federal act, he seems to have accepted the right of the several contracting parties to the constitution (the states) to see themselves as the highest guardians of the constitution.[44] What American history has subsequently denied has been any effective way for the states to act in this capacity. It can be seen from the list above that, apart from the right of protest, each of the options has either been denied (secession or revolt), ended (indirect elections to the Senate), effectively lapsed (the electoral college) or is extremely difficult to employ (impeachment or amendment). The net effect has been that states have been exposed to a gradual erosion of their powers through the actions of Union bodies (including the Supreme Court) while not having any point of entry into determining the interpretation given to Union powers. The end result has been an increasingly centralized Union.

If powers in Europe are to be delegated by the Member States to the Union it seems vital that the Member States should retain the role of authorizing constitutional change and blocking acts of the Union which infringe, in the view of the Member States, the intended distribution of powers. Even if powers were to be distributed in Europe as independent and coordinate powers, American experience strongly suggests that some method by which Member States can interpose their views on the constitution remains essential to avoid creeping centralization.

In the European context it therefore seems important:

- to have more than one method of constitutional oversight so that rule keeping does not rely solely on action after the event;
- in cases where judicial procedures of review appear appropriate (for example, in the case of conflicting interpretations by different courts) to look for judicial procedures that rest with a different court than that entrusted with applying Union laws;
- to look not just to judicial procedures but also to a more representative system of constitutional oversight;
- to look for ways that keep the contracting parties to any European constitution (the Member States and their peoples or representatives) as active players in overseeing the rules.

(ii) Alternative methods of oversight

In considering the use of non-judicial channels for oversight, whether it be a Union body, or the governments of the Member States, their assemblies or their peoples directly, the problem of deciding on the necessary majorities for effective decision taking would have to be confronted. For example, it will become increasingly difficult for the governments of the Member States to mobilize a high majority, let alone unanimity, for constitutional changes.

In this context, the distinction made earlier between the blocking of unintended changes to the rules and the carrying out of considered changes, remains important. Because constitutional rules are intended to provide stability, decisions to maintain the status quo should be easier to take than decisions to make changes. Thus, the blocking of unintended changes should be possible on the basis of a minority decision while decisions to make changes to the rules should require a high majority in favour. In both cases the minorities are given a privileged position.

The situation where rule changes are to be considered is easy to identify. It will involve amendments or language changes to the constitution. Much less easy to identify are those cases where it is alleged that the rules are being applied or interpreted in ways not intended by the contracting parties. There are, however, identifiable situations where disputes about interpretation are most likely to occur. It is in these situations that minorities might be specifically authorized to block acts. There may be other kinds of situations where the use of blocking minorities could be justified, but the principal situations are when there are disputes about:

- the appropriate constitutional basis for a Union act (for example, where there is more than one basis but with different decision rules attached to each);
- any Union measure that rests on implied powers;
- proposed acts that call into question the balance of powers between the Union and the Member States (for example, where there is no clear need for the Union to act).

An ability to mobilize a blocking minority would retain the contracting parties in a position to exercise continuing surveillance over key areas of the constitution. However, in the different situation of making changes to the rules, there is much to be said for avoiding frequent constitutional reviews. It introduces uncertainty into the basic rules. It also makes the constitution vulnerable to changes that simply reflect passing fashions or that enter into unnecessary detail. On the other hand, the advance knowledge that there will be a mechanism for periodic review may act as a discipline in the interim and may also act as a safety valve if there are discontents that are accumulating with the existing constitution. Moreover, it allows for the fact that the circumstances under which the constitution was drawn up will change and that rules may be needed where there was previously silence. There seems therefore much to be said for the Jeffersonian principle that reviews should be automatically provided at say twenty year intervals, if they have not been held in the interim.

The question remains as to where any power to block, or any power to make changes should reside, if it is not to be entrusted to a judicial body.

The four principal alternatives to judicial procedures for constitutional oversight consist of:

- referral to the governments of the Member States;
- oversight by a representative assembly;
- direct popular votes;
- review by a special body (such as a constitutional convention).[45]

(a) Referral to the governments of Member States The idea that the governments of the Member States should have a role in constitutional oversight appears in flat contradiction to the idea of government under the law or government under the rules. Whether there is such a contradiction depends in part on whether the

governments of the Member States remain involved in the government of the Union. If they do, for example through the European Council, then they cannot easily be entrusted with the keeping of the rules.

If the governments of the Member States remain active in the government of the Union, the case for their having a role also in constitutional oversight could, however, still be rested on the view that they themselves will not be the source of likely disturbances to the constitution. If challenges to the rules are seen as more likely to spring from other sources – such as from the Union assembly or from the rulings of the Court of Justice – there would remain a case for the governments of the Member States to act as the rule keepers. The question is which is the 'least dangerous' set of rule keepers.

A rather different way of looking at the role of the governments of the Member States would be to see their power to block, or their power to make changes, as being conditional on approval by the representative assemblies or peoples in their own Member States. In this case the governments could be seen as acting as agents triggering a process rather than as principals making the decision.

(b) Assemblies The great advantage of having a representative assembly involved in constitutional oversight is that it can act not only after measures have been taken by the government, but is also well placed to prevent proposed measures before they go ahead. It emphasizes the early historical role of a representative assembly in keeping a government in check, before the time when parliaments turned towards their modern role of providing support to governments. It is more easily reconcilable with the concept of making sure that governments obey the rules.

Madison objected to the idea of the legislature as guardian of the rules of the US constitution because he saw it potentially acting as a dangerous source of challenge to those rules. A directly elected European assembly (such as the existing European Parliament) can be ruled out of consideration essentially on the same grounds. The European Parliament has, and will inevitably continue to have, an expansive view of its own powers – not only in relation to the other institutions of the European Union – but, equally importantly, in relation to the prerogatives of the jurisdictions of the Member States.

There are however other representative bodies in Europe – namely the parliaments of the Member States. They have a critical self-interest in the maintenance of a system that maintains multiple jurisdictions. They are potentially placed to be able to act to prevent measures that threaten to transgress the rules before such measures are enacted. They are therefore extremely well suited to act as guardians of the rules at the point of prevention rather than after the event.

They would provide one means for the contracting parties to the constitution to play a continuing role in constitutional oversight. The core function would be to watch that the laws proposed by the government of Europe and sought by the directly elected assembly were in accordance with the constitutional distribution of powers and procedures.

One important difficulty is that national parliaments have no tradition of working together and no established procedures for so doing. The closest they have so far come to cooperation on European issues is through the meetings of the conference of the specialized European committees of the national parliaments (COSAC). This committee has not yet reached the point of being able to issue joint statements. If it, or a similar committee of parliaments, is to become a decision taking body, rules relating to voting power will be needed and the status of representatives on such a body would need to be clarified.

If national parliaments are to play an effective role in watching that the exercise of Union powers is kept within constitutional limits:

- either, a procedure would have to be set up so that parliaments giving separate consideration to a proposed Union measure were able to block it;
- or alternatively, representatives of national parliaments could meet together as a more formal body. Essentially, a second European chamber would be set up alongside the directly elected chamber to act as a rule keeping 'senate'.

In either case, thresholds would have to be established in order to determine what constituted a blocking minority against acts which were held to be unconstitutional. The voting weights of the different national parliaments (or their number of representatives) would have to be established. Different decision thresholds would also be needed if national parliaments were to be positioned, not just to block acts that they considered unconstitutional, but also to propose and carry amendments to the constitution. In this case a high majority would be required.

The power of the governments of Member States to block unintended changes to the constitution might exist alongside the blocking powers of their representative assemblies. But the representative assemblies will confer a greater legitimacy on the process and their ratification of any blocking powers exercised by their governments would seem in any case to be needed.

The ways and means for the parliaments of the Member States to play an 'interpositioning' role in constitutional oversight is considered further at a later point in the more general context of the role of representative assemblies in the legitimization of Europe's system of government.

(c) Direct popular vote (the referendum) Even if Member States exercise powers of constitutional oversight, and particularly the powers to block unintended changes, through their governments or through their assemblies, the people themselves will still be excluded from the most basic decisions about the framework for their political association unless they themselves are consulted. The possibility for their direct involvement essentially depends on the use of referenda, or popular initiatives, to block acts or to pass amendments.

In this connection there is an important distinction to be made between referenda which are made at the initiative of governments and referenda which are made at the initiative of the people.[46] There is a role for both. But it is the latter which are particularly important since their purpose is to enable people to block acts or resist amendments supported by their governments.

(d) Review by a special body Entrusting the oversight of the constitution to a special body is usually conceived in terms of the calling of a special constitutional convention. The difficulty with such procedures is that they are cumbersome and such bodies are unlikely to arrive at agreed interpretations or changes.

A more manageable alternative is to think of a quasi-judicial tribunal along the lines of France's *Conseil d'Etat* which would be answerable to the Member States. This would have the advantage of separating responsibility for the uniform application of the laws of the European Union from constitutional interpretation. It might have a particular mandate to look at those areas already identified where disputes are most likely to arise – any judgement of a Union court that relied on implied powers rather than those expressly conferred in the constitution, questions about the particular legal base on which a measure has been based or proposed acts of Union bodies, or judgements of a Union court, that appeared to upset the balance between Union powers and the powers of the Member States. Such a body might be seen to represent some kind of 'halfway house' between political and judicial methods of constitutional oversight. For this very reason it might not be seen to be satisfactory. It would be important in any event in setting up any such body to arrive at procedures which are fully transparent.

(iii) The core responsibility for oversight

The choice about where to locate responsibility for the keeping of the rules involves a decision about what is the least unsatisfactory method of oversight. Each potential location and method has its drawbacks. The people must be seen as the ultimate guardians. But even referenda can be manipulated. At the same time it is one of the most critical constitutional choices that has to be made.

Despite the achievements of the US Supreme Court as interpreter of the US constitution, there can be no presumption that it is a practice that should be incorporated without modification into Europe's own system of government. There are three principal doubts about the wisdom of transposition into the different circumstances of Europe. First, entrusting the same body to keep the rules of the constitution in addition to applying the law of the Union, risks confusing rule based government (*Rechtsstaat*) with law as the instrument of government (*Staatsrecht*). Second, a particular court with an interest in a particular jurisdiction cannot be seen as a neutral body for interpreting procedural values that aim to entrench multiple jurisdictions. The body responsible for Union law may itself pose part of the risk to the intended constitutional processes. Third, the method means that the keeping and the refreshing of the rules of political association in Europe would be unrepresentative in character and would exclude the contracting parties.

The analysis suggests that a European political union should not follow the American model of combining in the same judicial body a responsibility both for the uniform application of Union laws and for constitutional interpretation. If judicial procedures for constitutional oversight are seen to provide the least unsatisfactory method, a special court or tribunal would seem appropriate, instead of the European Court of Justice, which would remain charged with applying Union legislation. Possibly, as mentioned above, a court ruling on conflicts between the laws of the Union and the laws of the Member States could take on this role, or otherwise the Member States might set up a body analogous to the *Conseil d'Etat*.

However, in a system of government where the centre exercises delegated powers, it seems critically important to preserve the role of the contracting parties – the Member States – in the oversight of the rules. It also seems desirable to keep alive representative methods of constitutional oversight.

If any representative method of oversight is to be effective, whether triggered by the governments of the Member States (in the first instance), or exercised by their parliaments, or by their peoples directly, a distinction has to be made between the decision rules that block unintended changes to an existing constitution and those that amend and alter the language of the rules. Blocking actions can be based on qualified minorities. Changes to the language of the rules on the other hand will require high majorities.

A power to block could be located with the governments of the Member States themselves in the first instance. Periodic constitutional review by the governments of the Member States of the need for possible rule changes seems desirable in any event. But the governments could not act by themselves – only subject to ratification by their parliaments and their peoples. A more representative method of constitutional oversight, and one which is easier to reconcile with the concept of government under the law, could be provided by a 'senate' composed of the representatives of national parliaments. There is, in addition, a need to keep alive direct popular involvement in constitutional oversight as a check on government. Building in a clear link between the representative assemblies of the Member States and the representative assembly of the Union will help preserve the representative bodies of the Member States as the custodians of the constitution and, together with the right of popular initiative, should better ensure that the processes of the Union remain close to the ultimate guardians of the constitution – the people themselves.

Notes

1   See Lijpart, A. (1984), *Democracies*.
2   'Once undertaken, governmental programs are hard to terminate. Interests become vested, bureaucracies entrenched, constituencies solidified'. Higgs, R. (1987), *Crisis and Leviathan: Critical Episodes in the Growth of American Government*.
3   Dahl's account of democratic societies as 'polyarchies' is a theory that 'focuses primarily not on the constitutional prerequisites but on the social prerequisites for a democratic order'. See Dahl, R.A. (1971), *Polyarchy, Participation and Opposition*.
4   'The whole tendency to equate Community institutions with familiar national institutions (e.g. Council and European Parliament as the upper and lower houses of the legislature, Commission as the government), or to regard them as evolving naturally towards those models, seems thoroughly misconceived'. Dashwood, A. (1994), 'The Role of the Council' in *Liber Amicorum Henry J. Schermers*.
5   Bentham, J. (1830), *First Principles Preparatory to the Constitutional Code*.
6   Vile gives a history of each. See Vile, M.J.C. (1967), *Constitutionalism and the Separation of Powers*.
7   'Whether or not powerful minorities or mass-based dictatorial leaders have refrained from establishing tyranny is clearly not related to the presence or absence of constitutional separation of powers'. Dahl, R.A. (1956), *A Preface to Democratic Theory*.
8   'A state cannot fail to prosper where the sovereign retains those rights proper to his majesty, the senate preserves its authority, the magistrates exercise their legitimate powers, and justice runs its ordinary course. Otherwise, if those who have sovereign power attempt to invade the sphere of the senate or the magistrate, they only risk the loss of their own authority'. Bodin, J. (1576), *The Six Books of a Commonwealth*.
9   'When both the legislative and executive powers are united in the same person or body of magistrates, there is no liberty. For then it may be feared that the same monarch or senate has made tyrannical laws in order to execute them in a tyrannical way. Again there is no liberty, if the power to judge is not separated from the legislative and executive powers'. Montesquieu, C. de S. (1748), 'The Spirit of the Laws', Book VI, Chap. VI in Richter, M. *The Political Theory of Montesquieu*.
    Locke justified the division between legislative and executive powers, 'because it may be too great temptation to human frailty, apt to grasp at power, for the same persons who have the power of making laws to have also in their hands the power to execute them'. Locke, J. (1690), 'Second Treatise of Government' in *Two Treatises of Government*.
10   See *Federalist Paper*, no. XLVII, (Madison J.J.J.) 'The accumulation of all powers, legislative, executive and judiciary, in the same hands, whether of one, a few, or many, and whether hereditary, self appointed, or elective, may justly be pronounced the very definition of tyranny'.
11   'The Madisonian argument exaggerates the importance, in preventing tyranny, of specified checks to government officials by other specified government officials'. Dahl, op. cit.
12   Lijpart, op. cit.
13   The term 'consociational' democracy has been attributed to David Apter and the development of the theory is associated with Lijpart, Lehmbruch, Steiner and Stiefbold. See Daalder, H. 'On Building Consociational Nations: the Cases of the Netherlands and Switzerland' in McRae, K. (ed) (1974), *Consociational Democracy: Political Accommodation in Segmented Societies*. According to Lijpart the four characteristics of consociational democracy – grand coalition, segmented autonomy, proportionality and minority veto

– are recognizable in the more encompassing criteria of consensus democracy.

14 '... the majoritarian model is one of executive dominance, whereas the consensus model is characterized by a more balanced executive-legislative relationship'. Lijpart, op. cit.

15 '... there is no doubt that constitutional separation of powers tends to give the legislature more strength and independence vis à vis the executive than does fusion of powers'. Lijpart, ibid.

16 Madison wrote of Montesquieu's view of the separation of powers, 'His meaning... can amount to no more than this, that where the whole power of one department is exercised by the same hands which possess the whole power of another department, the fundamental principles of a free constitution are subverted'. *Federalist Paper*, no. XLVII.

17 The ambiguities that are made possible by the use of traditional terms are well illustrated in Kelsen's theory of the state where the constitution determines whether the executive or legislature or judiciary fulfils a 'legislative' role. See Kelsen, H. (1946), *The General Theory of the Law and the State*.

18 Vile notes that in the United States, 'Most major measures are prepared by the Administration'. Vile, op. cit.

19 Wheare has written of the term 'legislatures' that 'the use of the name is convenient and indeed justifiable, but it can mislead. For a large part of the time of these bodies is not devoted to law-making at all'. Wheare, K.C. (1963), *Legislatures*.

20 'To state that legislatures are to make laws is to refuse to recognize that most legislation... implies a preparation at the technical level and a modicum of agreement between interested parties which cannot be achieved in a legislature'. Blondel, J. (1973), *Comparative Legislatures*.

21 Hayek saw the term as a 'courtesy title'. 'If we are not to be misled by the word 'legislature'... we shall have to remember that it is no more than a sort of courtesy title conferred on assemblies which had primarily arisen as instruments of representative government'. Hayek, F.A. (1976), *Law, Legislation and Liberty*.

22 See Vile, op.cit.

23 Tribe notes, 'Arguments about the legitimacy of judicial review are ultimately meta-constitutional: the relevant considerations are political, philosophical, and historical in the broadest sense'. Tribe, L.H. (1978), *American Constitutional Law*.

24 Tribe suggests that, 'If the Constitution is seen as substantive law, as a translation of certain values into rights, powers and duties, then it may be possible to justify constitutional adjudication not by its methods but by its results. Decisions are legitimate, on this view, because they are right'. Tribe, ibid. This is a curious return of the view that systems of government can be justified by the outcomes they produce.

25 Bryce noted, 'This process of turning a League of States (Staatenbund) into a Federal State (Bundestaat) is practically certain to create a rigid constitution'. Bryce, J. (1901), *Studies in History and Jurisprudence*.

26 'No law ever was so written as to anticipate and cover all the cases that can possibly arise under it'. Bryce, ibid.

27 Mill argued against the idea of contracts in perpetuity. 'The presumption in favour of individual judgement is only legitimate, where the judgement is grounded on actual, and especially on present, personal experience; not where it is formed antecedently to experience, and not suffered to be reversed even after experience has condemned it'. He suggested that the practice of long binding contracts needed to be restricted and needed to contain a way out. Mill, J.S. (1848), *Principles of Political Economy*.

28 'There are sound reasons... for believing that the hard, confining, and yet enlarging context of a real controversy leads to sounder and more enduring judgements'. Bickel,

A. (1962), *The Least Dangerous Branch.*

29   For this kind of distinction see Dicey, A.V. (1915), *Introduction to the Study of the Law and the Constitution.*

30   Dahl notes, 'If the constitution permitted easy amendment by majorities, then most of the advantages of judicial review set forth by its advocates would disappear. Hence we cannot consider judicial review independent of the amending power'. Dahl, R.A. (1956), op. cit.

31   De Toqueville pointed to this dilemma and suggested that there was no alternative to union (federal) jurisdiction in such cases.

32   See Cox, A. (1976), *The Role of the Supreme Court in American Government.*

33   Madison saw the legislative department as much the most dangerous branch of government. 'Its constitutional powers being at once more extensive, and less susceptible of precise limits, it can, with the greater facility, mask, under complicated and indirect measures, the encroachments which it makes on the coordinate departments... . On the other side, the executive power being restrained within a narrower compass, and being more simple in its nature, and the judiciary being described by landmarks still less uncertain, projects of usurpation by either of these departments would immediately betray and defeat themselves'. *Federalist Paper*, no. XLVIII.

34   'A judge is one of the most deadly instruments in the hands of a tyranny of which others are at the head; but, while he can only exercise political influence through the indirect medium of judicial decisions, he acts within too confined a sphere for it to be possible for him to establish a despotism in his own favour'. Mill, J.S. 'De Toqueville on Democracy in America', *Essays on Politics and Society.*

35   Hayek referred to constitutional rules as providing a 'superstructure'. 'It would be more appropriate to regard them as a superstructure erected to secure the maintenance of the law, rather than, as they are usually represented, as the source of all other law'. Hayek, op. cit. He suggested that they provided something akin to Hart's rule of recognition. (See Hart, H.L.A. (1961), *The Concept of Law*.)

36   Ely, J.H. (1980), *Democracy and Distrust: A Theory of Judicial Review.*

37   For example, Dicey stressed the importance of conventions not reflected in the written text. 'Is it possible that so-called 'constitutional law' is in reality a cross between history and custom which does not properly deserve the name of law at all?'. Dicey, op. cit.

38   Kelsen's theory of the state denied this to be a problem because, 'the legal order cannot have any gaps'. What he meant by this is that the constitution prescribes the method for creating valid legal norms. If there is no general norm to fit the case, 'The court is authorized to create for the concrete case the norm of substantive law it considers satisfactory, just, or equitable. The court then functions as a legislator'. If, on the other hand, the determination of constitutionality rests with the legislator, 'in this case, no statute enacted by the legislative organ can be considered to be 'unconstitutional''. Kelsen, op. cit.

39   Ely, op. cit.

40   De Toqueville also praised judicial review as a defence against assemblies. '. . . the power vested in the American courts of justice of pronouncing a statute to be unconstitutional, forms one of the most powerful barriers that has ever been devised against the tyranny of political assemblies'. De Tocqueville, A. ((1835), *Democracy in America.*

41   For a brief description of the Virginia and Kentucky resolutions (1798) see Rutland, R.A. (1987), *James Madison: The Founding Father.*

42   See Madison's letter to Edward Everett (1830) contained in Padover, S.K. (ed) (1953), *The Complete Madison: His Basic Writings.*

43   'In the event of a failure of every constitutional resort. . . there can remain but one resort, the last of all – an appeal from the cancelled obligations of the constitutional

compact, to original rights and the law of self preservation'. Madison, ibid.

44   Referring back in 1836 to the Virginia resolution, Madison wrote, 'The course and scope of the reasoning requires that by the rightful authority to interpose. . . was meant, not the authority of the states singly and separately, but their authority as the parties to the Constitution, the authority which, in fact, made the Constitution; the authority which being paramount to the Constitution was paramount to the authorities constituted by it, to the judiciary as well as the other authorities'. See Madison's 1836 note on nullification in Meyer, M. (ed) (1981), *The Mind of the Founder: Sources of the Political Thought of James Madison*.

45   These alternatives were enumerated by Bryce and remain valid. Bryce, op. cit.

46   See Smith G. (1976), 'The Functional Properties of a Referendum', *European Journal of Political Research*, 4, No. 1.

8 The Government of Europe

'Intrigue and corruption are the natural defects of elective government'. Alexis de Toqueville, *Democracy in America*, 1835.

I The choice

At the apex of the Union is the need for a body that initiates and sets the direction of collective policy in the Union, bears responsibility for the measures needed to carry through policy, including the passage of legislation through the law making process, and which oversees the execution of policy. Within the Member States this is the task of the government. Within European political union it is the task of a Government of Europe.

Two bodies can potentially perform this function – the Commission or the Council of Ministers. Currently, the Maastricht Treaty assigns responsibility for the overall direction of policy in the Union to the European Council – the heads of government (or state).[1] In practice, heads of government can only decide on a few issues that have been well prepared in advance. Thus, for practical purposes, on most matters of public policy it is the Council of Ministers acting for the European Council that is the alternative to the Commission. In the discussion that follows the references are therefore to the Council of Ministers but this should be taken to include the possibility that they will refer the most important matters of public policy to the European Council for a final decision.

The Commission is a collegiate body consisting of the appointees of the Member States.[2] Historically, the founders of the original European Economic Community had wished the Commission to be a body with clearly supra-national authority over the governments of Member States, along the lines of the High Authority of the European Coal and Steel Authority. This was not acceptable to the governments. However, its powers in the Treaty of Rome (Art. 155) were defined to include much more than just the powers of implementation under the Council of Ministers. The Commission was given an exclusive right of initiative, the right to 'participate in the shaping of measures' taken by the Parliament as well as by the Council and was charged with ensuring that the provisions of the treaty were applied (the so-called 'guardian of the treaty' role). Its functions therefore include an administrative role, a policy making role, a role in parliamentary processes, a role as keeper of the rules and, in addition, it performs quasi-judicial functions in certain areas (such as competition and trade). Although Commissioners are formally independent of the Member State that nominates them, increasingly the Commissioners have taken on the role of conduit and intermediary between the Commission and their own Member State.

Since its establishment, the Commission has had periods of prominence and periods of eclipse. The Commission's proposals at the time of the Maastricht Treaty negotiations made clear that it aspired to see its role develop as the Government of Europe. The Member States, for the most part, resisted.

All governments should be treated with suspicion.[3] Nevertheless, the question of which body should be in charge of government in Europe must be resolved:

- The sharing of responsibility for key tasks in a system of government confuses the question of core responsibilities and accountability across the entire range of functions.
- The dispute makes it impossible to draw the clear distinction necessary between the governmental function of establishing public policy and the agency and civil service function of carrying it out. Underlying the dispute is a fundamental debate about who is best equipped to carry out government in Europe in a democratic and rule based system.
- Having two bodies involved with assemblies in the passage of legislation complicates the legislative process, muddles the relationship between assemblies and government and blurs responsibilities. The debate conceals a major difference about the varying ways in which the relationship between the government and the assemblies can be framed.
- Having two bodies jostling for the policy role (the Commission and the Council) enables the Council to treat the Commission as 'scapegoat' for errors of public policy and for the Commission to return the blame to the Council. This allows each to get off the hook, to the convenience of each. The victim is the public and the principle of public accountability.

II The Commission

The case for the Commission to be developed as the Government of Europe rests in the first instance on history. There are many who feel that the Commission has acted as an indispensable 'motor' of European integration to date. It has acted not just as the guardian of the rules but also as the guardian of an ideal. For the future, Europe faces challenges at least as great as those encountered in the past. At the same time, the much larger number of Member States will make cohesion and effective policy making in the Council of Ministers even more difficult. The Commission appears to be able to provide the effective centre of policy making and the commitment to Europe that will be required. Its members are appointed for a five year term and can be reappointed. Thus they can provide continuity in policy making. In addition, they can spend all their time on the particular dossiers they are charged with. By contrast, continuity and full time attention is absent in the Council of Ministers. Management responsibilities in the Council rotate under the different presidencies of different Member States. Ministers come and go – depending not only on the vagaries of elections in their country but also on any reshufflings in ministerial portfolios between elections. Their dossiers include matters of purely domestic concern so that, even in the best of circumstances, they cannot give full time attention to European public policy in the area of their responsibility.

If the choice of locating responsibility for the Government of Europe rested simply on choosing the most effective instrument to accomplish specific goals, then the case for locating that responsibility with the Commission, or a body like it, would be powerful and possibly overwhelming. The choice is not of that nature. The legitimacy of a democratic political Union rests on processes not on goals. The responsibility for government must rest with arrangements that are consistent with the processes desired. The implications of entrusting the Commission with the functions of government in Europe have to be based not on the effectiveness of the Commission as an instrument but on what it would mean for processes in the Union.

If the Commission were to be developed as the Government of Europe, it could either remain as an appointed body, or it could become an elected body. The implications of both models for processes within the Union are discussed below.

(i) The non-elected model

The Commission is an appointed body. Its head is chosen through a process of common accord by the governments of the Member States. Other members are nominated by individual Member States. As a result of the Maastricht Treaty, the appointees to the Commission are subject, en bloc, to an affirmative vote of the European Parliament. The Parliament also has a 'consultative' role in the approval by governments of the head of the Commission. In practice, it would be very difficult for the Council to persist with a nominee who did not receive an affirmative vote from the Parliament. Thus effectively the Parliament has the power to block a nominee to head the Commission.

The powers granted the Commission in the Treaty of Rome clearly envisaged the Commission as being able to set the direction of policy in the Economic Community. The powers set out in Art. 155 include, 'its own power of decision' and the obligation to formulate recommendations where the Treaty expressly provides, 'or if the Commission considers it necessary'. In the economic area of the treaty, the Commission has the sole right of initiative which provides the basis for it to set the policy agenda and, perhaps more important in practice, to filter out proposals coming from elsewhere, such as the Council of Ministers. In addition, the Commission has the so-called 'guardian role' to 'ensure that the provisions of this Treaty...are applied'.

In making these provisions the framers of the Treaty of Rome had two fears. First was the fear that if policy lay in the hands of an intergovernmental body the organization would never be capable of acting decisively. It was a fear based on experience with the League of Nations in the interwar period. Second, there was distrust of how governments would act if they exercised power.

These fears were not groundless. The intergovernmental precedent had been provided by the League of Nations. It had achieved few successes to set against the overwhelming perception of its failures. Equally, there was reason to fear how governments might act. Governments in the Council of Ministers typically act to protect their own national, sectoral and special interests. They can be seen as a cartel. The role of the Commission could be viewed as an anti-trust body needed to break up the cartel of national interests.

In the early days of the Economic Community, where the focus was on breaking down national barriers to trade, the analogy of the Commission with that of an anti-trust body may have been justified. However, in general, non-elected appointees are more likely to be 'captured' by special interests precisely because they do not have to submit to an electorate. Moreover, in the context of constitutional arrangements for a political union the analogy is completely inappropriate for other, more fundamental, reasons.

The analogy is inappropriate for two reasons. First, the combination of powers accorded the Commission as an 'anti-trust' body is incompatible with any democratic or rule based system of government. Second, the concept of the appointed Commission with wide ranging powers belongs to a tradition of elitism in government. Elitist approaches to government are also totally incompatible with a rule based or democratic system of government.

(a) The combination of powers The range of powers granted the Commission stem from the concept of the Commission as the 'guardian' of the treaties. As the guardian of the ideal of European integration it needed to have the power of initiative to act as the dynamo or 'motor' of integration. As the guardian against 'backsliding' by Member States in the implementation of Community policies it was seen to need its own power of decision and the capacity to see that Community measures were being carried through into practice.

There is a benign interpretation which can be given to the guardian role. The benign aspect can be seen in the many ways in which a body such as the Commission can act as a helpful intermediary between the Member States. An intermediary can help establish the real concerns of particular Member States and see that they get communicated to others. It can help find the common view point which represents more than just the lowest common denominator. It can act as a go-between in 'brokering' differences between the Member States. By possessing quasi-judicial powers, an intermediary can act on behalf of one Member State against another, without the complications to bilateral relationships that would ensue from bilateral suits and challenges. It can act on behalf of the smaller Member States whose viewpoint and interests might otherwise be overlooked by the larger. All are important tasks. If the guardian role is equated with the 'honest broker' role, it can genuinely be seen in a favourable light.

However, the powers granted the Commission go well beyond the 'honest broker' concept and they were intended to do so. In so doing they confuse concepts that need to be kept clearly distinguishable. They mingle functions that are best kept apart.

First, for reasons both of transparency and respect for the law, it is important to distinguish the regulatory and quasi-judicial functions involved in implementing policy from policy making itself and the setting of the policy guidelines. Regulation is better conducted at arms length from the policy making role of governments and judicial functions are better kept largely separate from government. Where political direction is to be given to an economic regulator, or a political 'override' to be applied to regulatory areas, the transparency needed to make clear what is happening, and who is responsible, is better achieved through the separation of policy making bodies from agency functions. By combining the power of 'own decisions' with quasi-judicial and regulatory functions, the political and the judicial are mingled in a way that damages these distinctions. If the Commission is to develop as the policy making Government of Europe, it will need to shed its quasi-judicial and regulatory functions. If, alternatively, it is to develop as a regulatory and administrative body it will need to shed its emphasis on the policy making role.

Second, and even more fundamental, the role of constitutional guardianship – the role of the 'keeper of the rules' – is quite separate from the role of the 'guardian of the ideal'. The guardian of the ideal is about driving forward new initiatives and new law making. The two cannot be combined in the same body. On the contrary, the guardian of the rules has the function of ensuring that those who propose new initiatives are acting within the rules and that any proposed exercise of powers is also within the rules. As has been discussed earlier, 'neutrality' is a vital aspect of the rule keeping function. Administrative bodies can act as keeper of the rules only in the limited context of carrying out any regulatory functions. The body seen as the motor of integration cannot be seen as a neutral keeper of the basic rules of a constitution. When the rules concern jurisdictional boundaries or, when the rules involve the interpretation of express or implied powers, a body that sees itself as 'the motor of integration' will likely lean always in the direction of the exercise of central authority. As guardian of an ideal of European integration, and as a source of policy initiative, the Commission will always be seen as likely to favour the Union jurisdiction and interpretations of express or implied powers that favour Union action. Whatever body is to act as guardian of the rules must have strong incentives to act to preserve a system of multiple jurisdictions as well as protect the methods needed to express diversified preferences. If the Commission is to act as the policy making 'motor' of European integration, the incentives work in a quite opposite direction from those needed for the guardian of the rules.

The combination of powers given to the Commission in the original context of carrying forward a limited economic agenda, where the breaking down of economic barriers was likely to encounter the resistance of Member States, cannot therefore be seen as providing the prototype for the functions of the Government of Europe. The policy making role has to be distinguished from the agency, administrative and judicial role. The policy making role also has to be distinguished from the constitutional rule keeping role. The bodies that are candidates for the Government of Europe are not at the same time candidates to be the keepers of the rules of the constitution.

The fundamental question relating to the future of the Commission is whether it should develop its policy making functions as the putative Government of Europe or, whether it should be seen in an administrative capacity, acting as the agent of the alternative body for the governmental function – the Council of Ministers. Technically, the Commission could be developed as the Government exercising the policy making role. It would mean shedding its 'guardian' role to a different keeper of the rules. It would mean placing its administrative, regulatory and quasi-judicial functions at arms length, or with independent agencies. The objections are not technical. The objections are to the concept of government by appointees.

(b) Elitism The idea that the Commission should develop its policy making and government role rests unfortunately on an underlying belief in the advantages of government by elites. In essence it enshrines a belief that a group of appointees can be found able to transcend selfish interests and suited to rule for the well-being of society as a whole.

Elitist theories of government have a plausible factual basis. Involvement in active politics, and in the making of public policy, is limited in most countries to a small fraction of society. But elitist theories of government go beyond this factual observation to make government by the few a virtue. The basis for a belief in the virtues of rule by an elite are as follows:

- a distrust of mass politics and government based on mass electorates;[4]
- a belief that elites can provide a social and political equilibrium in divided societies.[5]
- a belief that politics should be viewed in terms of the ends it achieves;[6]
- a belief that a group can be found with superior knowledge or skills who can

best judge what is in the general interest.[7]

Those who comprise the elite can vary. The elite might consist of a bureaucratic class drawn from the meritocracy; it might be formed by the members of a political party or other ideological group or it might be seen as a business elite. In the case of the Commission, the concept is of an elite drawn from the meritocracy and motivated by an ideal.

Elitist traditions in the theory of government go back to the classical world and theories of guardianship. In their modern form they received a boost from the failures of elected governments in the 1930s. It was probably not coincidental that the founders of the Economic Community had been seared by experiences of the failure of democratic governments in the 1930s. Elitism received a further boost from postwar perceptions of the disparities between the information and access of those privy to the formation of public policy compared with the poverty of information and lack of influence of the modern electorate.[8] More recently still, it has been perceptions of the role of political or bureaucratic elites in providing cooperative solutions (or for managing conflicting interests) in segmented societies, that have provided a common element in various formulations of 'consociational' democracy.[9]

The difficulty for elitist theories lies in trying to justify the transition from allegedly factual sociological observations about the roles that elites play in society and government to the normative conclusion that a political structure should be built around elitist structures. The idea of consociational democracy has been justified as a particular form of 'federalism' where a deeply divided society is unified at the top by cooperation among the elites representing the different divisions.[10] But even in this context, the model has been seen as mainly relevant (if at all) to small societies and as a transition stage for developing countries moving from colonial regimes to more fully articulated democratic systems.

There are good reasons to reject elitism as a normative theory of how a European system of government should be set up. Elitism ignores the advantages of 'process' claimed as virtues in a democracy – for example, the importance of participation and of voice.[11] It tries to evade the genuine difficulties of providing for political processes that allow for the expression of diversities, by relying on 'people at the top' to interpret what is best for the people as a whole. It sees government as a 'top down' process, where a hierarchical ordering of powers and relationships provides the easiest way to transmit the superior insights of the governing elite.[12] Views may differ on the components of right process, but in viewing systems of government mainly in terms of outcomes lies the path to centralized and unrepresentative government. There is no place in democratic practices for institutions that reflect the view that a few can govern on the basis of a claim to superior knowledge of what is right for the majority of others in society. Those who put their trust in a few will sooner or later be disappointed. There is equally no place for such a view in rule based systems of government. The rules will always be vulnerable to the few. It is precisely the lack of regard of elitist theories of government to politics as process that has led to the perception that elitism constitutes the main threat to democratic forms of government in the contemporary world.[13]

(ii) The elected model

The elitist model of the Commission is impossible to defend. If the Commission is to be considered for a continuing role in providing policy direction it has to rest on an electoral base. There are two ways in which this could be arranged. The Commission could be elected by the European Parliament. Alternatively it could be elected directly by the people. There are precedents for either procedure. The US President is directly elected (leaving aside for practical purposes the electoral college). On the other hand, the Swiss Federal Council is chosen by the Swiss Parliament. The position of the House of Representatives in choosing the US President if the electoral college is deadlocked reflects the relic of the Virginia Plan for an indirectly rather than directly elected US Presidency.

(a) Indirect election The idea that the Commission should be elected by the European Parliament seems, at first sight, to be an attractive idea. It would place the policy making body in Europe firmly under the control of the representative body. It appears to replicate the situation in most of Europe where the government and the representative assemblies are 'fused', rather than separated, and where assemblies carry out an important 'oversight' function. However, the idea of a Commission elected by the European Parliament means more than 'oversight' by the representative body and would lead to a very special type of 'fusion'.

- First, election of the Commission by the assembly would lead to a system of government where there would be 'dominance' of the representative body over policy making. The policy framework within which the Commission would be entrusted to work would be set by the assembly. Candidates for the Commission would be chosen for their willingness and pledges to carry out the programme.
- Second, in circumstances where a particular grouping possessed a majority in the Parliament, that grouping would essentially become the decisive source of policy making. Indirect election could therefore lead to a majoritarian style of government through the Parliament.
- Third, regardless of whether the electoral majority was formed by a single political grouping or by a coalition of groups, election by the Parliament would be highly centralizing. The core function of setting policy direction as well as any core functions of a legislative nature exercised by Europe's

representative body would rest in the hands of those with an interest in power exercised at the centre.

Each of these features of the relationship between the Commission as indirectly elected government and the representative assembly would be difficult to justify.

'Dominance' of the representative body over policy setting is not a role performed by any parliament in Europe, nor by Congress in the United States. It runs counter to the Madisonian interpretation of the separation of powers – that although the different branches of government might not need to be kept completely separate, nevertheless, one branch should not have 'overruling' power over the core function of another. There may be a good case for saying that the pattern of government dominance over parliaments in European Member States has gone too far. However, the effect of a parliamentary system of election would be to rest the responsibility for setting the policy framework in Europe with parliament. It would swing the fusion of powers to the other extreme.[14]

Majoritarian forms of government are seen to be most fitted to political societies where there is a high degree of pre-existing consensus in society on approaches to major areas of public policy and no great divergencies in the intensity of preferences for different policies. Europe does not have this degree of conformity. As previously discussed, decision taking in Europe is best built around the concept of special majorities. A majoritarian approach to the selection of the Commission would again be difficult to justify.

A system where the Union assembly dominated the policy making arm would be very difficult to reconcile with processes intended to maintain a system of multiple jurisdictions. The assembly has a self-interest in an expansionist interpretation of its powers. It would claim electoral legitimacy for any initiative or for any interpretation of its powers. The Member States delegating powers for collective purposes would have no avenue for an effective voice. Even if nominations were to be made by the Member States, the process would essentially be controlled by the Parliament.

The problems of 'majoritarianism' could possibly be overcome. For example, it is possible that Parliament could consider choosing members of the Commission that would reflect a coalition of interests rather than a reflection of majority strength (for example, along the lines of the so-called 'magic formula' in Switzerland which predetermines party make up of the Swiss Federal Council). This however is a convention that operates in a political setting that is already highly consensual and where the Council also sees its duty as being to maintain consensual policies.

The centralizing combination of indirectly elected Commission and Parliament could also possibly be mitigated by developing the Council of Ministers as a kind of second chamber. Yet, it is doubtful how effective the Council could be in influencing policy in a situation where it would be trying to deal with two tightly connected institutions with a common interest in wielding central powers to the maximum. As already mentioned, the idea of the Council of Ministers performing in the capacity of second chamber is based on a terminological confusion about the functions of government and the functions of a representative assembly.

The alternative approach would be to consider direct election of the Commission or of its head.

(b) Direct election The direct election of the Commission as Government of Europe would raise some important 'technical' questions. Would the contest just be for the head of the Commission or for all members of the body? Would candidates put themselves forward, or have to be nominated by governments or by parties? Would there need to be a selection process ahead of a run-off election, or more than one round of voting, in order to narrow down the number of candidates? Although these questions are 'technical', they are not unimportant. The American system of government has many virtues. The manner of electing the President is not usually counted among them.

Whatever method of direct election were to be chosen, some of the main implications can be identified.

First, direct election would provide a means of keeping largely separate the core function of setting public policy from the core functions of the representative assembly. Under a system of direct election, the Commission would hold office on the basis of popular consent and the Parliament would not possess power of appointment or dismissal (leaving aside the special circumstances of possible impeachment powers). The problem of the 'dominance' of the representative body over policy formation thus would be avoided. The separation of powers too would be largely observed.

Second, accompanying this separation of powers would be a likely impact over time on the character of the assembly. If the Commission or its head were to be elected on a 'European' platform, representatives in the assembly might increasingly define their role in terms of representing local or special interests, or be viewed by the electorate and lobbying groups in this way.

Both the separation of powers and, less easily perhaps, the change in character of the assembly, could be defended. The drawbacks rest with the other implications of direct election. If the head of the Commission is to be elected, it is difficult to avoid a final electoral choice that does not leave a large part of the electorate feeling excluded. It would be easier in theory for the Commission to be more representative if its entire membership is elected in a manner to reflect some system of proportional representation of voting preferences.[15] Yet it would remain very questionable as to how far direct election for the persons determining collective policy for Europe would be desirable. It could result in a person or a body that was overpowerful. It would personalize politics in a way that Europe's history warns strongly against.

An even more fundamental difficulty is that a system of direct election is unlikely to be compatible with a decentralized distribution of powers in the Union.

The idea of a directly elected body to determine public policy in the Union rests most comfortably with a hierarchical system of distributed powers where the major public issues are decided on the Union level and where consequently the electoral system must focus on Union bodies. This is not the form of distribution of powers desirable for Europe.

Direct election of the governmental head (or the Commission as a body) appears consistent (by analogy with the United States) with a system of independent powers for the Union. But, as has already been discussed, the way in which relationships between Union and state institutions have been arranged in the American system have led to an increasingly centralized Union. The accumulation of policy making powers in the US Presidency has been part of this development. A similar drift to centralized policy making would likely take place in Europe if the Commission were to be directly elected. A directly elected Commission could appeal over the head of governments in multiple jurisdictions. Direct election would also lead to the Commission being able to claim authority or legitimacy for acting within other jurisdictions. Neither development can be easily reconciled with a system of powers where there is a desire to maintain stable jurisdictional boundaries.

A directly elected Commission is unlikely to be compatible with a system where the powers to be exercised by central bodies are to be limited to those expressly delegated to Union bodies. In this system it would appear essential for the institutions of the Member States to play a continuing role in the affairs of the Union – including the main role in the direction of public policy.

The concept of the Commission being developed as the future Government of Europe and being given the core function of determining the direction of public policy in the Union thus presents major problems. As either a directly, or as an indirectly elected body, the Commission as Government of Europe would be difficult to reconcile with a system of multiple jurisdictions and the delegation of powers to the centre. Moreover, either a direct or indirect system of election could produce a system of government reflecting simple majoritarianism. As a non-elected, appointed body, the justification of the Commission as Government would rest within a tradition of elitism that has no place in a democratic, rule based system of government.

The implication of this analysis is that the Commission has a continuing role in a European system of distributed powers, but in an administrative and agency capacity and not as the principal policy making body – the Government of Europe. Its policy making influence would rest with the not inconsiderable power that can be wielded by bodies that perform the role of honest brokers and intermediation and that effectively manage the implementation of policy.

The case for choosing the Council of Ministers as the Government of Europe cannot just rest on the negative implications of choosing an elected or appointed Commission. There are drawbacks to the Council of Ministers evolving as the Government of Europe. As already indicated above, a large part of the case for the

Commission to be developed as the Government of Europe has rested on perceptions about the shortcomings of the Council. The merits of the Council also have to be assessed.

III The Council of Ministers

The Maastricht Treaty gives to the European Council the task of setting policy guidelines in the Union. In practice, heads of government are likely to delegate the formation of many of the details of policy to their ministers in line with the ministerial structure of European governments. Thus, as mentioned above, in terms of the core function of setting policy in a political union, the European Council and the Council of Ministers should be seen as one. A variation of this approach would be to develop the capacity of the European Council itself to develop policy or, to entrust a larger role to specially designated Ministers of Europe. These however, are variations on a common theme. The alternative to the Commission as the Government of Europe is that policy formation should rest with the governments of Member States in a Council.

(i) The implications

There are three important consequences arising from developing the Council as the Government of Europe:

First, the Government would reflect a coalition of interests. Unlike the typical situation within those Member States where coalitions are frequent, the basis of coalition would not be according to party affiliation but by geographical area – the Member State. The overall party (ideological) composition would be an indirect result of the outcome of elections for governments within each Member State. Party affiliations might, and probably would, affect the way in which subgroups coalesced on particular issues within the Council. Nevertheless, the basis of the Council's composition would be primarily geographical and only indirectly according to party.

Second, the Government would be collective rather than 'prime ministerial' – thus rather different from the shape taken by ministerial government within Member States, where the head of government tends to dominate. This is because the system of leadership would likely rotate and need not be vested in one head of government or minister. The current six monthly rotation has little to be said for it and the current sharing of leadership between three Member States may also need to be modified. Nevertheless, even with different arrangements to reduce the frequency of rotation, sustained dominance over ministerial colleagues by one person over a long period of time, as has happened in a number of countries in Europe in the postwar period, is unlikely.

Third, if the Council provides the Government of Europe there will be a separation of powers between the institutions of the Union. This is because the Council will owe its existence to an electorate different from that which elects the European assembly.

(ii) Assessment

There are important objections that can be made to a Government of Europe with the characteristics outlined above.

First, although the Council would represent a coalition of interests, there are doubts whether it could transcend the geographical basis of these interests to consider the interests of the greater community of Europe as a whole.

Second, the collective nature of Council government is seen as likely to lead to a very indecisive form of government unsuited to deal with the challenges in Europe.[16]

Third, there is the doctrine that a government cannot be responsible to two bodies. At first sight this doctrine is pertinent to the Council because the Council would need to have a relationship with Europe's assembly but, at the same time, the members of the Council would be responsible to their own national parliaments.

Fourth, there is the difficulty of getting rid of the Government. Electorates that are wanting to see a change in public policies in Europe may vote against their particular government and their own representatives on the Council, but they will have no chance of voting on the Government of Europe as a whole.

These are important reservations. On closer inspection however, they seem to rest on underlying assumptions that are themselves suspect:

(a) The wider European view The belief that the Council cannot take a wide view of where Europe's interests lie, downplays the extent to which the governments in Member States see their national self-interest as intimately bound up in Europe. As long as politicians view the likely success of their government in their own jurisdiction as tied to the success of political and economic association with the rest of Europe, they will have a self-interest in making a success of European political union. If there was not a concern to cement interrelationships and to consolidate ways of acting together, there would be no move to European political union in the first place.

It cannot be excluded that some political leaders will come along having gained electoral support on the basis of opposition to the Union and its policies. However, such sentiment in the electorate is always possible, whatever the form of government in the Union. The question is which form of government is best able to contain opinion that might challenge the legitimacy of political association in Europe. It is not obvious that a more centralized form of government would be better able to contain such sentiment. On the contrary, it might exacerbate it.

Fears of how the Council would act as Government of Europe may reflect more a disagreement with the possible content of the anticipated policy thrust of the Council, rather than its ability to provide policy direction that is in the interest of Europe. It is true that Member States in the Council often act to protect what they see as in their national interest, or to protect parochial economic interests, such as declining industries or uncompetitive occupations. However, such concerns will be voiced somewhere in a representative political system or the system itself will be discredited. A belief that the government should not be reflective of interests affected by its potential acts, either assumes that elitist government is better, or assumes that majoritarian government is better than forms of power sharing in a coalition of interests. Either assumption is suspect in the European setting.

A territorial basis for political power sharing may seem less desirable than other ways of reflecting diverse interests in a political association.[17] However, a territorial base to the Government of Europe does not exclude other ways of reflecting different interests. That possibility depends more on the procedural limits set on governments and the vitality of intermediate associations in society.

The geographical basis for power sharing may also seem less desirable than the party basis familiar from national practices. This is because political parties play an important role in integrating opinion in a political association. However, the connections between the Member States is also likely to grow over time. So too will the links between the parties in the Member States. More important, basing the Government of Europe on the governments of Member States provides a way for the traditional ties of identity in Europe to be harnessed to the new form of political association, rather than risking inflame a powerful and disintegrative form of potential opposition. It mobilizes the inherited legitimacy of existing systems of government.

(b) Indecisiveness The concern about the potential indecisiveness of the Council as government reflects in part the difficulty of arriving at rules which provide for speedy decision taking. Earlier discussion presented the rationale for decision procedures not based on simple majorities and described how decisions could be based on critical mass rather than on commonality. Complaints about the perceived indecisiveness of the Council ultimately reflect a disagreement with such decision rules and the diversities that they may allow.

The concern about indecisiveness may also reflect a lingering fondness for more personalized forms of government which rotation and changes in Council membership arising from national elections may together deny. Europe has suffered from too many allegedly great leaders this century. The fact that the Council, in contrast to an elected Commission, would reduce the impact of personalities is an advantage in a democratic and rule based system of government.

(c) Dual accountability The view that a government cannot answer to two representative bodies was a theory put forward in the context of Westminster style
parliamentary government.[18] It critically depends on a belief in the virtues of
majoritarian government.[19] Again, the assumption, either that Europe will have
the kind of parliamentary regime to be found in the Member States or, that
majoritarian forms of government are best suited for Europe, are highly suspect. A
separation of powers would arise not only from the choice of the Council as the
future Government of Europe but would arise also if the Commission were elected
directly. It remains, as discussed earlier, a valid way of organizing the functions of
modern systems of government. (The further implications of the separation of
powers between Council and Parliament for the role of the assemblies is discussed
in the following chapter).

(d) Changing governments The difficulty of changing the composition of the Council
of Ministers is an important consideration. An ability for the electorate to get rid of
the government is a vital attribute of a democracy. There are however two aspects
involved. One is the need for members of a government to know that they can be
voted out of office. This possibility will still apply to each member of the Council in
respect of their own electorate. The other aspect is the possibility for the electorate
to produce radical shifts in public policies when they are discontented with the
current set of policies.

In practice, the possibility of large and rapid shifts in public policy in Europe is
debatable, since governments are usually bound by the inheritance of past policies
and the exigencies of current circumstances which limit their real choices. Radical
shifts are difficult in any system of government where power sharing is the norm
(regardless of whether power sharing arises from coalition styles of parliamentary
government or from situations, in a system of separation of powers, where the
branches try to hold each other in check). To look at politics in terms of its capacity
to deliver abrupt change within a given constitutional regime is probably a
mistake.[20] This may be possible in small and homogenous political communities
faced with a crisis. It is unlikely to be possible, or desirable, in a large and varied
political community such as Europe. The slowness and complexity of mobilizing
support for public policies in the United States has sometimes been a source of
deep concern for other countries. If America were quick to move and the source of
more frequent abrupt changes in policy, the complaints would be several times
louder. Europe is likely to be best served by developing a limited number of
collective policies that aim at continuity and where abrupt change is probably to be
avoided. The sources of change should be sought, not in the electoral politics of the
Union, but arising from the greater flexibilities and capacity to experiment and
emulate within the different jurisdictions that make up the Union and from
decision rules that allow for such diversities.

Hence, when they are examined more closely, the various objections to the
Council developing as the Government of Europe are not compelling. On the

contrary, they rest on other underlying assumptions, about procedures or institutional roles, which are themselves either incorrect or at least highly questionable. Moreover, there are important advantages which weigh in favour of the Council as the core policy making body in a European system of government. They stem from the depersonalization of what will become an extremely powerful body. They also flow from the advantages of maintaining the Member State at the centre of policy decisions in the Union. Not only will this help maintain a decentralized system of power in the Union, but it will also help provide an extremely desirable and probably essential link between the old systems of government focused simply on the nation state and the new system for Europe as a whole.

Notes

1   Art. D.
2   For a description of the Commission see, Edwards, G. and Spence, D. (eds) (1994), *The European Commission*.
3   'The most impudent quacks in medecine are modest in comparison of the quacks in politics. For not to speak of corruption, the quacks in medecine have not in their hands any such instruments of delusion as have the quacks in politics'. Bentham, J. (1830), *First Principles Preparatory to the Constitutional Code*.
4   The distrust of the kind of government emerging from mass electorates has been shared by many liberals – but the solutions offered are different. 'Provided good intentions can be secured, the best government. . . must be the government of the wisest, and these must always be few. The people ought to be the masters, but they are masters who must employ servants more skilful than themselves'. Mill, J.S. 'De Toqueville on Democracy in America', *Essays on Politics and Society*.
5   One of the first of the more modern sociological theories about the relationships between elites and social equilibrium is to be found in Pareto, V. (1916), *The Mind and Society*.
6   Bachrach, P. (1980), *The Theory of Democratic Elitism*. Elitism conceives of man's political interest, 'solely in terms of that which accrues to him from government'.
7   'The emphasis, in short, is placed upon the attainment of enlightened public policy; the elite is enlightened, thus its policy is bound to be in the public interest'. Bachrach, ibid.
8   In the late 1950s C. Wright Mills gave the best known (albeit inaccurate) account of the US government as being in the charge of a corporate\military\political elite. He declared that the images of the public of classic democracy were, 'A set of images out of a fairy tale'. Wright Mill, C. (1956), *The Power Elite*.
9   Lijpart defined consociational democracy, 'in terms of both the segmented cleavages of a plural society and the political cooperation of the segmented elites'. Lijpart, A. (1977), *Democracy in Plural Societies – A Comparative Exploration*. Lehmbruch pointed to the bureaucratic arbitration model of conflict management which perhaps fits the original concept of the Commission most closely. See, Lehmbruch, G. 'A Non-Competitive Pattern of Conflict Management in Liberal Democracies; the Case of Switzerland, Austria and Lebanon' in McRae, K. (ed) (1974), Consociational Democracy: Political Accommodation in Segmented Societies.
10 'Federal theory can. . . be regarded as a limited and special type of consociational theory'. Lijpart, op. cit.
11 Dahl, for example, suggests two major features for measuring the degree of

democratization in a society – public contestability and participation. Of his eight more detailed requirements for a democracy, each concerns a feature relating to processes. See, Dahl, R.A. (1971), *Polyarchy, Participation and Opposition*.

12   'In practice, then, hierarchy is democracy's most formidable rival; and because the claim of guardianship is a standard justification for hierarchical rule, as an idea guardianship is democracy's most formidable rival'. Dahl, R.A. (1989), *Democracy and its Critics*.

13   'The ultimate question is not capitalism against socialism, but liberalism against elitism'. Ackerman, B.A. (1980), *Social Justice in the Liberal State*. See also the discussion of guardianship in Dahl, (1989), op. cit.

14   Dahl notes that movement towards more democratic societies ('polyarchies' in his terminology) is associated with an independent executive. 'In a general way, then, the movement in polyarchies has been from a dependent executive to what is de facto if not de jure an independent executive'. Dahl, (1971) op. cit.

15   Lijpart notes in discussing the US Presidency that 'the Presidency would have to be collegial in order to facilitate the consensus requirements of power sharing'. Lijpart, A. (1984), *Democracies*.

16   Dahl suggests that ineffectual governments are likely to lead away from democratic practices towards more authoritarian forms of government. Dahl, (1971), op. cit.

17   Powers do not necessarily have to be distributed on a territorial basis – for example, it is sometimes desirable to have autonomous groups within the same political space (for instance cultural associations handling education). For a discussion, see Friedrich, C.J. (1968), *Trends of Federalism in Theory and Practice*.

18   See Wheare, K.C. (1963), Legislatures.

19   'The unqualified assertion that strong bicameralism is incompatible with parliamentarianism reveals a majoritarian bias'. Lijpart, (1984), op. cit.

20   'The economist is accustomed to dealing with a world in which there is a more or less continuous relationship between inputs and outputs, or between efforts and achievements. The political literature. . . is pervaded by an all-or-none logic: a party wins an election, or it loses: a law is passed, or it is defeated. I wish to argue that our traditional economic logic is also more appropriate to the political arena'. Stigler, G.J. (1975), *The Citizen and the State*.

9 Assemblies

'While it is essential to representative government that the practical supremacy in the state should reside in the representatives of the people, it is an open question what actual functions, what precise part in the machinery of government, shall be directly and personally discharged by the representative body'. John Stuart Mill, *Representative Government*, 1861.

I Defining the setting

The role performed by a representative assembly in a European political union has to be seen in a different light from the role performed by parliaments in the context of individual Member States in Europe.

First, there are the differences that arise from the separation of powers between the government and the assembly. In the parliamentary systems of the Member States, governments depend on their ability to command a majority in the representative assembly. It is for this reason that the government and the parliament are often regarded as 'fused'. In Europe, by contrast, a government built around the Council of Ministers and European Council will not depend on commanding a majority in Europe's parliament. On the contrary, individual members of the European Government (the Council) will remain dependent for their position on their majority in their own assembly in their own Member State. If the fate of a government does not depend on support in the representative assembly, and if at the same time members of the assembly have not been elected primarily to support a particular government, then the task of making or breaking a government does not rest with that assembly. It thus removes from Europe's assembly one function that has been traditionally held important in parliamentary practice in the Member States in Europe. However, precisely because the fate of the government does not rest in its hands, the assembly is much freer in the way in which it carries out its other tasks.

Second, there are the differences that arise because the role of national parliaments has evolved in the context of the essentially unified and hierarchical systems of government that exist in most Member States (even in those with regional assemblies). In a European political union where powers are distributed so that Union bodies exercise delegated powers, the institutions of the Member State continue to play a role in the shaping of public policies in the Union. This too provides a quite different context in which the role of the representative assembly for the Union must be defined.

These two fundamental differences in the context mean that the definition of the role of the representative body in a European system of government is more likely to be confused than illuminated by perceptions of the need to transpose to the Union assembly the functions of the different national parliaments. The variety of parliamentary practices in individual Member States, the need to distinguish between outward appearances and the underlying reality, and between the formalities and the often more important informal conventions, are confusing enough. But, in addition, the desire for transposition reflects an unwillingness to recognize the extent to which a system of government for Europe will be different from that prevailing in any Member State. The differences are fundamental. The role of representative assemblies in Europe's system of government will be substantially different from the role carried out by parliaments in the national setting.

In the discussion which follows, these two fundamental differences shape the analysis. The role to be played by a representative body in the context of a separation of powers will be considered first. The ways in which the relationship between the representative assembly of the Union and the representative assemblies of the Member States (the national parliaments) are best formulated will be examined thereafter.

One way to analyze the relationship between the representative body of the Union and the national parliaments is in terms of bicameralism. In order to play a continuing role in European public policy the parliaments of Member States may cooperate in a more regular manner between themselves, or they may develop the role of a coordinating committee (or committees) holding periodic meetings, or, they may form a standing committee of their members (a chamber). Whichever path is followed, the end result is a system of representation where the role of one representative assembly (the directly elected Union parliament) has to be defined in relation to another representative body (national parliaments acting in concert or through a coordinating committee or through a chamber of national parliaments). The essential character of this relationship can be defined in terms of bi-cameralism.

II   The representative body in a separation of powers

Is there a common thread to the functions of a representative assembly? One attempt to find a common denominator is in the concept of 'assent' – the idea that the role of a representative body lies in its necessary involvement in the giving of assent to government measures.[1] However, assent can range from a power to shape public measures, to the power to block government measures, to no more than a 'rubber stamping' role. The more elusive, but most relevant underlying concept is that of 'legitimization'. In one way or another, the different functions performed by representative bodies help give 'legitimacy' to the acts of government. The opposite side of this coin is the role of assemblies in challenging the acts of government. The key question is in what ways, in a system of separated and distributed powers, Europe's representative assembly can help confer 'legitimacy' on the acts of Europe's government or, conversely, challenge their legitimacy.

The role of a representative assembly in legitimizing or challenging the acts of government cannot be defined in terms of the exercise of a single power.[2] Legitimization lies not in a single function but in a combination of functions. In the discussion below, the tasks of a representative assembly are defined against four different benchmarks:

- the holding of the government to account;
- the role in policy making;
- participation in law making;
- acting as a 'forum' for debate and expressions of view.

The measurement of the role of the representative assembly in a European political union in relation to these benchmarks suggests that the role will be important but limited. The Union assembly will be able to confer only a partial legitimacy on the acts of European government. A fuller legitimization will require the parliaments of the Member States and the European assembly to find ways of acting together.

(i) Holding government to account

There are two main methods by which assemblies may hold a government to account for its measures. First, through a capacity to approve the formation of or dismiss the government. Second, through inquiry and investigation.

(a) The power to approve or dismiss governments The capacity to approve or dismiss a government is not a necessary function of an assembly. It has been linked traditionally to whether a separation of powers exists or not. In a case such as the United States where Presidents are elected in their own right, Congress has no power to approve or dismiss (other than through the impeachment process). The parliamentary system, where the government and the assembly are connected, has usually been linked with the capacity of the assembly to approve or dismiss a

government. (Switzerland is an exception in that once appointed the Federal Council has a fixed term of office). In practice, however, this capacity often does not exist even in parliamentary systems.[3]

The reality over most of Europe is that members of parliament are elected as members of political parties to support a government, or a potential government. When the party or a coalition achieves a clear electoral majority, the government has control of the assembly. Parliament will 'register' a government and will not in practice have the power to dismiss it. Even in those cases where the result of an election does not produce a party or coalition with a clear parliamentary majority, the actual formation of a government is often done outside the assembly by a caucus of party leaders or other 'king makers'.

If the Government of Europe is to be provided by the Council of Ministers, the European assembly will have no capacity to approve or dismiss the Government. The membership of the Government will rest on a different electoral base. The European system of government will thus have moved to a system closer in principle to the separation of powers that exists in the United States. It will be one which reflects also the reality of substantial government independence in many European parliamentary systems.[4]

In the absence of the power to approve the installation of a government, or the means to dismiss it, the Union assembly will look to other means of holding the Government to account and restraining its actions. The popular mandate gives it the moral authority to act to restrain the Government. Restraint however will probably take a weak form. Members of the Council will have their own mandate through the electoral process and their own parliaments. The weaker means of restraint is provided, in particular, through the inquiry and investigation role of assemblies.

(b) Inquiry and investigation The ability of an assembly to restrain a government through the holding of inquiries and investigations into its acts is an important one. No government likes its shortcomings or venality to be exposed. On the whole it is a power that has been somewhat muted in the parliamentary settings of the Member States. This is because the parliamentary system achieves a correspondence between the party composing the government and representation in the assembly. By contrast, in the United States the party in charge of the Presidency does not necessarily, or even usually, control the Congress. The result of the correspondence between parliamentary representation and the government is that parliament may pull its investigatory punches. The government may effectively control the inquiries and investigations by means of its parliamentary majority. Furthermore, party members will not wish to carry too far the embarrassment of the government they have been elected to support. In addition, many members of parliament will have entered parliament with the ambition of eventual membership of the government and will wish to demonstrate party loyalty for the sake of personal advancement.

The possibility of a more hard hitting investigatory and scrutiny role for the European assembly arises, not just because of the separation of powers, but also because of the possibility that the pattern of party representation in the Government of Europe will differ from the pattern of party representation in the elected assembly (for example, left of centre governments preponderant in the Council but right of centre parties preponderant in the assembly or vice versa).

How far these party differences will extend must be uncertain. The possibility of differences stems from two factors. One arises from deliberate 'ticket splitting' where a voter will vote for one party to provide the government and for another party in the assembly. The other relates to party organization. The parliamentary system puts a premium on party discipline. If the fate of the government does not rest on the majority in the assembly then there is both less incentive to impose party discipline and less incentive to follow it.

It is likely that the European Parliament will never experience the tight party discipline expected in national parliamentary systems in Europe. In addition, voters may increasingly behave in different ways in European elections from the way they behave in voting for a party to govern in national parliamentary elections. Both factors will bring Europe closer to the situation that prevails in the United States.

On the other hand, it is unlikely that the situation in the United States will be entirely replicated. There are long habits of party discipline and voter loyalty in many European countries. More important, the relationship between a vote for parties in the assembly and votes for parties that will provide members of the Government of Europe (the Council) will be much less apparent. The voting for governments in the national context is not synchronized with voting for the European assembly. Instead of voting for a single head of government, as in the United States (for the President), the vote in any one Member State will be a vote only for one member of the government (the Council). That vote too will be swayed by domestic policy concerns.

The loss of means (even hypothetical means) to dismiss the government, combined with the possibility of different party compositions in the Council and the Union assembly, means that the assembly will be motivated to focus on investigation and enquiries as the principal way of holding the Government of Europe to account. Yet there are other factors at work which may limit the assembly in performing this role. One limitation arises from the fact that the results of many of the measures taken by the Government of Europe will show up in the Member States themselves and in some cases will show up clearly only in particular Member States. Neither the government of that Member State, nor the parliament of that Member State, may be keen on investigation or inquiry to be carried out exclusively by a Union body. In order to be effective there are going to be many areas of enquiry which, if they are to be effective and to be carried out with the cooperation of the Member State concerned, will probably have to be conducted jointly between the parliamentary inquiry mechanism in the Member State and the inquiry mechanism of the Union assembly.

It is also unfortunately the case that the motivation of the Union assembly to inquire and investigate will be limited by other concerns. A focus on the assembly's powers to inquire and investigate is one that will run counter to some of the Assembly's instincts. The Union assembly has an interest in measures being undertaken collectively in Europe. Thus it will not welcome those investigations – particularly into the effects of previously approved Union measures – that may expose the flaws in collective action. In such cases the Union assembly will be motivated to cover up rather than expose. Here the motivation in the Member States to investigate the shortcomings of European measures (other than when they involve the receipt of money) may be stronger.

The need to involve national parliaments in the scrutiny and review function for holding the Government of Europe to account is reinforced by the fact that members of the Government of Europe will still remain answerable to their own national parliaments. As mentioned above, as long as the parliamentary majority is secure, the parliaments of the Member States will not in practice be able to dismiss their government for any perceived mishandling of their part in the development of Union measures in the Council. Dismissal through the loss of a parliamentary majority on European issues is likely to be rare. But the other ways open to representative assemblies to pinpoint the responsibility of their government for the way it handles Union measures, such as through debate and questioning, will remain available and important. Thus, in the same way as the Union assembly will look to hold the Government of Europe to account through the means of investigation and inquiry, so too will the parliaments of European Member States look to the same means for holding their representative on the Council to account.

Although the means of holding governments to account will be the same, the perspectives of the Union assembly and the parliaments of Member States will differ. From the standpoint of the people, the voters, these differences are desirable – they will add to the sum of information made available. At the same time there will be some occasions where there will be advantages for the people if the Union assembly and assemblies in the Member States pool their investigatory efforts.

(ii) Policy making

In so far as assemblies provide a channel to reflect the wishes of the populace (in addition to the electoral preferences shown in choosing the party of government) they have a claim to have a say in the formation of public policy. As discussed earlier, the core responsibility for public policy in Europe rests with the Government (the Council) the members of which have their own electoral legitimacy. There is no case for Europe's representative assembly to try to exercise an 'overriding' influence in the formation of collective policy. However, this does not mean that the representative body should not try to influence it at all.

The most traditional and historic method through which representative bodies have tried to influence public policy is by withholding the supply of funds necessary to carry on government. In modern terms this relates to the power of assemblies over budgets. In any Member State a government that cannot get approval for its budget cannot continue in office. By contrast, in a system where there is a separation of powers, the assembly cannot bring down the government by refusing to pass the budget. This will be the situation in the European Union. The Union assembly will not be able to bring down the Government of Europe (the Council) by refusing to pass the budget. In theory, the assembly could still deny the legal base on which European financial programmes operate and thus bring them to a halt. In practice, assemblies are unlikely to wish to exercise such a draconian power and it constitutes a weak threat. The more important provision is that of the 'continuing resolution'. If the Union assembly does not wish to approve the budget, the Government of Europe would be able to continue existing programmes only at levels previously authorized. This too is a weak threat. The Union assembly is more likely to have a desire to spend than a desire to curtail the Union budget.

Although in practice the Union assembly is unlikely to wish to derail the Union budget, the fact that the Government of Europe does not depend for its existence on the vote of the Union assembly, means again that the assembly will feel much freer to shape the budget. It will have its own public policy objectives and its own client relationships to foster. Thus, within the overall budget total and timetable for approval it will try (within other restraints) to influence categories of expenditure. This is a stronger power than that exercised by many national parliaments over their budgets.

While the ability of the Union assembly to influence categories of expenditure may provide a check on the spending preferences of the Government of Europe, there are reasons to limit the influence of the Union assembly over Union spending and thus over the shaping of Union policies that depend on that expenditure. First, there is the inherent tendency of any European assembly to wish to expand Union expenditures. Thus the effective control on the Government of Europe in respect of overall spending can only come through other means. Such other means are provided by limits expressed in the constitution itself which restrict the total size of the Union budget (for example, in relation to the GNP of the Union or the net contributing countries). They are also provided through ensuring that resources for the Union budget flow through the Member States. In this way the governments of the Member States have to justify the allocation of funds for Union purposes to their own assemblies in the context of alternative domestic uses or of tax decreases. Second, there is the likelihood that the Union assembly will be a less than vigorous investigator of how monies are spent. Because of its interest in expanding Union activities the Union assembly is unlikely to wish to investigate too closely whether expenditures from the Union budget have been used productively or for the purposes intended. The Court of Auditors provides for an independent review of such questions. However its influence will be limited and its reports largely ignored unless linked more effectively to other mechanisms for expenditure control. Again there is a case for the parliaments in Member States to have a share in the oversight role – particularly those parliaments of the Member States that are net contributors to the budget.

Influence over the budget is not the only way in which the Union assembly will be able to influence the formation of public policy in the Union. But it illustrates the enhanced possibilities that a separation of powers brings. At the same time, it illustrates the need to recognize the shortcomings in the way in which influence will be used – shortcomings that can in part be made up by a continuing role for the parliaments of Member States. Outside the budget function, the main occasion for assemblies to influence public policy is in the context of particular pieces of legislation that a government wishes to carry through.

(iii) Influencing legislation

On the whole, the law making powers of most parliaments in Europe are weak. Usually draft laws are prepared and formulated in the government machine and legislation is initiated by the government. Furthermore, the amendment powers of parliaments and the power of parliaments to block legislation are restricted by the need for members of the governing party or coalition to support the government.

In theory the separation of powers in Europe enables the Union assembly to amend and defeat the proposed legislation of Europe's Government without destroying the Government. The assembly loses the power to approve or dismiss the Government but potentially gains the power to exercise much greater influence in the law making process.[5] As with the budget, it can change proposed legislation without bringing down governments. How much influence should it have and how should that influence be exercised?

There are four channels through which an assembly can influence the law making process: through the formation and initiation of proposed laws; through the amendment of laws initiated by the government; through the power to block or veto and through the review of the implementation, workings and impact of previous legislation.

(a) The right of initiative There are in fact strong reasons why the Union assembly should not have the power to initiate.

- First, large representative bodies are not well suited to the formulation and preparation of legislation. They are unlikely to contain the expertise or knowledge needed and will turn instead to organized lobby groups for assistance. This will undermine their claim to represent the electorate at large.

- Second, it is a power that is likely to be used too actively. There is no limit to imaginative proposals which a large body cannot dream up for a cause close to the heart of one member or another.
- Third, the Union assembly may not be the best body to judge whether legislation is actually needed since it is operating at a high level of generality. This can be mitigated if the assembly confines itself to the preparation of general 'framework' legislation. But this does not overcome the problem of legislative responses that are inappropriate to the circumstances. Moreover, framework legislation is, because of its generality, more likely to overstep jurisdictional responsibilities.
- Fourth, it confuses where responsibility lies for the overall direction of policy. In the United States the responsibility for the preparation and initiation of legislation is in practice shared between the President and Congress. As a device to prevent rapid or abrupt changes in legislation and the policy framework, the sharing of responsibilities is a success. But as a means to make clear where responsibility lies for a measure, it is a weakness. It allows for endless evasion of responsibility. It provides the pass key for the lobbyists.
- Finally, initiatives from the Union assembly are likely to provide a constant testing of the limits of the jurisdictional domain of what should be a matter for collective European legislation and what should be left either to the international domain or to the Member States. Members of the Union assembly will be predisposed in one way – to favour the Union domain.

An alternative approach is to allow the Union Assembly the right to initiate but with a strong 'filter' mechanism that allows initiatives to be severely pruned or even stopped. Such a filter mechanism could be provided if the Government of Europe had a procedure to decide whether to include the assembly initiative in its programme. The need for this kind of filter adds to the complications of the legislative process while leaving untouched the fundamental reasons why the Union assembly should not possess the right of initiative.

(b) The right of amendment An assembly that does not have the power to make or break governments, or the power to initiate legislation, has little means left to influence public policy unless it has the power to amend legislation. The case for saying that the core function of the Union assembly should lie in the power to amend legislation is that it gives teeth to its investigation of proposed Union laws and cause for its other functions to command attention. It takes advantage of the greater scope available to an assembly when a government does not depend on the assembly's approval of its laws for its survival.

At the same time the right of amendment is probably a power that should be framed for only occasional and sparing use. Many of the arguments why the Union assembly should not possess the right of legislative initiative apply also against the over frequent use of any power to amend legislation. Moreover, in the case of Europe, the assembly may not have sufficient knowledge of the background in the individual Member States to be able to propose sensible amendments. The importance of the Permanent Representatives in relation to the proceedings of the Council of Ministers is linked to the need to bring administrative expertise from each Member State to bear on the preparation of Union measures. If the power to amend is to be framed only for occasional use, then a high majority and not just a simple majority, should be needed for amendments to pass.

(c) The power to block The key aspect of an assembly's power to block concerns where the 'last word' in the legislative process should lie – with the assembly or with the government. If the government is to carry the main responsibility for the direction of policy there is much to be said for the government having easily exercisable powers to veto amendments with which it is not in agreement. Here too the Union assembly might be required to muster a special majority (say three quarters) in order to prevail. This would ensure that the power to block would be used only on rare occasions and for issues of the greatest importance. In this way its use would not cloud perceptions that as a general practice the Government would be responsible for policy. The need for a high majority for the blocking of the Government's legislative proposals would also act as a deterrent to special interests aiming to block policy.

There is a case for saying that constitutional arrangements that provide for habitual stalemate between the representative assembly and a government bring about a generally desirable state of affairs. It prevents the system of government from doing anything. However, gridlock can also lead to frustration and contempt for a system of government. This is not a risk to be taken in Europe by conferring any routine power to block on the Union assembly.

There are important organizational consequences for an assembly with the power to amend and block legislation, even when such powers are to be used sparingly.

One is the resulting importance of the committee structure since it will be committees, rather than the assembly as a whole, that will be suited to investigate and amend legislation. Most of the work of the existing European Parliament is carried out in committee. This tendency will become even more pronounced.

A second implication is the need for a management process that steers the legislation in the assembly and manages differences with the government. In a system with a separation of powers, the management process for steering legislation lies in the first instance with party leaders in the assembly as a whole and in the committees. In the United States it is a role carried out by congressional leaders with seniority in the relevant committee or in the House or influential with blocks of votes. However, on contentious or major pieces of legislation, congressional leaders will be in direct liaison with the President's 'point men' at the White House or elsewhere in the administration. At present in Europe the role of managing the relationship between Council and the existing European Parliament is in most part carried out by the Commission. This role for the Commission is inappropriate. It further confuses which body is responsible for legislation. It is a relic of the Commission's aspirations to become the Government of Europe. It is a role to be performed by the Presidency of the Council in direct liaison with leaders of the assembly.

The third important implication is that the assembly will become the target of organized pressure groups and all those who wish to influence the content of the legislation. In this respect the Union assembly will again become much closer to the American Congress. In the case of Congress the activities of lobby groups have done much to undermine public confidence in Congress. Among the techniques which could help prevent the Union assembly falling into disrepute because of the perceived powers of lobby groups is the use of term limitations. If members were made subject to term limitations (of two to three terms maximum) this would remove the re-election constraint on members in their final term but it would also severely reduce the extent to which it would pay a lobby group to 'invest' in a member.

(d) The review of the impact of legislation The ability of the Union assembly to amend or block the legislative proposals of the Government of Europe, even if limited to rare occasions, will place it in a stronger position than many national parliaments whose ability to amend or block the initiatives of their own governments is usually restricted by the need to sustain a government in office. The framing of new legislation is always a more glamorous occupation than the review of whether past legislation is working in the manner intended or not. Yet it is the less glamorous activity that may be the more important. It is the review of past legislation that reveals the mistakes and unintended consequences of legislation. It is the short-comings of past approaches which motivates and frequently shapes the form of new initiatives. As with the review of the impact of European budget expenditures, the parliaments of the Member States will be better placed to judge the impact of European legislation within their own Member State. It is this experience that will often influence the position carried by their own government into the Council in proposing or considering new initiatives. It is important to mobilize this experience in framing the role of representative assemblies in a European system of government.

(iv) The forum role

The 'forum' or 'tribune' role of a representative assembly consists in the power to hold debates on matters of public concern, or of concern to the assembly, and to give vent to grievances.[6] It provides a way of educating or preparing public opinion, channelling demands, signalling injustices, flagging problems or generally warning government when it is stepping on toes. In carrying out this set of functions, a modern representative assembly is coming close to the traditional view of an assembly as intermediary between the government and the people. The assembly acts as a channel of communication.[7] In modern societies this role is mainly carried out by the media, as long as the media is not deferential to those who govern. Nevertheless, this function remains important for an assembly because it provides a way in which the representative body can act to mobilize support for a system of government and to integrate the concerns of the people.[8]

In the context of European political integration, the Union assembly has an important part to play in exercising this traditional role. In bringing together elected representatives in one body it performs a highly visible integrative function. By encouraging the formation of pan-European political parties, or other groupings that themselves act as channels of communication, it encourages the integrative process in other ways as well.

The influence that an assembly will have in exercising its forum role will crucially depend on the actual powers the assembly will have on public policy formation and the passage of legislation. Otherwise there is very little reason for any notice to be taken of the assembly's debates or investigations.[9] It is this consideration that underlies the need for the Union assembly to have some real powers to influence the policy making and legislative process. Moreover, the separation of powers gives the Union assembly a freedom of action not available to national parliaments. It is sensible to take advantage of this freedom in Europe's system of government. Even so, it remains the case that the powers of the Union assembly should be limited. It is important not to confuse the core responsibility of the Government of Europe for policy. It is equally important to recognize that the powers of the Union assembly must be framed in the context of a system for distributing powers between jurisdictions that provides the parliaments of Member States with an ongoing role in holding members of the Council to account. It is also clear from a review of the functions of representative assemblies that many of the key functions that can be performed by representative bodies are best seen in Europe as roles more effectively performed when undertaken together by the Union assembly and the parliaments of the Member States.

The sharing of roles occurs across each of the main functions that are performed by representative bodies:

- in the investigative and inquiry role for holding governments to account;
- in the policy making role, including budget formation and expenditure review;
- in the law influencing role, in particular in the review of the impact of past legislation;
- in the forum role. Even in the case of the 'integrative' function national parliaments will remain important for shaping attitudes about Europe.

It follows from this that the Union assembly should not be seen in isolation as the means to legitimize a European system of government by itself. In many respects its legitimizing role as a representative body will be shared with the parliaments of the Member States. Moreover, there is one fundamental task in the legitimization of a system of government to which the Union assembly is not well suited at all. That task is in the 'constitutional' role of keeping Union institutions within the rules. As discussed earlier, in a system of distributed powers in Europe the Union assembly is likely itself to be a major source of challenge to the rules. In so far as representative bodies have a role to play in the keeping of the rules of a constitution, the incentives favour a role for the parliaments of Member States.

Parliamentary legitimization of a European system of government is thus not a matter of giving as much power as possible to the Union assembly. It is a matter of arranging the relationships between the Union assembly and the parliaments of the Member States in ways which respect their comparative advantage in perform-ing the different functions of representative assemblies. Legitimization rests on being able to bring together their roles. The question of how this relationship can best be expressed is discussed next.

III The relationship between assemblies

The strength which the representative bodies of the Member States can bring to the legitimization of a European system of government lies potentially in the rule keeping function, in the inquiry and investigation function (particularly in respect of the review of past legislation and expenditures) and, in addition, as contributors to the policy formation function, where parliaments will influence opinion gener-ally and their representatives on the Council in particular. Moreover, they have a necessary role to play in the provision of financing.

The weakness of the representative bodies of the Member States is that each of these functions is performed at present by each parliament in isolation from the other parliaments in the other Member States. As a collective force their influence is diffused and often invisible. In addition, the relationship with a Union assembly is often seen as a competing one. Similarly, the existing European Parliament is inclined to see roles as competitive. Thus the gains to be achieved from viewing the roles of representative assemblies in combination are lost from sight.

In order to strengthen the role which representative assemblies can play in the legitimization of Europe's system of government, the representative assemblies of the Member States must develop ways of working together. In addition, for certain purposes, the assemblies of Member States and the Union assembly should carry out some functions jointly. The mechanisms to achieve either have not yet been found. The attempt to hold a 'grand assize' between the parliaments of Member States and the existing European Parliament was not a success. It is a misconceived formulation of the relationship. Large meetings are inappropriate for the functions suited for sharing. At the same time, cooperation between the parliaments of

Member States has advanced only as far as the periodic meetings of members of European scrutiny committees (COSAC).

The avenues available for redressing this situation are as follows:

- increased liaison between the parliaments of the Member States;
- increased use of coordinating committees between the parliaments of the Member States;
- joint committees of the Union assembly and some or all of the parliaments of the Member States;
- a standing committee of the parliaments of the Member States.

These arrangements represent different degrees of formality in working together. The standing committee approach essentially involves the setting up of a chamber of parliamentarians drawn from the parliaments of the Member States. It thus would bring the arrangements in the Union to a bicameral system. It is therefore discussed below in these terms.

(i) Increased liaison

The advantages of the parliaments of Member States increasing their liaison on European measures are undeniable. At the same time, there is a case for a 'minimalist' approach that does not interfere with their different working habits, traditions and structures and which creates no new institutions. The disadvantage is that minimalism is unlikely to lead to effective results. First, unless working habits on European issues are in some way aligned, and consideration by the relevant committees or full assemblies more formally coordinated, individual review and scrutiny by each parliament acting separately will fail to reap the advantages to be derived from the sharing of experiences or from better knowledge of the attitudes of others. Second, unless the attitudes of the parliaments of Member States can be expressed collectively, their viewpoints can only be expressed through their government representatives on the Council. This severely diminishes the role of representative bodies.

(ii) Coordinating committees

The next step up in formalizing relationships on European issues would be to develop a system of coordinating committees meeting as needed on particular topics. The existing committee (COSAC) could meet more frequently so as to bring together the views of the European scrutiny committees in each parliament. Furthermore, such meetings need not be limited to COSAC. Other relevant specialized committees in the parliaments of Member States (for example, on agriculture, the budget, immigration or on foreign policy) could also meet from time to time. This system too would have the advantage of trying to make as much use as possible of existing structures. In so far as the committees were important in their own parliamentary structures a joint committee statement representing the committees of all or several parliaments would carry some collective weight.

Again there must be some doubts about the effectiveness of such a system. The influence of committees in the different parliaments varies – as too does their exact relationship with their parliament as a whole and with the government of the Member State. Moreover, the collective impact of a coordinating committee will not be clear unless the status of each of its members and of their collective deliberations is clear.

Clarification of 'status' has two rather different aspects. One aspect of 'status' is whether a parliamentarian attending a coordinating meeting does so purely in a 'personal' capacity or whether the parliamentarian in some way carries a 'representative' responsibility in speaking on behalf of a committee, or a parliamentary party, or on behalf of the parliament as a whole. The second aspect concerns the status of the outcomes of such meetings. Is each member to carry back into their own parliament their own impression from such meetings, or are there to be 'agreed' statements. If positions are to be agreed, is the aim to reach a consensus, or to reach an agreement weighing the views of the representatives on an equal basis, or according to the voting weight of their government in the Council or on some other basis?

Even if members on the committees perform a representative role and agreed outcomes can be reached on an agreed weighted voting system, there remains still the question of whether the outcome will be heeded or not. Yet unless the outcome has to be taken into account in some visible and effective way it is most unlikely that the incentives will be present to resolve the status of representation or the status of collective 'decisions' of the coordinating meetings.

(iii) Joint committees with the Union assembly

The difficult issues connected with the status of coordinating committees of the parliaments of Member States can perhaps be sidestepped in the formation of joint committees of national parliaments and the Union assembly. In all matters relating to the review of past legislation, the implementation of legislation, and the review of expenditures there is much to be said in favour of joint committees consisting both of members of the Union assembly together with members of the parliaments, or their committees, of the Member States. The members from national parliaments are more likely to bring a critical eye to the acts of the Union and their cooperation is in any event likely to be helpful in the preparation of relevant analysis. Not all parliaments in all Member States may wish to be represented on all inquiries. A committee that includes parliamentarians from all

Member States plus members of the Union assembly will, in any event, become rather cumbersome. But considerable flexibility would be possible in defining representation for particular investigations.

There will again be a question as to whether any attention will be paid to the findings of such joint committees. On the other hand, they will carry more authority than the inquiries either of an individual parliament of an individual Member State or of an inquiry of the Union assembly by itself.

The drawback of such committees is that their use is necessarily limited to those areas, such as the review of past expenditures, where there is a clear advantage from a shared review. They are not suited to those areas where the parliaments of Member States may wish to coordinate their views at the stage of influencing their governments on the Council when a measure is at the formative stage. Here there may be considerable differences between the views of members of national parliaments and the views in the Union assembly. There will be differences both as to whether Union measures are needed and, if so, in what form. Nor are joint committees suited to the most fundamental task of all – the desirable role of the parliaments of Member States in reviewing whether the measures proposed by the Union are consistent with the jurisdictional responsibilities set out in the constitution.

(iv) Bicameralism

In the final analysis, the parliaments of the Member States will be able to exercise an effective collective voice only if Europe's constitution provides them with a formal role in Union procedures. This means a mechanism must be found to overcome the procedural obstacles in the way of effective cooperation on European issues. It also means that the results of cooperation must have a specific place in constitutional procedures. In effect, this means that some kind of standing committee is needed on which the status of representatives from the various parliaments of the Member States will be clear, and where the status of the outcome of the committee's deliberations will have to be taken formally into account by other bodies. To all intents and purposes it means establishing a committee of parliamentarians of the Member States as some kind of second chamber. The role of the representative bodies in the Union would be formalized in a bicameral system.

In the discussion that follows the two chambers will be referred to as the assembly of parliamentarians or as the directly elected assembly. This avoids the use of terms such as 'upper' or 'lower' assemblies and 'first' or 'second' chambers which can reflect a variety of different functions and relationships in different national contexts.

Most European countries have two representative assemblies. In a bicameral system where the basis of representation is the same and the functions are the same, the likely result is to add to the time and costs of activities for no obvious gain. Unless there is a clear division of functions, a system of primacy to establish which assembly shall prevail becomes necessary. Thus, a bicameral system that adds value to the deliberative process offers either a clearly different basis of representation, or the assemblies perform somewhat different functions, or preferably they differ in both respects. As mentioned above, in cases where the interests of the Union assembly and the parliaments of the Member States are shared, the formalities of a bicameral system can be avoided by setting up joint committees. The purposes of a bicameral system are to address those situations where interests and functions differ.

(a) Differences in interests The representation of the parliaments of Member States in a bicameral system is not the only basis available for reflecting different interests in the Union. Differences in interests could be represented by different economic and social interests, such as agriculture and industry or business and labour, or by different geographical interests. The former pattern is reflected in embryonic form by the Economic Community's ECOSOC. The latter pattern could be reflected by developing the representation of regional interests in those countries with a strong regional or state articulation.

Corporatist The representation of economic and social interests is subject to the same criticisms as can be made of corporatist theory. It entrenches transient interests. It is difficult to reflect interests other than those that are most organized – but they may not necessarily be representative. Organized interests are well placed in society to make their views known anyway. They will be the most active lobbyists of a directly elected assembly – the case to give them additional influence is weak. A second chamber thus should not be chosen on the basis of organized economic and social interests. The case for ECOSOC to remain in any shape or form among Union structures is poor.

Regional The case for developing the representation of regional interests in Europe is much stronger than for developing corporatist interests. However, not all Member States have strong regional identities. Even where they do exist, the basis is sometimes of quite recent origin. Moreover, regional identities exist in most cases alongside the identities of the Member State. What seems important is to make constructive use of what otherwise can be the most destructive force in Europe – national identities. This means looking to use the representative bodies of the Member States as the best way of reflecting diversities in Europe.

(b) Differences in function In order that the functions of the two chambers should be distinct and not duplicative, the assembly of parliamentarians would have a core function in vetting Union measures to ensure that they fell within the rules governing the distribution of powers. This would mean that its review of

legislation should come before proposals were finalized. A similar procedure would operate with the budget. Before final approval of spending plans under the Union budget, the assembly of parliamentarians would check that the budget had been drawn up in accordance with the expenditure limits and revenue raising procedures allowed for in the constitution. Its decision rules would be based on blocking minorities since its essential function would be to prevent unintended changes to the rules of political association in Europe.

There is a possibility of conflict between the two assemblies (of parliamentarians and the directly elected assembly) and also between the assembly of parliamentarians and the Government of Europe. This could happen wherever the measures proposed by the Council and approved or amended by the directly elected assembly were seen to overstep the jurisdictional limits. The final word on rule keeping would however have to rest with the assembly of parliamentarians.

Not all questions on which assemblies are called to approve or disapprove the actions of government involve legislation or finance. Notably there are powers to approve appointments and powers to approve treaties.

In some countries of Europe where the tradition of crown prerogatives remains strong (such as the UK) the parliament may not be involved in treaty ratification at all, except to the extent that it involves changes in legislation.

In Europe, treaties on subjects such as external trade, foreign affairs, security and defence matters involve two types of question. One is the matter of jurisdiction. They may involve matters of international rules and international law where the Union is not the optimum domain and where Member States wish to retain direct involvement. Second, they involve matters where a high qualified vote is likely to be needed in government decision taking – i.e. matters where the voice of the Member State will remain particularly strong. For both these reasons the function of approving treaties should properly rest with the assembly of parliamentarians.

(c) Status in the assembly of parliamentarians As mentioned above, the creation of a formal standing committee (or chamber) of national parliamentarians, with clearly defined functions suited to the parliaments of the Member States but not easily exercised by the parliaments of the Member States acting on their own, would need to overcome the issues concerning the basis of representation in the chamber. A deliberate tilt towards the overrepresentation of smaller Member States (as in the Senate of the United States) can be justified.[10] The smaller Member States, no less than the larger, are agreeing to delegate powers in specified areas. In respect of the standing of individual members of the chamber, different practices could be followed. Some might come with instructions from their parliaments. Others might be given much greater flexibility by their parliament, or by their parliamentary party, to act in a representative capacity. Recall should always be possible at any time.

One possible objection to a bicameral system for Europe, where one of the chambers represents the parliaments of the Member States, is that it gives the parliaments of the Member States an influence at two stages in the representative process. They influence the position taken by their ministers in the Council of Ministers. They subsequently watch over the rules in the law and treaty making process. However, such a system recognizes that the different facets of the legitimization of European government within a system of distributed powers cannot be encompassed by the directly elected Union assembly alone. In one way or another the role of the parliaments of the Member States has to be recognized in a formal way in Europe's constitution. It provides an avenue for keeping government close to the people. It provides also one of the few institutional means to ensure that the role of the representative bodies of the Member States in a system of multiple jurisdictions can be recognized and sustained.

IV Institutional overview

This discussion of how Europe's constitution should define institutional arrangements started by establishing the importance of defining the core functions of the different branches of a system of government as well as the importance of identifying key relationships in a system of distributed powers.

The analysis has suggested that the role of governments should be defined around their policy making function. The Government of Europe should be provided by the Council of Ministers acting in conjunction with the European Council. The Commission should perform an agency function, with its ability to influence policy resting on how well it can act as intermediary and honest broker in facilitating the work of the Council. The analysis also suggested that the different tasks of representative assemblies centre around the concept of legitimization. This legitimizing role is best seen as provided by the parliaments of the Member States and the Union assembly together – not as a function that can rest on the Union assembly alone.

In the discussion of the core function of constitutional oversight, a distinction was made between the rule keeping role and the role of ensuring the uniform application of Union law. It was suggested that Europe should maintain a representative system of oversight rather than follow the American example of judicial oversight. A distinction was also made between arrangements aimed at blocking unintended changes to the rules and arrangements which centre on amendments to the rules. It was suggested that areas of interpretation where unintended changes were most likely to occur could be identified in advance (for example, over the use of implied powers) and that unintended changes should be preventable by blocking minorities. By contrast, changes to the rules should require high majorities. While the governments of the Member States (for example, by a vote in the European Council) might trigger a blocking procedure, it seems important that their parliaments should also be involved. This can be achieved either by

parliaments acting individually to endorse or deny a blocking procedure instigated by the Government, or, if a chamber of parliamentarians were established,
the chamber could exercise such a role. There would, in any event, be a case for
allowing for popular initiatives, outside the discretion of governments, as a means
of blocking unwanted changes of for triggering amendments to the rules.

This definition and attribution of core functions illuminates the key relationships to be defined by Europe's constitution. The Government of Europe will
reflect a coalition of interests of the Member States and entail a separation of
powers between the Government and the Union assembly. Legitimization of the
system of government is best expressed in a bicameral relationship between the
representative bodies in those instances where the responsibilities cannot be
carried out jointly. The discussion of the constitutional oversight function also
highlighted the need to maintain a continuing relationship between the contracting parties to the constitution and subsequent rule keeping and rule changing
arrangements.

In its broad pattern, a European system of government arranged along these
lines would fit within a spectrum of constitutional experience in plural societies
around the world.[11] Its particular shape and the articulation of particular components however, arise from trying to ensure that institutional arrangements are not
regarded as independent choices but are fully consistent with non-coercive constitutional processes and with a rule based system of government. The suggestions
necessarily have grown from Europe's own traditions and historical environment.
If Europe's institutions are to endure, they must continue to draw support from the
best parts of that tradition and history.

Notes

1   'What such bodies have in common is that they are constitutionally designated
    institutions for giving assent to binding measures of public policy, that assent being
    given on behalf of a political community that extends beyond the government elite
    responsible for formulating those measures'. Norton, P. (ed) (1990), 'General Introduc-
    tion' in *Legislatures*.

2   The focus of much traditional analysis was on the 'law making role' of parliaments,
    leading to inattention to other functions. See Norton, P. 'Parliaments: a Framework for
    Analysis', in Norton, P. (ed) (1990), *Parliaments in Western Europe*.

3   'This traditional way of distinguishing between the two systems is more theoretical
    than real, for the right of dissolution did not exist even in some of the best known
    'parliamentary' systems'. Blondel, J. (1973), *Comparative Legislatures*.

4   'It is no more reasonable to expect legislatures to be involved in making and unmaking
    governments in a detailed and recurrent fashion. It is true that there should be a
    relationship between the legislative and the executive. . . But the dependence of the
    executive on the legislature cannot be expected to be very strong, for if it were, the
    consequence would be a series of upheavals'. Blondel, ibid.

5   'There is no doubt that constitutional separation of powers tends to give the legislature
    more strength and independence vis à vis the executive than does fusion of powers'.

Lijpart, A. (1984), *Democracies*.

6   'I know not how a representative assembly can more usefully employ itself than in talk, when the subject of talk is the great public interests of the country, and every sentence of it represents the opinion of some important body of persons in the nation, or of an individual in which some such body have reposed their confidence. A place where every interest and shade of opinion in the country can have its cause even passionately pleaded, in the face of the government and of all other interests and opinions, can compel them to listen, and either comply or state clearly why they do not, is in itself, if it answered no other purpose, one of the most important political institutions that can exist anywhere, and one of the foremost benefits of free government'. Mill, J.S. (1861), *Representative Government*.

7   'The function of the legislature is to provide a means of ensuring that there are channels of communication between the people and the executive'. Blondel, op. cit.

8   See, Norton, P. (1990), *Legislatures in Western Europe*.

9   'Assemblies cannot achieve their communication functions unless they have legal powers of decision, any more than they can do so if they try to insist on exercising these decision powers often'. Blondel, op. cit.

10   In the US Senate the small states of the Union remain overrepresented in proportion to their population. The most favourably represented five per cent of the population in the United States have twenty eight per cent of representation in the Senate. See, Lijpart, A. (1977), *Democracy in Plural Societies*.

11   These institutional arrangements, together with constitutionally protected procedures relating to the limits of political action, and together with the decision rules described, would bring Europe's system of government close to the eight characteristics of Lijpart's consensus model of democracy for a plural society:

- the government will represent a broad coalition of interests;
- there will be a separation of powers between government and assembly;
- there will be bicameralism with minority representation;
- Europe's multi-party system will continue to evolve;
- parties will likely remain multi-dimensional and not be divided simply on a left-right spectrum;
- proportional representation will likely outnumber 'first past the post' methods of voting;
- multiple jurisdictions will be protected both by territorial and non-territorial mechanisms;
- there will be a written constitution requiring a special majority for amendments.

See, Lijpart, (1984). op. cit.

10 Conclusions

"'Troglodytes'", dit le roi, "les richesses vont entrer chez vous; mais je vous déclare que, si vous n'êtes pas vertueux, vous serez un des peuples les plus malheureux de la terre. . . Nous pouvons être unis par un beau lien; si vous êtes vertueux, je le serai; si je suis vertueux, vous le serez'". Charles de Secondat Montesquieu. *Lettres Persanes*, 1721.

Since the end of the Second World War, a tacit political agenda has existed in Europe – the search for a political framework to contain the rivalries of the nation states of Europe. Initially this search centred on the relationship between France and Germany and grew to include most of the countries of western Europe. The collapse of communism means that this search can now be conducted on a wider scale to include all countries in Europe. Because of its central geographical location, its size and its economic strength, the position of Germany is pivotal and the search must include its neighbours in central and eastern Europe.

An overt political agenda has always been seen as likely to be divisive. Political integration has thus been sought through other means – above all through the means of economic integration. There are some who feel that continued pursuit of the economic agenda – in particular monetary union – still provides the way ahead to political union. Moreover, new objectives, notably the need to refashion security and defence arrangements in Europe, are also seen as additional vehicles for sustaining the momentum towards the underlying goal of political union.

The assumption that political integration in Europe can continue to be pursued through indirect methods is a false one. It insults the instincts and intelligence of the peoples of Europe. It provokes a myriad of ill-defined and contradictory fears. It stimulates irrational opposition. It aggravates the tensions between the ties of the old political order that are under challenge and the ties of the new order of political association which have yet to be firmly established.

The task of putting in place a durable political union in Europe must be confronted openly. In order to bring out the issues involved, this book has placed them in the context of a discussion about the shaping of a constitution for Europe.

Whether, in practice, European political union should be approached step by step, or through the pursuit of a more ambitious constitutional settlement, is a secondary question. Even incremental change needs to be guided by an informing vision. Otherwise, even small steps may be in the wrong direction. In the meantime, the existing treaties act as a surrogate constitution, built for the different purpose of economic integration and unsuited as a foundation for political union.

The analysis has suggested that the approach to political integration should rest on the following ten elements:

(i) A clear statement of values

If a political union in Europe is to command assent it must reflect values that themselves command assent. It must do more than appeal to mutual interest. A sense of mutual interest is a necessary tie for political association but the ties of political union must also possess a deeper resonance.

A reluctance to engage in debate about what values are important in a constitution has led to a proliferation of expressions of value in the current treaty base. The existing approach to values is a muddle – it has been easier for treaty negotiators to 'throw everything in' rather than to sort out what the key values are, and in what particular contexts other expressions of value find their place. 'Consistency', 'solidarity', 'cohesion', 'social progress', 'social cohesion', 'the rights and interests' of citizens, 'ever closer union', maintaining the *acquis communautaire*, 'respect for the national identities of the Member States', and 'the principles of democracy' are among the values expressed in the present Treaty on European Union in the first title alone.

'Throwing everything in', is convenient for midnight political compromises but is not a lasting foundation for a political union. On the contrary, the net effect of such confusion is to put at risk all the essential elements of political association:

- one set of values can be set against another.
- some values will be used as a reason to override other values, without clear consideration as to whether there is an appropriate ordering and, if so, what that ordering should be.
- values that are about 'end states' (the desired outcomes of political union) are not distinguished from those that are about the processes to be upheld in the political union as it strives to attain its peoples' aspirations.

This confusion can only be resolved if it is recognized that the most important values in a constitution are those that underlie the processes of political association. Processes themselves must be valued.

(ii) Political union based on rules of restraint

A political association which gives primary emphasis to the processes of doing things together has to be based on a system of rules. These rules incorporate procedural values – the value to be attached to such qualities as participation, dialogue and transparency. They do not emphasize the attainment of outcomes. No system of government can guarantee outcomes. People would be foolish to believe that they can. A concentration on outcomes results in the processes by which the intended outcomes are to be reached being devalued.

Association in Europe rests at the present time on the basis of three treaties – the Treaty of Rome, the Single European Act and the Maastricht Treaty – each of which was constructed to achieve particular outcomes – the creation of a Common Market, the attainment of the Single Market and the basis for monetary union. The setting of such objectives may well have been the right approach for achieving economic integration in Europe. The treaties set out the mutual gains from unimpeded economic exchange for all to see. But targeting outcomes is the wrong approach to building a political union in Europe. The existing treaty base, its institutions and its procedures cannot serve as a basis for political union without substantial modification.

In a European political union, rules which emphasize procedural values can reflect the value of cooperation and the value of settling differences through exchange and bargaining, but they must also address the problem of the coercive powers of government. Here, as in the early United States, prudential values should prevail. The rules that establish the powers of government in a European political union should be framed as rules of restraint.

In a political union, people can willingly accept those rules of association which help bring about the gains from cooperation, or which encourage the settling of differences through bargaining. However, political association also involves rules that enforce and rules that impose solutions when interests and preferences conflict. Here the gains are not mutual – some interests will be winners and others losers. The dangers in any system of government lie in that same power to impose choice – whether it be a majority that imposes on a minority, or a minority that uses the power of government to impose on a majority. The danger is both from intolerant majorities and from dedicated minorities.

The fears about the processes in a political union in Europe centre on this power of coercion. Are the rules going to allow for a distant government to impose its preferences and the particular interests it reflects, into a society that seeks to combine, where combination makes sense, but which also holds dear a diversity of values, preferences and interests? This fear can only be put at rest if the rules of political association rest on prudential values that restrain the coercive powers of European government. The principle that summarizes the value of rules of restraint is that the processes in a European political union should minimize the coercive powers of European government.

Rules of prudence are not the same as moral rules. The reason prudential values should command respect is partly pragmatic – a political union that attempts to impose choice in an area of such diversity as Europe is likely to fail. The mutual gains from politics will thus also be lost.

However, rules of prudence in political association can be justified in relation to ethical standards. Rules that restrain government allow for ethical standards in society to be the subject of choice not the result of coercion. They recognize that moral choice is not imposed choice. Systems that do not coerce, allow for the evolution and reinterpretation of ethical relationships in society. Political processes that reflect rules of prudence help ensure that moral standards will not themselves become the victim of political association. They allow for the rules of political association to be constantly evaluated by ethical standards. They recognize that the ethical base of government must always be open to challenge. Government is never due unquestioned obedience.

(iii) Minimizing coercion

In a political order in Europe that values the processes of political association there are three areas vital to restrain the powers of government and to minimize imposed choice:

- a system of multiple jurisdictions must be maintained as a way of expressing differences, for determining the true costs and benefits of public policy and for establishing 'best practice';
- decision rules should be graduated around a system of voting that recognizes the differences in the relative importance of different decisions and which protects both small and large Member States. The system should offer protection to Member States against the risk that choices will be imposed in the areas of greatest concern to them;
- the limitations of politics as a means of resolving disputes about values should be recognized and limitations placed on politics in Europe's system of government in those areas where political choice is weakest.

(iv) A system of multiple jurisdictions

Europe's constitution needs to redefine the role of the nation state. This redefinition is to be found within a system of multiple jurisdictions. The nation state becomes the anchor for jurisdictions where national, regional and local preferences can be expressed robustly but, at the same time, a vehicle for the making of collective choices in Europe where necessary. Multiple jurisdictions provide a framework for a more accurate reflection of preferences in Europe, a means of testing the merits of different approaches to public policy and for establishing their true costs. The key task for the rules of the constitution in organizing the distribution of powers is to express the relationships between the different jurisdictions in a way that maintains distinction of choice between them but which eases collective action where that is needed.

In the present treaty base the relationship between jurisdictions remains unclear. The subsidiarity clause can be interpreted in two quite contrary ways. It can be seen as a doctrine about powers flowing down from the Union to subordinate jurisdictions, or about powers flowing upwards from the Member States and their regions. References to 'exclusive competence' of the Union (Art. 3b.) can be interpreted as trying to establish a hierarchy of powers headed by the Union, or as an attempt to establish an area of independent authority for the Union, or simply as an area where the Member States have agreed to delegate their powers for joint action. References to the maintaining and building on the *acquis* (Art. B) and to 'ever closer union' (Art. A) suggest a one way dynamic in the rules which can only erode the value to be attached to multiple jurisdictions. The main inspiration has been to extend the prerogatives of Union jurisdiction rather than to articulate a system of multiple jurisdictions.

The maintenance of a system of multiple jurisdiction means:

- a hierarchy of jurisdiction with powers cascading from the European level to subordinate lower levels should be avoided – lower level jurisdictions will soon find their responsibilities emasculated;
- the Union should not have independent powers and authority – they will be used to encroach progressively into the jurisdictional responsibilities of the Member States;
- powers exercised in Europe collectively should be only those expressly delegated by the Member States;
- those powers that are properly exercised by Europe collectively but which fit within a broader international domain, such as in respect of international trade or monetary arrangements or in respect of security or peace keeping arrangements, should be framed in a way to reflect this broader domain;
- jurisdictions with shared responsibilities should be minimized because they introduce the disadvantages of confused responsibilities and accountability at the same time as denying the advantages of different approaches in different jurisdictions.

The allocation of tasks between different jurisdictions should be seen as subordinate to the system of powers and power relationships that is intended. What is much more important is to articulate the relationship between the jurisdictions and to allow for specific functions to be exercised collectively where some or all of the Member States decide it is best to pool their efforts, and to be withdrawn when collective efforts do not work out. Specifying tasks in any too detailed way and on any permanent basis is a mistake. What can be done by the markets and what needs to be done through political choice will change over time. So too will what is done best collectively in Europe and what is done best by jurisdictions acting independently. The temptation to strike political compromises will lead to power sharing proposals which will undermine any clear system of responsibility and accountability. Politicians may gain but the people will lose.

(v) Decision taking methods based on concurrent majorities and critical mass

The way in which collective decisions are taken in Europe will be crucial to the acceptability of European political union by public opinion and for all other jurisdictions within the Union whether national, regional or local. Within a system of multiple jurisdictions, decision taking at the European level will have to take account of inequalities between Member States. The range of choice which will require collective decisions in Europe also involves great variations in the degree of importance of the choices – some will be routine economic regulations, others could involve the commitment of troops. These differences in choice mean that the jurisdictions delegating powers to the Union will regard the risks of having their own preferences outvoted as being very different in different areas.

Unanimous voting will be impractical and create a bias against action. Simple majorities fail to reflect inequalities between the choosers and between the choices. The decision taking rules will thus need to be centred on a system of qualified majority voting. The general approach will be one which minimizes the risks to participants of having choices imposed in the areas of the greatest importance to them. A system of concurrent majorities will be required reflecting both the number of Member States needed to block a decision or to form a decisive group, as well as the proportion of the population for which they account. For the most important decisions, both the small Member States and the large will need to have additional means to block an unwanted decision. This means that an additional third measure for the concurrent majority will be needed, which gives further protection to both small and large Member States.

Decision taking rules need not, and should not, insist on common action except in those rare cases where the opting out of one participant, even a small one, fatally undermines collective policy. Such instances will be rare. The problem of 'free riders' is a real one – but also one whose importance is often exaggerated. In most cases the relevant concept will be that of 'critical mass' – that necessary minimum of Member States needed to try out a collective policy. Collective policy in the Union will not be linked with one particular territorial boundary or with static boundaries.

Collective policy in a European political union is best suited to a relatively limited agenda where continuity in policy is important. Even with a limited agenda, collective policy in the Union will remain difficult to change and difficult to unwind. The decision rules can help counteract the tendency of powers to accumulate in the centre and for the Union institutions to ratchet up their authority. This can be done by making decisions which are deregulatory, or which do not impose costs, easier to take than those that do. In addition, it should be easier to return Union powers to the jurisdictions that have delegated them than it is to add to powers to be exercised collectively.

In cases where any Member State finds that the balance of attraction of membership no longer outweighs the attractions of independence, however illusionary that 'independence' may actually be, the possibility of secession should always be open. The Union must always remain a voluntary one.

(vi) Limits on collective choice

Not all values are shared across Europe. Even those values that are held in common are not always held with the same intensity. If politics provided a perfect means for expressing and settling such differences, political processes could be relied on to manage relationships between those holding different values. However, political processes are crude and can be manipulated. Not only can they not be relied upon to settle differences but political processes must themselves be limited.

Europe's constitution should therefore recognize in advance in its rules to:

- exclude the most contentious areas of choice, such as religion and language, from European political processes;
- limit declarations of rights to those that create a reserved area that separates individual life and civil liberties from politics;
- maintain specialized judicial procedures for the area reserved for individual and civil liberties so that their protection does not involve a general erosion of jurisdictional boundaries;
- provide specialized arrangements that counteract the pressures of the short term on political choice. This means having strong fiscal constraints as well as monetary constraints. If a constitutional protection could be found, the importance to be attached to the long term in decisions relating to the environment would also be desirable.

The alternative of entrusting a long list of social and human rights to the jurisdiction of the Union is to look to European government as the means to realize every human aspiration and to permit the processes of politics or the law to become the means of enforcing what is correct in the eyes of the majority of the moment. Such a Union will mismanage its economic and social choices. More important, where value differences involve ethical or moral questions, the identification of what is ethically correct with what is politically correct will inflame both law and politics, obliterate the boundaries between jurisdictions and blur the borders between individual choice and collective choice. Unless society has a high degree of uniformity in its choices the effect will be to overload political and judicial processes. Europe does not have that degree of uniformity.

In the present treaty, the limits that need to be placed on political processes remain poorly articulated. Limits on politics are recognized in some areas, such as monetary policy, but in other areas, such as the rights of citizens, the concept appears to be being developed as a reason for expanded political activism rather than the recognition of the need for a 'reserved' area. The tendency is to try to develop the concept of Union 'citizenship' to increase the grounds for intervention to cover all social aspirations. In addition, the rules of the market order are inconsistent – an attachment to free and open markets is 'balanced' by other criteria which modify the rules. Instead of reflecting a social concern that can be met through income support in the appropriate jurisdiction the result is to build political discretion into the rules of the market for Union bodies to exercise. The fiscal constitution is incomplete and leaves the way still open for the future to be mortgaged by the present.

Recognizing the limits of politics means that, along with an agreeable expression of diversities, there will also be values expressed that are disagreeable. Disagreeable values can be countered in part by the rules that establish thresholds for membership. There is, however, a contradiction between setting standards that must be met and allowing for plural values. The standards themselves therefore can legitimately relate to political pluralism such as freedom of expression but they cannot impose, either through political or judicial processes, any broader set of values. Acknowledging a diversity of values, beliefs and preferences within the Union means accepting that sometimes, and in some areas of the Union, there will be values expressed that are disagreeable to the majority. They will not only be expressed but, in a system that provides for multiple jurisdictions, they may also be acted upon in particular jurisdictions.

(vii) Institutions consistent with processes

The institutions of the European Union require composition, powers and relationships consistent with the value attached to getting the processes of political union right. Institutional choices are not free standing. The wrong institutional choices will destroy the processes that are valued.

The institutional debate is confused by a natural tendency to try to transpose the institutions of the Member States to Europe and by trying to fit European institutions into some mould that is familiar from national institutional arrangements. In practice, Europe's arrangements will be different and there is a need to return to look again at the principles of representative government.

There are two general theories about how powers and relationships might be arranged in Europe – a theory of mixed government and a theory of the separation of powers. The prevailing approach has been to emphasize the virtues of mixed government (where there is a fusion of powers between the government and representative assemblies) rather than the importance of the doctrine of the separation of powers. Theories of mixed government provide a convenient pretext for each major institution, Council, Commission and Parliament, to lay claim to their share in any activity without the need to clarify who should be doing what. However, the doctrine of the separation of powers remains crucial. This is because it emphasizes the need to define core functions precisely in Europe's system of government. Equally important is its emphasis on the need to define in a precise way the exact relationships between those bodies exercising core functions. It creates a presumption against one body having too much influence in the core responsibilities of another. It provides a means to ensure that institutional roles and relationships are specified in ways consistent with fundamental procedural values.

In the present treaty base, unfortunately, fundamental weaknesses remain in each of the basic areas where constitutional clarity is most needed. The definition of core functions and key institutional relationships remains grossly inadequate – disputes about the core functions of the Commission and the Council of Ministers have been papered over rather than resolved. 'Codecision' procedures confuse responsibilities between Council, Commission and Parliament in the legislative process because of a more fundamental failure to sort out the proper relationship between the Government of Europe and the assembly. The relationships between the institutions of the Member States and the institutions of the Union – particularly in respect of parliaments and constitutional oversight remain unarticulated. How to establish constitutional oversight of the rules of a European political union has never been addressed in depth.

Moreover, so far in the current treaty arrangements, institutions in the European Union have been approached primarily as instruments to achieve ends. The interrelationship between institutions and processes has frequently been ignored. A single clause in the Treaty of Rome (Art. 235) allows the institutions to take action in any area of the Common Market; under the Maastricht Treaty the Union is defined primarily in terms of its objectives (Art. B) and once again a single clause (Art. F3) gives the Union a general latitude to 'provide itself with the means necessary to attain its objectives and carry through its policies', without any reference to checks or balances or due process. As a result of viewing institutions simply as instruments to carry out certain ends, the Commission has been entrusted with a combination of functions quite incompatible with rule based systems of government. A similar approach to viewing institutions primarily as implementing bodies also inspires the opening provisions dealing with both the Council of Ministers and the Court of Justice. European political union requires a fundamentally different approach to defining the core functions of the main institutions and to clarifying their relationships.

(viii) Policy direction under the Council

It is the function of Europe's government to set and carry through the direction of public policy in the Union in those cases where collective action is warranted and to be in charge of the legislative programme where legislation is needed. It should be the responsibility of the European Council and Council of Ministers to reflect the coalition of interests involved in determining collective policy in the Union. The conception of the appointed Commission belongs to an elitist tradition of government that has no place in Europe. An elected Commission would lead to a centralization of politics in the Union incompatible with a diversity of jurisdictions.

(ix) Legitimization based on bicameralism

In a modern system of government, representative bodies perform a number of functions which centre on a core role in helping to legitimize or to challenge the legitimacy of government action. The European Parliament will not have the possibility of dismissing the Council of Ministers. Individual members on the Council will remain answerable to their own parliaments. National parliaments thus will need to keep involved in activities which help legitimize or challenge the legitimacy of acts of the Council.

The European assembly will gain the freedom of action allowed by a separation of powers. In principle this allows for a more balanced relation to develop between government and assemblies. In particular, the European assembly has an important 'integrative' function to perform. Yet, in looking at the different functions that can be performed by a European assembly it is clear that certain functions, particularly those of scrutiny and review, will be better performed jointly with the representative bodies in the Member States.

In addition, there is an important function of 'rule keeping' for which the European Parliament is not a safe pair of hands. This different function involves checking whether collective measures are needed, that they fall within the powers expressly delegated for the purposes of collective action and that correct procedures for their exercise are being followed.

For these different reasons it is important for methods to be found which will give national parliaments, as well as the European assembly, a formal and an effective voice in legitimizing the acts of the Union government. This can be achieved either by arrangements to coordinate national parliaments acting individually, or by their coming together in a standing committee or chamber. Whichever means is chosen for formalizing the role of national parliaments, essentially a bicameral system of legitimization will be established.

(x) Representative methods of oversight

The function of constitutional oversight means both preventing unintended change and allowing for a process of considered change. Judicial methods are not appropriate in Europe for this purpose. Europe cannot risk any confusion between the role of courts in implementing laws and the different task involved in overseeing a rule based system of government. Courts have an important role in keeping governments within legal bounds. But the rules of a constitution are not the same as laws – they set out the political and legal framework for association including (in Europe's case) that of defining the scope for Union law.

The least unsatisfactory method of oversight is to ensure the continuing involvement of the contracting parties to a constitutional agreement. Governments need to be able to trigger a process involving their parliaments and their peoples. The process of preventing unintended changes under the rules should be through the use of blocking minorities (either in the European Council or by a sufficient number of national parliaments or their chamber) in those areas where interpretative difficulties can be expected to arise (for example, in relation to implied powers). The process of considered changes to the rules should take place at periodic intervals of, for example, twenty years and involve high majorities to approve changes.

Ultimately, the maintenance of constitutional rules and values must depend on the people themselves. Elements of direct democracy need to be incorporated into the arrangements for European political union. Their place lies not only in relation to the arrangements for periodic constitutional review but also in allowing for popular initiatives if constitutional provisions appear to be being ignored.

* * * * *

The evident shortcomings of the present treaties as a basis on which to found an enduring political union in Europe are regarded by the opponents of European political union with equanimity. To those hostile to, or fearful of, political union the shortcomings guarantee the ultimate failure of the endeavour. There is, however, another alternative – not that political union will fail but, instead, that Europe will tread a gradual and unwitting path to a form of political union where freedom will not prosper. The virtues of political compromise will be extolled; the most admirable objectives will be held out as goals; an array of praiseworthy values will be expressed; the most benign labels will be attached to the arrangements. But amidst these benign appearances the most important lesson will be lost. Politics is not benign. Governments fail their peoples. People fall short of their best intentions.

Constitutions stand as a barrier against the frailties of the political process. They are a narrow barrier. They cannot alter human nature. They can at best provide a thin line of defence against the effects of weaknesses in human behaviour.

Constitutional restraints on political behaviour have all the imperfections of self-imposed constraints. But the defences are needed. The mutual benefits to be derived in Europe from the processes of political cooperation, as well as the gains to all shades of opinion in Europe if differences can be reconciled through political bargaining, are too great to ignore. If the gains are to be harvested then the risks of political union must be run. The risks lie in the coercive powers of political association – the powers of government to impose choices where differences cannot be reconciled. The overriding task of a constitutional settlement for Europe is to define those processes that will enhance the prospect of mutual gains but minimize the scope for choices to be imposed.

Over the next decade the peoples of Europe have the chance to build a political union that will bind together all the countries of Europe. It will not be an association limited just to economic objectives. Neither need it be limited to just a few countries. The existing treaties of the current European Union do not provide the base for that political union. On the contrary, if carried over from the economic purposes they have served well to the political purposes to which they are not suited, the approach embodied in the treaties will endanger freedoms in Europe. They need to be modified from a constitutional perspective. Sooner, rather than later, a complete constitutional settlement will be needed. The rules of the constitution must value, above all else, the processes of political association. It is only through finding those processes that will minimize coercion in the Union that the peoples of Europe will reap the mutual benefits of political association while, at the same time, retaining their individual freedoms.

Bibliography

Ackerman, B.A. (1980), *Social Justice in the Liberal State*, Yale University Press, New Haven, Conn.

Arkes, H.R. and Hammond, K.R. (eds) (1986), *Judgement and Decision Making: An Interdisciplinary Reader*, Cambridge University Press, Cambridge.

Arrow, K.J. (1974), 'Limited Knowledge and Economic Analysis', *American Economic Review*, 64.

Arrow, K.J. (1951), *Social Choice and Individual Values*, Wiley, New York.

Axelrod, R. (1984), *The Evolution of Cooperation*, Basic Books, New York.

Bachrach, P. (1980), *The Theory of Democratic Elitism*, University Press of America, Lanham, Md.

Barry, N.P. (1986), *On Classical Liberalism and Libertarianism*, Macmillan, Basingstoke.

Becker, G.S. (1962), 'Irrational Behaviour and Economic Theory', *Journal of Political Economy*, 52, February.

Becker, G.S. (1974), 'A Theory of Social Interactions', *Journal of Political Economy*, 82.

Beitz, C. (1989), *Political Equality*, Princeton University Press, New Haven, Conn.

Bell, D.E. Raiffa, H. and Tversky, A. (eds) (1988), *Decision Making*, Cambridge University Press, Cambridge.

Benn, S.I. (1988), *A Theory of Freedom*, Cambridge University Press, Cambridge.

Bentham, J. (1789), *An Introduction to the Principles of Morals and Legislation*, Burns, J.M. and Hart, H.L.A. (eds) (1970), Athlone Press, University of London, London.

Bentham, J. (1776), *A Fragment on Government*, Wilson and Pickering, London, 1823.

Bentham, J. (1830), *First Principles Preparatory to the Constitutional Code*, Schofield (ed.) Clarendon Press, Oxford, 1989.

Berglas, E. (1984), 'Quantities, Qualities and Multiple Services in the Tiebout Model', *Journal of Public Economics*, 25.

Berman, H.J. (1983), *Law and Revolution*, Harvard University Press, Cambridge, Mass.

Bickel, A. (1962), *The Least Dangerous Branch*, The Bobbs Merrill Co. Inc., Indianapolis.

Black, D. (1958), *A Theory of Committees and Elections*, Cambridge University Press, London.

Black, A. (1984), *Guilds and Civil Society in European Political Thought from the 12th Century to the Present*, Methuen and Co, London.

Blaug, M. (1980), *The Methodology of Economics*, Cambridge University Press, London.

Blondel, J. (1973), *Comparative Legislatures*, Prentice Hall, New Jersey.

Bodin, J. (1576), *The Six Books of a Commonwealth*, trans. Tooley, Basil Blackwell, Oxford, (1955).

Bonner, J. (1986), *Introduction to the Theory of Social Choice*, Johns Hopkins University Press, Baltimore.

Boulding, K.E. (1977), *The Image – Knowledge in Life and Society*, University of Michigan Press, Ann Arbor.

Braithwaite, R. B. (1955), *Theory of Games as a Tool for the Moral Philosopher*, Cambridge University Press, Cambridge.

Brams, S.J. (1976), *Game Theory and Politics*, Free Press, New York.

Bratman, M.E. (1987), *Intention, Plans and Practical Reason*, Harvard University Press, Cambridge, Mass.

Brennan, G. and Buchanan, J.M. (1980), *The Power to Tax: Analytic Foundations of a Fiscal Constitution*, Cambridge University Press, Cambridge.

Brennan, G. and Buchanan, J.M. (1985), *The Reason of Rules*, Harvard University Press, Cambridge, Mass.

Breton, A. and Scott, A. D. (1978), *The Economic Constitution of Federal States*, University of Toronto Press, Toronto.

Breton, A. (1987), 'Towards a Theory of Competitive Federalism', *European Journal of Political Economy*, Special Issue 3.

Breton, A. (1974), *The Economic Theory of Representative Government*, Aldine Publishing Co., Chicago.

Bryce, J. (1901), *Studies in History and Jurisprudence*, Oxford University Press, Oxford.

Buchanan, J.M. (1975), *Limits of Liberty: Between Anarchy and Leviathan*, University of Chicago Press, Chicago.

Buchanan, J.M. (1991), *The Economics and Ethics of Constitutional Order*, University of Michigan Press, Ann Arbor.

Buchanan, J.M. (1990), 'The Domain of Constitutional Economics', *Constitutional Political Economy* I.

Buchanan, J.M. and Tullock, G. (1962), The Calculus of Consent, University of Michigan Press, Ann Arbor.

Burke, E. *Works*, (ed.) Langford, Clarendon Press, Oxford, (1981).

Cappelletti, M., Seccombe, M. and Weiler, J. (eds) (1985), *Integration Through Law*, de Gruyter, Berlin.

Chamberlin, J. (1974), 'Provision of Collective Goods as a Function of Group Size', *American Political Science Review*, 68.

Coase, R.H. (1937), 'The Nature of the Firm', *Economica*, 4.

Coase, R.H. (1960), 'The Problem of Social Cost', *The Journal of Law and Economics* III.

Coase, R.H. (1974), 'The Lighthouse in Economics', *The Journal of Law and Economics*, 17.

Coase, R.H. (1988), *The Firm, the Market and the Law*, University of Chicago Press, Chicago.

Coase, R.H. (1992), *The Institutional Structure of Production*, American Economic Review, vol. 82. no. 4.

Coleman, J.S. (1990), *Foundations of Social Theory*, Harvard University Press, Cambridge, Mass.

Cornes, R. and Sandler, T. (1986), *The Theory of Externalities, Public Goods and Club Goods*, Cambridge University Press, Cambridge.

Cox, A. (1976), *The Role of the Supreme Court in American Government*, Oxford University Press, Oxford.

Cukierman, A. (1992), *Central Bank Strategy, Credibility and Independence*, The MIT Press, Cambridge, Mass.

Dahl, R.A. (1956), *A Preface to Democratic Theory*, Chicago University Press, Chicago.

Dahl, R.A. (1971), *Polyarchy, Participation and Opposition*, Yale University Press, New Haven, Conn.

Dahl, R.A. (1989), *Democracy and its Critics*, Yale University Press, New Haven, Conn.

Dashwood, A. (1994), 'The Role of the Council in the European Union' in *Liber Amicorum Henry J. Schermers*, Kluwer, Amsterdam.

Demsetz, H. (1967), 'Towards a Theory of Property Rights', *American Economic Review*, 57.
Demsetz, H. (1970), 'The Private Production of Public Goods', *Journal of Law and Economics*, 13.
Dicey, A. V. (1915), *Introduction to the Study of the Law and the Constitution*, (ed.) Wade, Macmillan & Co., (1959).
Dietze, G. (1973), *Two Concepts of the Rule of Law*, Liberty Fund, Inc., Indianapolis.
Downs, A. (1957), *An Economic Theory of Democracy*, Harper and Row, New York.
Dworkin, R. (1977), *Taking Rights Seriously*, Harvard University Press, Cambridge, Mass.
Eggerton, T. (1990), *Economic Behaviour and Institutions*, Cambridge University Press, Cambridge.
Elster, J. (1984), *Ulysses and the Sirens*, Cambridge University Press, Cambridge.
Elster, J. (ed.) (1986), *The Multiple Self*, Cambridge University Press, Cambridge.
Elster, J. and Hylland, A. (eds) (1986), *Foundations of Social Choice Theory*, Cambridge University Press, Cambridge.
Elster, J. and Slagstad, R. (eds) (1988), *Constitutionalism and Democracy*, Cambridge University Press, Cambridge.
Ely, J.H. (1980), *Democracy and Distrust: A Theory of Judicial Review*, Harvard University Press, Cambridge, Mass.
Eucken, W. (1948), 'What Kind of Economic and Social System?' in *Germany's Social Market Economy: Origins and Evolution*, Peacock, A. and Willgerodt, H. (eds), Macmillan Press Ltd., London, (1989).
European Constitutional Group, (1993), *A Proposal for a European Constitution*, European Policy Forum, London.
Farquharson, R. (1969), *Theory of Voting*, Yale University Press, New Haven, Ct.
Fried, C. (1981), *Contract as Promise: A Theory of Contractual Obligation*, Harvard University Press, Cambridge, Mass.
Friedman, M. (1953), *Essays in Positive Economics*, Chicago University Press, Chicago.
Friedman, M. (1962), *Capitalism and Freedom*, Chicago University Press, Chicago.
Friedrich, C.J. (1968), *Trends of Federalism in Theory and Practice*, Pall Mall Press, London.
Fudenberg, D. and Tirole, J. (1992), *Game Theory*, The MIT Press, Cambridge Mass.
Fuller, L. (1981), *The Principles of Social Order*, Duke University Press, Durham, NC.
Gaus, G.F. (1990), *Value and Justification: The Foundations of Liberal Theory*, Cambridge University Press, Cambridge.
Gauthier, D. (1986), *Morals by Agreement*, Clarendon Press, Oxford.
Geertz, C. (1973), *The Interpretation of Cultures*, Fontana Press, London, 1993.
Gewirth, A. (1981), *Reason and Morality*, Chicago University Press, Chicago.
Gierke, O.v. (1900), *Political Theories of the Middle Age*, trans. Maitland, Cambridge University Press, Cambridge.
Gray, J. (1989), *Liberalism*, Routledge, London.
Griffin, J. (1986), *Well-being: Its Meaning, Measurement and Moral Importance*, Oxford University Press, Oxford.
Hampton, J. (1986), *Hobbes and the Social Contract Tradition*, Cambridge University Press, Cambridge.
Hart, H.L.A. (1961), *The Concept of Law*, Oxford University Press, Oxford.
Hart, H.L.A. (1963), *Law, Liberty and Morality*, Oxford University Press, London.
Hayek, F.A. (1944), *The Road to Serfdom*, Routledge, London.
Hayek, F.A. (1960), *The Constitution of Liberty*, Routledge, London.
Hayek, F.A. (1976), *Law, Legislation and Liberty*, 3 vols, University of Chicago Press, Chicago.
Hayek, F.A. (1978), *New Studies in Politics, Economics and the History of Ideas*, Routledge and Kegan Paul, London and Henley.
Hegel's Philosophy of Right, (1821), trans. Knox, T.M., Clarendon Press, Oxford, 1952.

Higgs, R. (1987), *Crisis and Leviathan: Critical Episodes in the Growth of American Government*, Oxford University Press, Oxford.

Hirschman, A.O. (1970), *Exit, Voice and Loyalty*, Harvard University Press, Cambridge, Mass.

Hirschman, A.O. (1982), *Shifting Involvements. Private Interests and Public Action*, Martin Robertson, Oxford.

Hirst, P. (1994), *Associative Democracy*, Polity Press in association with Blackwell Publishers, Oxford.

Hobbes, T. (1651), *Leviathan*, (ed.) Tuck, Cambridge University Press, Cambridge, (1991).

Hobbes, T. (1651), *De Cive*, (the English version), (ed.) Warrender, Clarendon Press, Oxford, (1983).

Hogarth, R. M. and Reder, M. (eds) (1987), *Rational Choice*, Chicago University Press, Chicago.

Humboldt, W.v. (1792), *The Sphere and Duties of Government*, trans. Coulthard, J., John Chapman, London, (1854).

Hume, D. (1740), *A Treatise of Human Nature*, (ed.) Rhys, Everyman's Library, J.M. Dent & Sons, London, (1930).

Hume, D. (1748), *An Enquiry Concerning Human Understanding*, (ed.) Selby-Bigge, Oxford University Press, Oxford, (1975).

Kant, I. (1790), *Kant's Critique of Teleological Judgement*, trans. Meredith, Clarendon Press, Oxford, (1928).

Kant, I. (1797), *The Metaphysics of Ethics*, (ed.) Calderwood, T. and T. Clark, Edinburgh, 1871.

Kant's Political Writings, (ed.) Reiss, H., Cambridge University Press, Cambridge, (1970).

Kelsen, H. (1946), *The General Theory of the Law and the State*, trans. Wedberg, A., Harvard University Press, Cambridge, Mass.

Kelsen, H. (1973), *Essays in Legal and Moral Philosophy*, trans. Heath, D. Reidel Publishing Co., Dordrecht.

Kelsen, H. (1986), 'The Function of a Constitution', trans. Stewart, in *Essays on Kelsen*, Tur, R. and Twining, W. (eds), Clarendon Press, Oxford.

Lewis, D.K. (1986), *Convention: A Philosophical Study*, Basil Blackwell, Oxford.

Lijpart, A. (1977), *Democracy in Plural Societies*, Yale University Press, New Haven, Ct.

Lijpart, A. (1984), *Democracies*, Yale University Press, New Haven, Ct.

Locke, J. (1690), *Two Treatises of Government*, (ed.) Everyman's Library, J.M.Dent & Sons, London, (1955).

Lomanski, L.E. (1987), *Persons, Rights and the Moral Community*, Oxford University Press, Oxford.

Madison, J. Jay, J. and Hamilton, A. (1788), *The Federalist*. (ed.) Everyman's Library, J.M. Dent & Sons, London, (1934).

McClennan, E.F. (1990), *Rationality and Dynamic Choice: Foundational Explorations*, Harvard University Press, Cambridge, Mass.

McClennan, E. F. (1990), 'Foundational Explorations for a Normative theory of Political Economy', *Constitutional and Political Economy*, I.

McMillan, J. (1979), 'The Free Rider Problem: A Survey', *Economic Record*, 55.

McRae, K. (ed.) (1974), *Consociational Democracy: Political Accommodation in Segmented Societies*, McLelland and Stewart, Toronto.

Mill, J.S. (1848), 'Principles of Political Economy', (ed.) Robson, *Collected Works of J.S. Mill*, University of Toronto Press, Routledge and Kegan Paul, (1977).

Mill, J S. (1859), *Utilitarianism, On Liberty and Representative Government*, (ed.) Everyman's Library, J.M. Dent & Sons, London, (1960).

Mill, J.S. 'Essays on Politics and Society', (ed.) Robson, *Collected Works of J.S. Mill*, vol. XVIII, University of Toronto Press, Routledge and Kegan Paul, (1977).

Minogue, K.R. (1976), *Nationalism*, B.T. Batsford Ltd., London.
Mises, L.v. (1933), *Epistemological Problems of Economics*, Van Nostrand, Princeton, N.J. (1960).
Montesquieu, C de S. (1721), *Lettres Persanes*, (ed.) Vernière, P., Garnier Frères, Paris, (1960).
Montesquieu, C.de S. (1748), 'The Spirit of the Laws' in *The Political Theory of Montesquieu*, Richter, M., Cambridge University Press, Cambridge, (1977).
North, D.C. (1990), *Institutions, Institutional Change and Economic Performance*, Cambridge University Press, Cambridge.
Norton, P. (ed.) (1990), *Legislatures*, Oxford University Press, Oxford.
Norton, P. (ed.) (1990), *Parliaments in Western Europe*, Frank Cass, London.
Nozick, D. (1974), *Anarchy, State and Utopia*, Basil Blackwell, Oxford.
Nozick, D. (1981), *Philosophical Explanations*, Clarendon Press, Oxford.
Oakeshott, M. (1975), *On Human Conduct*, Clarendon Press, Oxford.
Oates, W. E. (1972), *Fiscal Federalism*, Harcourt, Brace and Jovanovitch, New York.
Olson, M. (1969), 'The Principle of Fiscal Equivalence: the Division of Responsibilities Among Different Levels of Government', *American Economic Review*, 59.
Olson, M. (1971), *The Logic of Collective Action*, Harvard University Press, Cambridge, Mass.
Olson, M. (1982), *The Rise and Decline of Nations: Economic Growth, Stagflation and Social Rigidities*, Yale University Press, New Haven, Ct.
Ordeshook, P.C. (1986), *Game Theory and Political Theory*, Cambridge University Press, Cambridge.
Ostrom, V. (1987), *The Political Theory of a Compound Republic*, University of Nebraska Press, Lincoln.
Pareto, V. (1916), *The Mind and Society*, trans. Livingston, A., Harcourt Brace & Co., New York, (1935).
Peacock A. and Willgerodt. H. (eds) (1989), *German Neo-Liberals and the Social Market Economy*, Macmillan (for the Trade Policy Research Centre), London, 1989.
Pears, D. (1984), *Motivated Irrationality*, Clarendon Press, Oxford.
Polanyi, M. (1951), *The Logic of Liberty: Reflections and Rejoinders*, University of Chicago Press, Chicago.
Popper, K.R. (1957), *The Poverty of Historicism*, Routledge and Kegan Paul, London.
Popper, K. R. (1960), *The Open Society and Its Enemies*, Routledge and Kegan Paul, London.
Purcell, E.A. (1973), *The Crisis of Democratic Theory*, The University Press of Kentucky.
Rae, D.W. (1969), 'Decision Rules and Individual Values in Constitutional Choice', *American Political Science Review*, 63.
Rand, A. (1964), *The Virtue of Selfishness*, Signet, New York.
Rawls, J. (1955), 'Two Concepts of Rules', *Philosophical Review*, 64.
Rawls, J. (1972), *A Theory of Justice*, Clarendon Press, Oxford.
Raz, J. (1979), *The Authority of Law*, Oxford University Press, Oxford.
Raz, J. (1986) 'The Morality of Freedom', Clarendon Press. Oxford.
Riker, W.H. (1987), 'The Development of American Federalism', Kluwer, Boston.
Rothbard, M.N. (1982), *The Ethics of Liberty*, Humanities Press, New Jersey.
Rousseau, J.J. (1762), *The Social Contract and Discourses*, trans. Cole, Everyman's Library, J.M. Dent and Sons, Ltd., London, (1961).
Schelling, T. (1960), *The Strategy of Conflict*, Harvard University Press, Cambridge, Mass.
Schelling, T. (1984), *Choice and Consequence*, Harvard University Press, Cambridge, Mass.
Schotter, A. (1981), *The Economic Theory of Social Institutions*, Cambridge University Press, London.
Schwartz, T. (1977), 'Collective Choice, Separation of Issues and Vote Trading', *American Political Science Review*, 71.
Schwartz, T. (1981), *The Logic of Collective Choice*, Colombia University Press, New York.

Sen, A.K. and Williams, B. (eds) (1982), *Ethical Theory and Utilitarianism*, Cambridge University Press, Cambridge.

Sen A.K. (1970), *Collective Choice and Social Welfare*, Holden-Day, San Francisco.

Sen. A.K. (1973), *On Economic Inequality*, Clarendon Press, Oxford.

Shubik, M. (1984), *A Game Theoretic Approach to Political Economy*, MIT Press, Cambridge, Mass.

Simon, H.A. (1986), 'Alternative Views of Rationality' in Arkes, H.R. and Hammond, K.R. (eds), *Judgement and Decision Making: An Interdisciplinary Reader*, Cambridge University Press, Cambridge.

Simon, H.A. (1985), 'Rationality in Psychology and Economics' in *Rational Choice*, (eds) Hogarth, R.M. and Reder, M.W, University of Chicago, (1987).

Smith, A. (1762–4), *Lectures on Jurisprudence*, Clarendon Press, Oxford, (1978).

Smith, A. (1776), *An Inquiry into the Nature and Causes of the Wealth of Nations*, (eds) Campbell and Skinner, Clarendon Press, Oxford, (1976).

Smith, A. (1778), *The Theory of Moral Sentiments*, (eds) Raphael and Macfie, Clarendon Press, Oxford, (1976).

Smith, G. (1976), 'The Functional Properties of the Referendum', *European Journal of Political Research*, 4, no. 1.

Stigler, G. J. (1975), *The Citizen and the State*, University of Chicago Press, Chicago.

Tiebout, C.M. (1956), 'A Pure Theory of Local Expenditures', *Journal of Political Economy*, 64.

Toqueville, A. de (1835), *Democracy in America*, trans. Reeve, Saunders and Otley, London.

Tribe, L. (1978), *American Constitutional Law*, The Foundation Press, Mineola, New York.

Ullmann-Margalit, E. (1977), *The Emergence of Norms*, Clarendon Press, Oxford.

Vile, M.J.C. (1967), *Constitutionalism and the Separation of Powers*, Oxford University Press, Oxford.

Wicksell, K. (1896), 'A New Principle of Just Taxation' in Musgrave, R.A. and Peacock, A.T. *Classics in the Theory of Public Finance*, Macmillan, London, (1958).

Weber, M. (1947), *The Theory of Social and Economic Organisation*, trans. Henderson and Parsons, Oxford University Press, Oxford.

Weber, M. (1978), *Economy and Society*, (eds) Roth, G. and Wittich, C. University of California Press, Berkeley and Los Angeles, Ca.

Wheare, K.C. (1963), *Legislatures*, Oxford University Press, London.

Wiseman, J. (1989), *Cost, Choice and Political Economy*, Edward Elgar, Cheltenham.

Wright Mills, C. (1956), *The Power Elite*, Oxford University Press, Oxford.